FEASTING OUR EYES

FEASTING OUR EYES

Food Films and Cultural Identity
in the United States

 LAURA LINDENFELD
FABIO PARASECOLI

Columbia University Press
New York

Columbia University Press
Publishers Since 1893
New York   Chichester, West Sussex
cup.columbia.edu

Library of Congress Cataloging-in-Publication Data
Names: Lindenfeld, Laura, author. | Parasecoli, Fabio, author.
Title: Feasting our eyes : food films and cultural identity in the United
States / Laura Lindenfeld and Fabio Parasecoli.
Description: New York : Columbia University Press, [2016] |
Includes bibliographical references and index.
Identifiers: LCCN 2016008166| ISBN 9780231172509 (cloth : alk. paper) |
ISBN 9780231172516 (pbk. : alk. paper)
Subjects: LCSH: Food in motion pictures. | Motion pictures—United States—
History. | Food—Social aspects—United States.
Classification: LCC PN1995.9.F65 L56 2016 | DDC 791.43/6564—dc23
LC record available at http://lccn.loc.gov/2016008166

Columbia University Press books are printed
on permanent and durable acid-free paper.

Printed in the United States of America

c 10 9 8 7 6 5 4 3 2 1
p 10 9 8 7 6 5 4 3 2 1

Cover design: Lisa Hamm
Cover image: Courtesy of Photofest

CONTENTS

ILLUSTRATIONS

ACKNOWLEDGMENTS

Many hands, minds, and hearts provided important contributions to this book. I am deeply grateful to all who shared ideas, emotional support, recommendations for foodie flicks, and—of course—great food over the years.

If writing a book is anything like making a meal, working with Fabio Parasecoli was like planning the most sumptuous banquet one can imagine—even better than *Babette's Feast* or *The Big Night*. Fabio can whip up words and ideas with the ease that Julia Child brought to the creation of a magnificent soufflé. Fabio, I will forever be grateful for your friendship and collegiality. This book would not have come to be without you. May others have the pleasure and joy of the ease, integrity, fun, and focus that I experienced in working with you.

Portions of this book struck their original roots in my dissertation. Although the book has evolved significantly since that time, its advancement was possible because of the kind and steady support I received from Jay Mechling. Jay, I still miss going to lunch with you and talking about food. How lucky was I to have you as my doctoral adviser. Gratitude goes to Kent Ono and Sarah Projanksy, who read, reviewed, and offered feedback on this work in its earliest phases of development. It was such a pleasure and an honor to work with you.

The University of Maine's Office of Research supported this book with a summer research fellowship. The University of California, Davis supported the dissertation out of which parts of this book grew with a Dissertation Year Fellowship. I am deeply grateful for the support provided to me by both institutions.

My sincere appreciation and affection go to the colleagues and friends who supported this book. Many gave input and shared ideas over the years at meetings of the Association for the Study of Food and Society, National Communication Association, Conference on Communication and the Environment, Cultural Studies Association, and American Studies Association. Alice Julier, Psyche-Williams Forson, Charlotte Biltekoff, Anita Mannur, Carole Counihan, Warren Belasco, Arlene Voski-Avakian, and Netta Davis provided moral support and helped me to advance my thinking about identity and food in critically important ways. Special thanks to Davis-era friends Anna Kuhn, Dave & Jen Nachmanoff, Kelly Nelson, jesikah maria ross, and Erin MacDougall. Laurie Nickel, the many miles running and hours spent talking have been fundamentally influential in all that I do. At UMaine I have so many people to thank. Kathleen Bell and Shaleen Jain (my Mod Squad sustainability siblings), Gisela Hoecherl-Alden (sister coauthor of a food film paper), Jen O'Leary, Annie Langston, Nate Stormer, Naomi Jacobs, Kristin Langellier, Mike Socolow, Amy Blackstone, and Jeff St. John, you have been such steady sources of strength and kindness over the years. I have had the privilege of working with so many amazing students who have helped to enrich the thinking that went into this book. Beth, Mike, Eli, and Zeke, thank you for providing creative space for writing and wonderful food over the years.

Thanks to Rich Kilfoyle and Lucy Quimby from the bottom of my heart. You have no idea how much you have meant to me and how influential you have been in my life. Grace Noonan-Kaye, you stepped in to support me at a critical phase and offered wise guidance for focusing on the work that resulted in this book. Thank you.

To our editor, Jennifer Crewe, we are grateful for the support you provided that made this book so much better. We feel privileged to have received such supportive feedback from our reviewers and are grateful for your time and care. Jen St. John, our special thanks go out to you for your detailed edits, enthusiasm about this project, and general joie-de-vivre.

I am blessed with a supportive family that loves great food and movies. Thank you Mom and John, Katie and Kevin, Dan and Shannon, Dad and Ann, David and Lorraine, Mike and Beth, Robin and Michael for your endless support. The many meals and conversations I shared with you enrich me and my work every day. Vic and Lee, you hold a special place in my heart when it comes to food, wine, music, and friendship.

My work on this book is dedicated to Roger and Micah, my foodie guys. Micah, you were born around the time my dissertation was done, and now you can read this book and talk about food, film, and identity like an adult with dad and me. I am so incredibly proud of the person you have become. Roger, thank you for all the wonderful meals, talk of food, piles of food magazines, willingness to watch food movies (good and bad), partnership, constant source of love, and tolerance of me staring at a screen. I love you two more than words can express.

The ideas about cultural citizenship in this book were initially fleshed out in 2011 in "Feasts for Our Eyes: Viewing Food Films through New Lenses," which appeared as a chapter in *Food as Communication, Communication as Food*, edited by J. Cramer, C. Greene, and L. Walters (New York: Peter Lang). Portions of chapter 6 appeared in 2007 in "Visiting the Mexican American Family: *Tortilla Soup* as Culinary Tourism," *Communication and Critical/Cultural Studies* 4, no. 3 (2007): 303–320. Other portions were published in "Digging Down to the Roots: On the Radical Potential of Documentary Food Films," *Radical History Review*, no. 110 (2011): 155–160; and "Can Documentary Food Films like *Food Inc.* Achieve Their Promise?" *Environmental Communication* 4, no. 3 (2010): 378–386.

—Laura Lindenfeld

First of all, I want to thank my coauthor and friend Laura Lindenfeld, with whom I have swapped ideas and insights about media in general and cinema in particular since we first met, years ago, through the Association for the Study of Food and Society. Who would have thought we'd be writing a book together when I was enjoying lobster and seafood with her wonderful family (hi Roger and Micah!) in her Maine home! Working with her has been a pleasure. Neither of us has been proprietary about our work, and we've always felt free to cut, add, and edit as we felt was best. A rare and precious experience.

Thank you also to Anne Bellows, my dissertation adviser at Hohenheim University, Germany (now at Syracuse University, New York), who allowed me to write about food and masculinities in blockbuster films and offered crucial guidance through the whole doctoral process.

A special thank you goes to my family and friends in Rome, as well as to Doran Ricks, who sat through many films he may not have been necessarily interested in.

I want to acknowledge all the students with whom I have shared my passion for food and film at Città del Gusto, New York University, the University of Gastronomic Sciences, and now the New School. Over the years they have pushed me to examine topics that would not have occurred to me, making me aware of new material and keeping me on my toes. Those courses helped me think through many of the issues we discuss in this book.

Much gratitude and affection goes to my friends in the Association for the Study of Food and Society, which I have always considered my intellectual (and emotional) home in academia, as well to my colleagues at the New School, who have provided a great working environment for me to grow as a teacher and a scholar. In particular, I want to thank Bea Banu, my partner in crime in the Food Studies program, who had my back when I had to double down on writing and revising the book, and Laura Di Bianco, who taught Food and Film at the New School, with whom I had great and useful conversations.

Portions of this book were part of my doctoral dissertation, "Food and Men in Cinema: An Exploration of Gender in Blockbuster Movies." Parts of chapter 5 were published in May 2013 in *Projector: A Journal of Film, Media, and Culture* as "When a Weirdo Stirs the Pot: Food and Masculinity in *Ratatouille*." Other portions appear in the journal *Semiotica* in an article titled "Starred Cosmopolitanism: Celebrity Chefs, Documentaries, and the Circulation of Global Desire"; in the chapter "From Stove to Screen: Food Porn, Professional Chefs, and the Construction of Masculinity in

Films," in *What's Cooking? Food, Art and Counterculture*, edited by Silvia Botticelli and Margherita D'Ayala (forthcoming, University of Arkansas Press); and in "Kitchen Mishaps: Performances of Masculine Domesticity in American Comedy Films," in *Food, Masculinity, and Home*, edited by Michelle Szabo (forthcoming, Bloomsbury).

—Fabio Parasecoli

FEASTING OUR EYES

INTRODUCTION

Food passes across any boundary you care to mention.

Salmon Rushdie, *The Satanic Verses*

Big *Night. Ratatouille. Julie & Julia.* Besides their commercial success, the common element that unites these films is that they are all about food, prepared in the kitchen, served at the table, and offered to global audiences for visual and emotional consumption. Above all, cooking and eating shape the characters' lives and adventures, while dishes and ingredients, luscious and appealing, often steal the scene. Food looms large in contemporary cinema, even when it is not the main narrative engine, in comedies like *Spanglish* (Brooks, 2004), dramas like *The Help* (Taylor, 2011), and even gangster movies like *Goodfellas* (Scorsese, 1990) and *Eastern Promises* (Cronenberg, 2007). The presence of food in commercially successful films is far from being an exclusively U.S. phenomenon: Hollywood operates within a well-established trend that is visible at the global level. We can mention, among others, films like the Brazilian *Estomago* (*Estomago: A Gastronomic Story* [Jorge, 2007]), the French *Haute Cuisine* (*Les saveurs du palais* [Vincent, 2012]), the Japanese *The Chef of South Polar* (*Nankyoku ryôrinin* [Okita, 2009]), the Indian *The Lunchbox* (*Dabba* [Batra, 2013]), and the Spanish *Mediterranean Food* (*Dieta mediterránea* [Oristrell, 2009]).

Their themes vary, respectively, from the culinary world of a prison inmate to the story of the female chef for a French president, the adventures of the cook in an all-male scientific research base in the South Pole, the lonely existence of a widower, and the struggle of a female chef to assert herself both in her business and in her private life.

The evocative potential of the moving image is reinforced when cuisine and ingestion are used to convey dynamics and feelings that would otherwise be difficult to express visually or verbally. For this reason food has always been present in cinema, long before the release of seminal works like *Tampopo* (Itami, 1985) and *Babette's Feast* (Axel, 1987)—often hailed as the first "food films"—and even before Hollywood fully embraced food as a legitimate and lucrative theme. Yet, since the early 1990s, cooking and eating have acquired unprecedented visibility in American cinema, reflecting a growing interest among moviegoers and in the movie industry. What changes in audiences, the media, and the film business have made the cinematic and narrative focus on food viable and successful? Do these developments reflect deeper trends in culture and society? In other words, why do Americans long for food on the silver screen, and what does that desire say about U.S. society? Can we talk about "food films" as an emergent genre focused on the topic of food, cooking, and eating that includes works as varied as Hollywood and independent narrative films, documentaries, and docufictions? And finally, how does this U.S. trend relate to larger global phenomena about food, film, and media?

These are some of the questions that *Feasting Our Eyes* addresses. These complex issues can be unpacked from many points of view, all legitimate and interesting, ranging from visual style to communication strategies, from business concerns to audience reception. Without ignoring any of these aspects, we pay particular attention to what food films can reveal about the production and negotiation of identity, relationships of power, and ultimately citizenship in contemporary U.S. society. More specifically, we focus on the connection between these media products and the cultural and social negotiations around class, gender, race, age, and political affiliation, even when at first blush they may seem unrelated to food and eating. Although these debates influence each other, allowing for the emergence of heated and contested identity politics, we focus on specific aspects of identity to provide a more accessible analysis, while making frequent references to their mutual connections. We zoom in on films released from the early 1990s to the present, a period that marks a watershed in the use and presence of food in media in general and cinema in particular. Are food films just harmless reflections of current trends, or do they rather participate in shaping them? Do they simply respond to the shifting interests of audiences, or are they at least partially responsible for generating those very preferences? Ultimately, to what degree do they influence our understanding of ourselves as individuals and as members of various communities?

Food has explicitly become part of how U.S. citizens talk about themselves. America, the *New York Times* wrote in 2009, is "in the midst of a feeding frenzy. . . . The Food Network holds 65 million monthly viewers in its thrall, and sales of gourmet foods and beverages are expected to top $53 billion next year."[1] The marketability of food—its pervasive and lucrative representation on television and in magazines, advertising, film, and literature—and a plethora of self-help and cooking books suggest that narratives about eating constitute a highly contested arena in which cultural, social, economic, and political tensions converge. As with other kinds of consumption, food choices play an increasingly relevant role in defining the cultural stance, the social status, and the political worldviews of Americans. Shopping at a farmers' market, patronizing a farm-to-table establishment, or buying one's groceries at a local cooperative communicates specific information about individuals who embrace these behaviors. Eating at a fast-food restaurant on the way to the local big box store could be interpreted as the expression of a very different set of stances on issues ranging from labor to the environment. Along a varied and complex spectrum of values and actions, Americans adopt diverse and fragmented practices.

Academic and journalistic exposés into food production, consumption, and politics have received widespread attention. Eric Schlosser's investigation into fast-food production structures, Marion Nestle's uncovering of the complex connections among food, politics, and nutrition, and Michael Pollan's exhortations to change the food system have set the stage for increasingly relevant conversations in civil society and in the media.[2] Specialized events such as the Food Film Festival in New York City and Charleston, South Carolina, San Francisco's Food & Farm Film Fest, and many others confirm this increased visibility. The growing interest in food matters, both from a cultural and a political point of view, is part of larger global phenomena, as the presence of food festivals in Amsterdam, Seoul, and the Italian Alps suggest.[3] Self-proclaimed "foodies" with solid financial backgrounds enjoy a cosmopolitan lifestyle that exposes them to restaurant and culinary trends all over the world, priming them to look for and appreciate food films, no matter their origin.

Yet the discussion about the nature and motivations of food films is still quite limited. Scholarly research has not frequently addressed the intricate connections among cinema, food, eating, identity, consumption, and their relationship to power and politics. In their engagement with liberal themes—including ideological pluralism, ethnic and racial acceptance, gender equality, and class flexibility—at face value food films seem to approach culture and identity through a critical and progressive lens. For instance, *Big Night* portrays the struggles of new immigrants trying to make it in the United States, while *Julie & Julia* lightly prods viewers to reflect on changes in gender roles. If, however, one pays enough attention to go beneath the surface, it quickly becomes clear that these films consistently undermine these progressive efforts by reasserting conventional approaches to nation, gender, race, sexuality, and social status. Mainstream media frequently enable dominant U.S. culture to celebrate its supposed commitment to diversity, while simultaneously positioning women and people of color as objects of consumption and pushing unruly and unsightly bodies—fat bodies, old bodies, disabled bodies, unfit bodies—to the margins. It comes as no surprise that the sort of films we examine emerged with the rise of liberal multiculturalism and ethnic identity politics in the United States in the 1980s and 1990s.[4] Their complicated relationship to diversity mirrors the strategy of "political correctness" that promotes seemingly tolerant behavior and attitudes while undermining that very same progressiveness. Much food media purports to "teach" about otherness, but we have to consider how power operates along the lines of ethnicity, race, gender, sexuality, and national identity within the United States when we take these "lessons" in. Indeed, our consumption of food media tends to render ethnicity as novel and exciting, while also ensuring that we as viewers engage with worlds that are safe and clean.

Despite the progressive veneer, food films may mask conservative politics, as the need for commercial success prevails over the ability to advance any effective social critique. Participating in the reproduction of the existing cultural and social order, food films play an important role in defining our sense of what is normal, natural, and appropriate, while keeping their mechanisms and strategies invisible. The virtual experience of eating while exploring different lifestyles and unfamiliar cultures provides audiences with seemingly safe and ordinary spaces to play out anxieties about racial differences, alternative sexualities, class distinctions, and all sorts of power issues. Food films, however, often end up highlighting consumption behaviors and lifestyles that privilege mainstream value systems while offering a virtual, vicarious touristic experience of various kinds of otherness. Food films help to draw lines between who does and does not belong to mainstream society, an issue central to any notion of citizenship.

Throughout this book we refer to the concepts of race and ethnicity. It is worth a brief discussion of these concepts in this introduction, without forgetting that they constantly interact, overlap, and often complicate issues of gender, class, and age. *Race* refers to the idea that groups of people can be differentiated from each other based on biological characteristics like skin color, hair texture, and facial and body structure.[5] The term *ethnicity*, in contrast, categorizes groups of people based on cultural commonalities, like nationality, language, ancestry, and identification with each other. The way that we use the term *ethnicity* rejects the notion of a biological basis for race and therefore the idea that certain groups of people inherently embody particular traits *because* of their biology (for example, the stereotype that African Americans can dance or sing better than whites because of their biology). When we use the term *race* in this book, we are deliberately referring to the way the films themselves impose biologically deterministic characteristics on specific characters and groups. Our use of the term *ethnic food* implies a range of cuisines, and we deliberately contrast ethnic to mainstream white food, not because white people don't have ethnic differences but rather because the films themselves demark "white" culture from the culture of nonwhite groups. We emphasize this because of the distinct privilege that whiteness holds in the United States.

Race and ethnicity issues cannot be fully appraised without examining their complex interplay with gender, which we approach as a cultural construction and a performance rather than a fixed position related to an individual's biological sex. By doing this, we build on reflections that developed in the late 1960s, following and partly inspired by the civil right movement, when traditional gender relations were scrutinized and criticized by social movements that focused on the rights of oppressed members of society, such as blacks, women, and LGBT persons. Gender, patriarchy, family, and even sexual desire revealed their character of ideological formations. They reproduce the existing cultural and social order within institutions such as the state, the school, the workplace, and the military. Masculinity does not develop in absolute opposition to femininity but rather can be considered as the expression of a gender continuum that includes different, but sometimes overlapping, categories. In fact, different models of masculinity and femininity may prevail at certain points in time, but their dominance is always implicitly critiqued and even threatened by alternative gender models. Food films clearly indicate how food can become an arena where identities are negotiated, influencing the ways we perceive, represent, and perform ourselves as gendered individuals and as members of social groups.

These preliminary observations about food films lead us to argue that in the past two decades, food media, including movies, have become an important platform for the formation and contestation of U.S. American identity. What is the context in which these films emerged? How are they connected to broader cultural trends related to food?

A BRIEF ARCHAEOLOGY OF THE FOOD FILM

Although the films discussed in this project were produced and distributed between the early 1990s and 2015, food has appeared in cinema since its inception. One of the first films, the 1895 *Le repas du Bebé* by the brothers Lumière, focused on the meal of a baby, surrounded by its attentive parents. In silent movies food often served as a pretext for physical action: characters throwing whipped-cream pies at each other or slipping on banana peels offered opportunities for visual comedy at a time when audiences were not yet entertained by the actors' voices.[6] Even then, food managed to steal the spotlight. D. W. Griffith's *A Corner in Wheat*, produced in 1909, focused on how stock market control over wheat led to the exploitation of farmers and the destruction of the social fabric in rural U.S. areas. The production, sale, and consumption of food connect the six tableaux that form the fifteen-minute silent film, offering a political commentary about social inequalities. In an unforgettable scene a ruthless finance tycoon falls into a wheat chute and is suffocated by the very goods on which he built his financial empire. Later, in Charlie Chaplin's 1925 *Gold Rush*, the main character famously cooks and eats a shoe, establishing an iconic image that still reverberates today. In *Modern Times* (Chaplin, 1936) Chaplin makes us laugh and think by showing us a worker disastrously force-fed by a machine meant to save time and increase efficiency. As it focuses on a blue-collar male being stripped of his agency and autonomy, the scene hints at social class and gender identity issues.

Although U.S. filmmakers were aware of its dramatic potential as symbol or metaphor, food was seldom used as more than a prop, also owing to cost and logistic complications. Commensality—from dinners to drinks at a bar—offered filmmakers and scriptwriters the opportunity to have their characters convene and talk with each other, providing important information about themselves and the story. Food served as a transitional device; when we see somebody starting to eat, the camera then cuts to an empty plate.[7] The representation of food objects and practices from specific times and places also provided elements of realism. Yet despite its recurring presence, food was seldom the protagonist. It was expensive and tedious to prepare appetizing-looking food that could appear consistently enough to maintain the illusion of reality across the many takes required to shoot a scene. Besides, actors loathed eating again and again for each take.[8]

Some notable exceptions appeared before the emergence of food films in the late 1980s, mostly outside the States. In *Tom Jones* (Richardson, 1962) the male protagonist and his female counterpart engage in the consumption of an abundant meal as a sensual, albeit unusual, form of courtship. The two characters gnaw bones clean and slurp oysters as an introduction to more carnal pleasures. In the 1970s, food appeared in European movies as a symbol of the moral bankruptcy of the bourgeoisie, touching at the same time on social class and gender issues. In his 1973 *La grande bouffe* Marco Ferreri depicted eating in wealthy social contexts as obsession and overindulgence, closely related to gender exploitation, to the extreme of self-destruction. In *Sweet Movie* (Makavejev, 1974) the revolutionary Anna, who makes candy in her boat while sailing through the canals of her city, uses her confections to seduce young boys, whom she then destroys. Food and eating appear in black comedies such as *Who Is Killing the Great Chefs of Europe?* (Kotcheff, 1978), in which chefs are killed in ways inspired by their most famous dishes. A conspicuous absence of food marks Luis Buñuel's 1972 *Le charme discret de la bourgeoisie*, in which a meal is consistently postponed to the point where food never actually appears. In doing so, the filmmaker uses food as a vehicle for social criticism to denounce the inconsistencies and the limits of bourgeois sensibilities. In all these European works, food cannot be isolated from intricate and mutually influencing issues of class, gender, and age, while race does not emerge yet as an urgent topic.

The 1980s films that focus on cooking and eating, often viewed as the founding works of the new "food film" genre, tended to treat food with a more ambivalent display than the glorifying and often utopian approach that became prevalent in the 1990s. In 1985 *Tampopo* brought to the screen an unforgettable ensemble of picaresque characters that gravitate around a young single mother and her dream to produce a perfect bowl of ramen (fig. 0.1).

Filmmaker Jûzô Itami uses food and irony to explore the complexities and contradictions of Japanese society, introducing viewers to yakuza gangsters and homeless gourmets, stuck-up etiquette teachers and insensitive family men. Two years later *Babette's Feast* focused on a female French chef who, after the Paris commune, takes refuge among the members of a severe religious community in a tiny Danish hamlet. Despite the glorious scenes featuring cooking and eating, the story let viewers reflect on themes such as religion, sacrifice, and the saving value of earthly sensuality. *Babette's Feast* marked a major shift in the United States, as critics began to use the term *food film* when discussing it. *The Cook, the Thief, His Wife, and Her Lover* (Greenaway, 1989) echoed some of the critical themes of the 1970s, connecting food with conspicuous consumption, cultural identity,

FIGURE 0.1 In *Tampopo* a single mother dreams of creating the best ramen recipe to transform her run-of-the-mill shop into a unique culinary destination.

gender, and class. At the end of the film the "lover" is cooked and served to the "wife," a cannibalistic representation intended to evoke feelings of disgust and discomfort in the viewer.

These early "food films" were not produced in the United States and tended to circulate through the art-house and foreign-film crowd, often playing at small theaters in metropolitan centers. These works, followed by *Like Water for Chocolate* (Arau, 1992) and *Eat Drink Man Woman* (Lee, 1994), gained increasing popularity among U.S. spectators to the point that restaurants began offering meals to "recreate" notable food scenes. Furthermore, they introduced new ways to represent food onscreen, laying the basis for the visual style that is now often called "food porn," which we discuss later in this introduction.

The success of these foreign films stimulated American filmmakers to adopt a different approach toward food, moving it from the periphery to the core of their work. In the latter part of the 1990s, the film *Big Night* (Scott and Tucci, 1996) emerged in the independent film scene in the United States. *Big Night* opened on art-house screens and eventually made its way to mainstream theaters across the country, where it attracted a growing audience. Complete with marketing tie-ins (a cookbook and film soundtrack), *Big Night* was the first U.S. food film to be produced and consumed extensively. As the genre gained popularity, larger-scale independent and Hollywood productions emerged.

In this same period food became increasingly visible in American media. Although pioneers like James Beard, Dionne Lucas, and Julia Child had presented cooking on TV since the mid-1950s, it is the success of Martha Stewart and the launch of the Food Network in 1993 that placed food fully on the radar of mainstream American viewers.[9] Over the years the Food Network shifted from traditional cooking shows that gave audiences tips and advice to more spectacular fare. Although this approach, exemplified by Emeril Lagasse, has become prevalent, the Cooking Channel, which focuses more on actual cooking and recipes, was launched in 2010. Furthermore, food has colonized the Internet through a plethora of specialized websites, videos, blogs, photos, and social media that allow web users to post information and pictures about their meals and the dishes they cook, exchange tips about restaurants and stores, and discuss recipes and techniques. This false sense of democratization maintains that anyone is entitled to claim some form of culinary expertise in communication and media, generating illusions of empowerment in a field of cultural and social action that is now at the forefront of public debates and private preoccupations. At the same time, food appeared in academic conversations as a legitimate object of study and research, as the development of food studies programs across the country indicates.

Scholars and authors have explored the ever-growing presence of food in media and the reasons behind it. In his seminal 1977 essay Alexander Cockburn introduced the expression "gastro porn," pointing to "curious parallels between manuals on sexual techniques and manuals on the preparation of food; the same studious emphasis on leisurely technique, the same apostrophes to the ultimate, heavenly delights. True gastro-porn heightens the excitement and also the sense of the unattainable by proffering colored photographs of various completed recipes."[10]

Molly O'Neill, exploring the concept of "food porn," associated food writing with "a world that exists almost exclusively in the imagination, the ambitions, and the nostalgic underpinnings of American culture."[11] Andrew Chan compared cooking shows to pornography as well, arguing that they arouse viewers' senses without any physical participation, messy food preparation, or annoying cleanup.[12] Pauline Adema interpreted food media as a form of surrogate pleasure and a response to the perception of time as a prized commodity, which increases the value of homemade meals. The irony is that viewers do not actually want to spend time cooking. For Adema, "a safer way to benefit from the comfort inherent in food is to increase consumption vicariously, by ingesting food television. . . . Food television is a way to consume food without consequence."[13]

Other scholars interpret many of the tensions and ambivalence surrounding food as related to anxiety: anxiety about otherness and difference; anxiety about the constitution and maintenance of national identity; anxiety about gender and sexuality; anxiety about racial and ethnic difference; anxiety about health and safety; and anxiety about body image and fatness, as overweight people are often stigmatized for a supposed laziness, lack of will, and scarce adherence to those physical ideals that mainstream culture has embraced as a symbol of its belief in personal choice and as a marker of social relevance.[14] For Signe Rousseau the consumption of food media constitutes a distraction from real life, providing solutions for widespread preoccupations with health, body image, and status that frequently coalesce around food. In this context celebrity chefs become authorities that relieve audiences from responsibilities, both private and social, and from uncomfortable choices.[15] We recognize an important relationship between this anxiety and the emergence of the food-film genre, where preoccupations around food itself as well as about issues of identity like race, class, gender, and sexuality can be played out through narratives about food and identity. Any discussion of food films and cultural citizenship must consider the relationship between food as beautiful, sexy, desirable, and even utopian and food as a possible source of anxiety, foregrounding issues of identity, consumption, and power. We acknowledge that viewers consume films in a variety of ways and for a wide range of purposes. While this ambivalence may not stand at the core of every viewer's experience, the connection between pervasive anxiety about food and the emergence of ever more food media, especially comforting, beautiful films, begs for deeper conversations.

The emergence of food films in American cinema has taken place precisely when representation of gender, sexuality, race, and ethnicity are rapidly changing on the silver screen. Susan Jeffords identified what she defined as the "remasculinization" of American men in mainstream media in the 1980s, which developed in response to feminism and positioned men as oppressed and therefore in need of social attention. This move pointed to a shift in the margin of power relationships that hid the actual social predominance of masculinity.[16] Similar analyses of mainstream masculinity emerged in film scholarship around this time.[17] At the same time as this debate about masculinity developed, representations of women and food tended to place women back in the kitchen. The United States witnessed a resurgence of conservative gender politics, a backlash against feminism that disguised itself in a progressive veneer.

It comes as no surprise that the eroticization of food should be coupled with the guilt that has traditionally accompanied sexuality in Western culture. More important, sexuality and eating are interwoven with each other in many of these films. Food, like sexuality, can be experienced "virtually" and vicariously through films, a seeming escape from the guilt and anxiety experienced with actual eating, actual bodies, actual identities, and actual social conflicts. Furthermore, food has acquired relevance as an important aspect of material and social life. These phenomena have developed as income inequalities are growing among Americans, increasing the disparity between haves and have-nots.[18] Food plays an enormous cultural and economic role in this context, allowing for greater distinction among consumers—affluent people are often involved in the establishment of alternative food networks that respond to their priorities but may not take into account equality, justice, and the need for political intervention to usher structural change in the food system. Similarly, food films provide a productive site of inquiry for issues related to race and ethnicity in the United States. Within this broader context, the increasing visibility of food in media and the growing success of food films need to be examined as a response to widespread anxieties and a confirmation of cultural capital for segments of the population that can claim full access to cultural citizenship.

A NEW FILM GENRE?

Do food films constitute a new genre? And, more generally, is the concept of genre useful to understanding these films? Film criticism has often employed genre as a way to identify a group of works that present a recognizable set of similar narrative elements, images, setting, mood, format, and relationship to the audience.[19] From this vantage point genres provide templates for the film industry and filmmakers, while at the same time creating expectations and interpretive grids for viewers.[20] In this sense genres constitute a powerful ideological weapon that instructs audiences in proper behaviors, including social and political beliefs.[21]

Theorists have debated the definition of genres, oscillating between considering them social conventions based on the accepted cultural consensus within audiences and defining them as elements that are specified in advance on the industry side.[22] In other words, as film scholar Robert Stam observed, the main question is whether genres really exist in the world or whether they are just the constructions of critics and theorists and, as a consequence, if the study of genres should be considered prescriptive or descriptive.[23] Other authors have used genre analysis to examine the movie industry's response to cultural changes.[24]

When it comes to defining food films, a study on food in Stanley Kubrick's work from 2001 distinguished between movies where food is used merely as a prop to enhance the realism of the action, the setting, or the characters, and movies where food plays a central role as a powerful symbolic cinematic element.[25] Several scholars have asserted that the more recent body of food films points to an emerging genre or subgenre.[26] In the edited volume *Reel Movies* Anne Bower identifies food's role as star in terms of camera attention, the specific settings (kitchens, dining rooms, restaurants, etc.), and the film's narrative arc, which represents "characters negotiating questions of identity, power, culture, class, spirituality, or relationship through food." Bower notes that the boundaries of what belongs and does not belong to the food film genre are subjective.[27] The genre is too recent to be sure if it will maintain itself over the years or if it will be transformed through a process of variation and invention.

Touching on the genre issue, film scholar Cynthia Baron points out the relevance of the way food is woven into the plot in terms of the order of scenes, time allotted to characters and story elements referring to food, narrative voice, general mood, and cinematic choices (editing, framing, camera movements, lighting, mise-en-scène).[28] In contrast, James Keller, when describing food films as a subgenre in *Food, Film, and Culture*, insists on narratives and images in which the filmmakers as chefs or artists "exploit the audience's visceral response to the imagery of food in a fashion similar to the manipulation of sex on screen."[29] Zimmerman and Weiss, in *Food in the Movies*, organize the book around themes and categories such as belly laughs, killer meals, food for thought, and romantic and unromantic meals. In the last chapter, "Visual Feast," they acknowledge the presence of something that could be defined as a "food genre."[30]

Contemporary genre theory has expanded the study of film genres beyond the text-driven analysis of similarities to think about the relationship of audiences to the production and marketing of films. Drawing on neogenre scholarship based on the work of Rick Altman and Stephen Neale, we include the films' production and reception configurations as distinctive elements of a genre.[31] First, our concept of the food-film genre responds to film critics' and viewers' groupings of and responses to these movies. A number of examples serve to illustrate this point. Customers on websites like Amazon.com create lists of their favorite food films, thus helping to articulate which films belong to the food-film genre. Similarly, as we have already noted, professional film critics deploy the term *food film* to discuss this body of movies.

Even when they do not explicitly use this expression, film critics and online listserv participants group certain films and compare them to each other. Roger Ebert's comments on *Big Night* exemplify this tendency: "I was reminded of other movies where food suggests the possibility of an ideal state: 'Like Water for Chocolate,' 'Babette's Feast,' and 'Tampopo' in which the whole universe is reflected in a perfect bowl of noodle soup."[32] Some critics have alluded to the niche audiences attracted to food films, often implying an overlap with the art-house movie crowd. The *Los Angeles Times* wrote, "Featuring a pair of competing Italian restaurants, 'Big Night,' like 'Babette's Feast,' 'Like Water for Chocolate' and 'Eat Drink Man Woman' before it, capitalized on the increasing overlap between the audiences for independent films and sophisticated restaurants."[33] Repeatedly, reviewers of *Big Night*, *Eat Drink Man Woman*, and later films such as *Woman on Top* (Torres, 2000), and *Chocolat* (Hallström, 2000) compared and contrasted these films with other members of the food-film family, further developing the perception of an emerging, autonomous genre. An example from the *San Francisco Chronicle* illustrates this trend: "'Big Night' is both a delightful story and a great food movie that ranks with 'Like Water for Chocolate' or 'Babette's Feast.'"[34] Reviews of *Julie & Julia* consistently compared the film to *Babette's Feast*, *Eat Drink Man Woman*, *Big Night*, and other food films.[35] As these films grew in popularity and visibility within the fragmented landscape of popular culture, the industry increasingly aligned these films with each other and referred to them as food films. Furthermore, although this book focuses mainly on U.S. productions, it is important to recognize that from the beginning, the genre developed globally, with authors, critics, and viewers constantly referring to films from different origins.

We can now attempt to identify the elements that seem to lead both critics and consumers to consider a movie a food film. First of all, food tends to function as a driving force in the films' narrative structures. It connects the characters with each other and often emerges as a character itself. The protagonists are often domestic or professional chefs or at least individuals with strong connections to food and cooking. The camera spends a great deal of time focusing on images of strikingly beautiful food, which takes center stage, bolstered by elements in the mise-en-scène. Frequent food close-ups, ornamented and sensual, display the visual "food porn" style we mentioned earlier. This visual style has become so commonplace that an episode of celebrity chef and author Anthony Bourdain's TV show *No Reservations* entitled "Food Porn" aired in November 2009. The episode satirizes tropes that have come to dominate the way we see food in mainstream media since the early 1990s: extreme close-ups, amplified sounds, and fetishistic attention to glistening and textured ingredients.[36] As Frederick Kaufman observed in his conversation with porn still photographer Barbara Nitke, from a technical point of view food and porn representatios do seem to have recourse to the same bag of tricks in terms of engagement of the viewers, shots, lighting, and sound. (fig. 0.2).[37]

FIGURE 0.2 *Babette's Feast* is one of the first films in which the filmmaker used food shots, lighting, and editing solutions that would later become mainstays in culinary representations across different forms of media.

Cooking scenes have developed a clear visual language with recognizable shots, from the ingredient detail to highlight its material qualities to the handheld shots that glorify dexterity and skills, moving to larger shots that include table, instruments, and dishes, as well as the face of the cooking character, all the way to wide shots that reveal the cooking environment and the interaction with other characters. Editing can vary from meditative, slow takes to frantic rhythm, depending on the intention of the camera artist.

Through these techniques food is sexualized and intertwined with desire, frequently functioning as a vehicle for experiencing a utopian state of bliss, pleasure, and contentment. Food and eating are narrative agents that instigate key turning points that frequently occur in the context of a large, elaborate meal served to characters in the film. Food is the means through which conflict and resolution transpire. While these films share important similarities with each other, their generic conventions overlap with other (sub)genres, particularly the romantic comedy. Even though we consider these films part of a group, we acknowledge their differences as much as we consider their similarities.

The use of the term *food film* is appropriate in yet another sense. A number of movies like *Simply Irresistible* (Tarlov, 1999), *Woman on Top*, and *Chocolat* build on earlier films, including *Babette's Feast* and *Like Water for Chocolate*, referencing them in a variety of ways and placing already existing narrative and visual elements in new plots. These connections reveal themselves in the films' reception and in the context of their production and distribution. Video/DVD covers, inserts, trailers, and publicity campaigns frequently reference earlier food films, aligning themselves with the genre. Moreover, the diffusion of digital media has allowed an even greater global diffusion of films among audiences in very disparate contexts, often through piracy and illegal downloading. This phenomenon begs the questions of how viewers from diverse geographical locations and cultural backgrounds may interpret and react to food films from different countries. This is an important topic for further research, which goes beyond the scope of this book but should take into consideration the development of a cosmopolitan community of "foodies" that exchange information and ideas through travel and social media.

FOOD, FILM, AND THE VIEWER'S BODY

As food increasingly functions as a sign and symbol for numerous and different kinds of meanings, it becomes all the more compelling to critically evaluate how narratives condition the consumption of food and how food conditions the consumption of media. Mediated narratives of food are especially important objects of analysis because they provide insight into food's signifying power, the interconnected and interdependent pleasure of consuming food via media, and the commercialization of basic necessities. Representations of food have emerged across a wide variety of media, and U.S. food media have a profound influence not only in the States but also all over the world. As such, they play a crucial role in the constitution of the global *foodscape*, that is to say the totality of representations, values, and practices that underline the spatial nature of foodways as seen through the eyes of those who inhabit that specific environment.[38] These mediated representations are interconnected, mutually influencing and engaging in dialogue with each other. Film, television, advertising, cooking magazines, websites, and blogs participate in the broader landscape that constitutes food discourse and interact with practices and behaviors. Although this book focuses specifically on films, it carefully considers the larger tapestry of media culture and the place that film holds within it.

There is still work to be done on the specific processes of how cinema creates meaning and contributes to the formation of identity through food. For instance, what processes of identification with characters and objects are activated in the viewer when food is involved in cinematic action? Eating is a truly universal activity, and its emotional and cultural power is enormous; food is able to elicit visceral reactions and strong feelings. Does the recognition of food and actions related to it help viewers to identify with the characters and events they see on the screen, making the movie experience more intense? As early as the 1930s, Walter Benjamin had discussed in the essay "The Mimetic Faculty" the physical and almost tactile nature of cinema, which he defined as "a sensuous and bodily form of perception."[39] But for decades, under the influence of structuralism and psychoanalysis, film theory demonstrated little interest in the spectator's body and its reactions, often writing them off as a metaphorical expression and focusing rather on their cognitive aspects. It is within the feminist critique to the psychoanalytic approach that we find one of the first calls to put the body back into the theoretical reflection about movies. In her 1981 essay "Film Bodies: Gender, Genre, and Excess" Linda Williams defined horror, porn, and melodrama as "body genres," focusing on violence, sex, and emotion, which provide physical jolts and "sensations that are on the verge of respectable."[40] Williams wondered whether the body of the spectator is caught in an almost involuntary mimicry of the emotions and sensations shown by the body on the screen when exposed to these "body genres." Since the early 1990s, a reflection about the body's participation in the movie-watching experience has developed in film and media theory, reinforcing academia's growing interest in embodiment.[41]

Among others, Vivian Sobchack has offered a very stimulating new approach to the issue, analyzing the experience of what she refers to as "the kinesthetic subject," whose senses are blurred. "At the movies our vision and hearing are informed and given meaning by our other modes of sensory access to the world: our capacity not only to see and to hear but also to touch, to smell, to taste, and always to proprioceptively feel our weight, dimension, gravity, and movement in the world. In sum, the film experience is meaningful *not to the side of our bodies but because of our bodies*. Which is to say that movies provoke in us the 'carnal thoughts' that ground and inform a more conscious analysis."[42] Interestingly, in her reflection Sobchack does refer to food films such as *Tampopo, Babette's Feast*, and *Like Water for Chocolate*.

Do similar dynamics take place with these so-called food movies? And how do food-related scenes influence receptions of movies that do not necessarily focus on food? In *Food, Film, and Culture* James Keller argues that "the cinematic hunger artists manipulate gustatory imagery in order to increase the sensory response of the film audience to a medium that cannot access smell or taste, but, nevertheless, seeks to create a full sensory response to a strictly visual and auditory medium. Food cinema thus invokes the gustatory appetite in a fashion similar to the arousal of the libido through romantic and sexual imagery, accessing the full sensory experience of the actor and, subsequently and vicariously, of the audience."[43] Keller, however, seems to condemn food images when they are purely a ruse used by film-makers to increase the spectators' involvement through the excitement of their appetites, which will not be physically satisfied.

What Keller fails to account for is the possibility that food can actually be consumed visually and that this constitutes an act of ingestion that shapes and conditions our sense of taste alongside the actual food we consume. By its very title, *Feasting Our Eyes* suggests that we can no longer think of the virtual and actual consumption of food as totally separate. Our enjoyment of food images in film makes us hungry for "real food," just as "real food" makes us hunger for mediated images of food. When we feast our eyes, we feast.

FOOD FILMS, IDENTITY POLITICS, AND CULTURAL CITIZENSHIP

Why does food resonate so deeply with filmmakers and audiences? Is it just a reflection of the desire for food as a source of nourishment and pleasure, or does it tap into deeper currents of contemporary life? At the hinge of the biological, the emotional, and the social, food crosses boundaries of many sorts as its preparation and consumption are not just material practices but rather are always invested in and influenced by meaning that individuals and communities attribute to objects and acts.

In particular, food shapes and is shaped by cultural hierarchies and power structures, providing insights into marginalization and disenfranchisement. For centuries conspicuous consumption of food has been used to display wealth and worldliness, by marking clear distinctions between haves and have-nots. Food production and preparation played an important role in marking class, racial, ethnic, and gender identities. At the same time, communities all over the world identify themselves not only based on what they eat but on how different what they eat is from what their neighbors consume. For these reasons food is an important site to explore how cultures debate about citizenship. This is of particular interest in the concept of how we shape cultural citizenship, the kind of citizenship that appears in everyday life in the consumption of goods and services, including leisure activities and entertainment.[44] The concept of cultural citizenship stresses that culture is central to our participation in society, and it reminds us that citizenship is much more than voting (political citizenship) or purchasing goods (economic citizenship).[45]

Classical definitions of citizenship divorce the concept of the citizen from the consumer, positing citizenship as exclusively political. In his analysis of different definitions of cultural citizenship, social scientist Toby Miller concludes that commodities themselves have become central to the process of constructing cultural citizenship, with "good taste" functioning as an arbiter of who can claim cultural, political, and economic belonging.[46] Cultural citizenship moves beyond formal and abstract concepts of equality to achieve recognition and empowerment of segments of the populations perceived as different. In other words, in an increasingly multicultural nation the question of who belongs and who does not is built on the complex connections among political rights, economic power, social relationships, and cultural practices. To remove the issue of culture and consumption from citizenship is to ignore the ritualized practices that constitute our quotidian, mundane, and often unconscious acts of belonging.

Whereas policy scholars have traditionally separated citizenship from entertainment, our analysis aligns with those who affirm the centrality of culture and everyday life to citizenship. In their work on new media and civic engagement Jean Burgess, Markus Foth, and Helen Klaebe write, "Bona fide citizenship is practiced as much through everyday life, leisure, critical consumption, and popular entertainment as it is through debate and engagement with capital 'P' politics."[47] They draw on recent feminist scholarship to argue that commercial culture and everyday practices are as "constitutive of cultural citizenship for particular social identity groups as are the spaces of formal politics."[48] Indeed, the exclusion of entertainment, pleasure, and everyday life from concepts of citizenship loses sight of some of the most powerful pathways of citizenship engagement.[49] From this perspective, studying the intersection of food and media becomes especially important because it provides insight into both ritualized daily practices and commercially based popular entertainment industries. Food, with the practices that surround it and its complex symbolic meanings, plays an important role in helping to define cultural citizenship.

In the United States, as across the globe, the production, distribution, and consumption of food have shifted dramatically over the past century. While food overproduction is a normal occurrence in the States, many struggle to put food on their tables, and even obese individuals are often malnourished. Hundreds of new food products enter the market each year, many geared toward weight loss. Mainstream American culture obsesses about fat, carbohydrates, gluten, food safety, and genetically altered foods. Public policy efforts to stem childhood obesity, diabetes, and other food-related illnesses have increased, and alternatives to established systems are identified in the switch to local, organic, or artisanal products. But the cost of high-calorie, low-nutrient foods is significantly lower than healthier foods, which makes them appealing to middle- and low-income families who have seen their living wages diminish over time and often are considered objects, rather than subjects, of policies, marketing, and educational efforts.[50] At the same time, representations of food in different forms of media narrate, provoke, tone down, reinforce, and disrupt this paradoxical relationship to a basic necessity.

The purchase and consumption of goods has turned into a driving force for the formation of individual, group, and national identities in U.S. society, through the embracing of lifestyles that are more and more personalized. As consumers define themselves increasingly by what they buy, they enjoy the illusion that they are making choices for themselves by expressing their own taste and personality even when the available options are predetermined and prepackaged by marketing and production constraints. Elspeth Probyn describes this shift in consumption as the emergence of "choiceoisie," and she attaches this concept to women, in particular, emphasizing that the idea that women often receive social validation for their consumption choices based supposedly on individual motives rather than on economic or social pressures.[51] We broaden this term to think about consumption in general in the United States. *Choiceoisie* means that we can determine what our new car will look like by selecting options and styles, but unless we are able to afford huge sums, our choices are limited by what carmakers actually offer. Similarly, individuals, families, and even communities might want to express their personal and political beliefs through food preferences and purchases, opting for local, organic, artisanal, sustainable, and other kinds of food that, despite being more expensive, are perceived as better for one's health, for the environment, and for society as a whole.

The popularity and success of food films appears intrinsically linked to their ability to present material that challenges cultural norms while also adhering to what Raymond Williams refers to as "emergent culture," by which he means, "first, that new meanings and values, new practices, new significances and experiences, are continually being created. But there is then a much earlier attempt to incorporate them, just because they are part—and yet not a defined part—of effective contemporary practice. Indeed it is significant in our own period how very early this attempt is, how alert the dominant culture now is to anything that can be seen as emergent."[52] The food films we examine navigate between what Williams calls "effective dominant culture" and "oppositional culture."[53] They provide a sense of how this negotiation operates within the parameters of mainstream tastes and values. In this sense the films allow for a certain degree of potentially empowering diverse readings, readings that, however, to a large extent reaffirm effective dominant culture. The power and creativity of the individual to create meanings of one's own, to which, some would argue, media texts open themselves, is overshadowed by ideological elements in the film that affirm mainstream, dominant culture.[54]

Focusing on food films provides a close look at how one type of media functions in relationship to citizenship, multiculturalism, globalization, and dominance. On the surface food films seem to embrace progressive politics and the goals of liberal multiculturalism. They often feature families from diverse ethnic groups, present gay and lesbian characters, introduce unusual male figures, and represent women as chefs in professional kitchens. Yet focusing on representation is not enough. It is necessary to examine the industry that produces the movies and the context in which they acquire their cultural meaning. It is precisely this move that enables a deeper understanding of how food films, identity, and cultural citizenship are linked to each other.

Food films, like advertising and television, have become part of the terrain that determines how food is consumed, what meanings this consumption carries, and how consumption both produces and reflects the formation of identity. While they might appear apolitical, food narratives perform, critique, and establish dominant cultural and social attitudes about citizenship, especially as these relate to the debates on diversity, multiculturalism, and marginalization in the United States. The physical necessity to eat assumes a cultural dimension that, in its seeming naturalness and normality, appears to provide stable meanings and acceptable social practices. Food can offer a privileged point of view to look at the way various models of gender, race, ethnicity, identity, community, trade networks, economic interests, and political alliances are created, negotiated, questioned, and, sometimes, eliminated in the global network of mass media.

Food films embody many of the same contradictions that form the basis of liberal multiculturalist ideologies, and they enact tensions fought out in the culture wars in the 1990s by taking up potent political debates only to tame them. Furthermore, these films enhance the marketability of difference by participating in what Canadian scholar Deborah Root describes as a "cannibal culture" that appropriates and commodifies otherness.[55]

We already see this tension in the consumption of food, but these debates manifest themselves even more clearly in the formation of narratives about food by avoiding straightforward conversations about the political and economic nature of culture. If food itself becomes a commodity fetish, then media about food amplifies this tendency. Our analysis seeks to understand the degree to which American food films establish a fixed sense of "we" or "us" despite their attempts to celebrate diversity. The films tend to affirm corporate multiculturalism and advance a watered-down, depoliticized version of feminism that ultimately undermines pluralism and privileges assimilation. Grounded in whiteness, heterosexuality, Euro- or American-centric, and middle-class values, food films provide a remarkable space for studying how the debate about citizenship and belonging is articulated in popular culture.

THE TOOL KIT AND THE MENU

In this book we consider food films as part and parcel of the larger context of mainstream U.S. media and food cultures. Furthermore, we draw connections between food films and other manifestations in popular culture, such as popular television chef programs. We shed light on the films themselves, while furthering the discussion of film as part of a larger cultural landscape. Although the book focuses on the U.S. production, frequent references to films from different origins and their impact are inevitable, as the food-film genre has developed, since its inception, in a globalized fashion. Films provide representations within a media culture that offers the possibility of producing multiple, diverse meanings. Yet this same media culture often absorbs what seem to be individual interpretations and choices into the framework of mass production and consumption. Looking at reviews of the films by critics and at Internet discussions, we acknowledge that they can be interpreted in various ways and generate apparently unrelated readings. We connect the assertions that individuals make about these films to close textual analyses of the films themselves and look to the mass marketing of these films to determine how the media industry positions them to encourage further consumption. As an interdisciplinary project, the analyses of the films, their marketing, and their treatment in the United States draws on fields as diverse as food studies, cultural studies, media criticism, film theory, critical theory, and feminist psychoanalysis, as well as sociological and anthropological studies. We believe that this approach enables us to approach this body of films from a richer, more nuanced perspective than a singular discipline-based focus would allow.

Our methods include filmic analysis that draws on ideological criticism, together with textual and contextual investigation of these films. In other words we look closely at the content (narratives, stories, character development) and at the formal elements of the movies themselves (visual style, shots, framing, editing, lighting, sound), while simultaneously assessing the meaning these elements acquire in the wider context in which the movies were produced, released, and consumed. Additionally, we study the films' relationships with other forms of food media (television, advertising, websites, video games, newspapers), food performances, and food marketing through an analysis of discourses of national identity, sexuality, race, ethnicity, social class, and gender. Analysis of the film and media industry informed by theories of political economy guide our investigation of the films' production and distribution histories. We also examine the audience and film critic responses to the films through the analysis of film reviews, websites, and blogs. Throughout the book we focus on hypothetical spectators who do not read the films "against the grain" but rather who consume these films in alignment with the films' preferred readings, as embedded in the narrative and in the visual material themselves.

As we occupy the dual positions of consumer and critic of food films, our goal is to explore the viewing pleasure alongside the political, social, and economic stakes inherent in that very pleasure. Our overarching assumption is that we feast our eyes on the visual medium of food films with consequences for the production of cultural belonging and marginalization. What these films express about food and identity is as significant as what they *fail* to represent. For this reason we have dedicated each chapter to a specific aspect of these debates about the meaning of cultural citizenship and belonging in the United States. This book is organized to highlight a particular aspect of identity in each chapter, honing in on specific groups of films that cluster around these respective aspects.

This means that films that feature female chefs in a leading role, for example, are grouped in one chapter, while films about lead male chefs in domestic roles are discussed together in another. This analytical strategy enables us to move across a large body of films, but it also mirrors how audiences group the films in their online communications and how reviewers reference the films. We recognize that this poses both challenges and opportunities. Organizing the book according to chapters that focus on distinct issues of identity as a primary focus enables us to group the films in a meaningful, structured way, but these groupings may emphasize one marker of identity over others at times and forgo a more intense analysis of how diverse markers of identity interact. This choice reflects our commitment to ensuring that this book is accessible to readers who come from a range of disciplinary backgrounds.

While the chapters respectively prioritize a focal lens, they do so in such a way that highlights what cultural critics refer to as the "intersectionality" of different markers of identity. Feminist scholars have long pointed to the idea that combined markers of identity operate differently together than alone. Combined markers of identity are often greater in their ability to marginalize and disempower people. Here, the whole has a more profound impact than simply as the sum of individual parts. Being African American *and* female *and* disabled produces a different experience of marginalization than, for example, being white and female and disabled does. Elizabeth Spelman wrote that, in the case of women's issues and feminist theory, "the problem has been how we weigh what we have in common against what differentiates us." The difficulty, she continues, is "how feminist theory has confused the condition of one group of women with the condition of all."[56] But simply adding up different markers of identity eclipses how these very markers interact and influence people's lived experiences. Spellman describes this as the "ampersand problem in feminist thought" that "can work against an understanding of the relations between gender and other elements of identity."[57] Gloria Anzaldúa summarizes this problem beautifully when she defines identity as a process rather than a set of markers: "Identity is not a bunch of little cubby holes stuffed respectively with intellect, sex, race, class, vocation, gender. Identity flows between, over, aspects of a person."[58] We are committed to understanding how intersectionality functions as a process of how "social inequalities are formed and maintained," as Patrick Grzanka stresses. Like Grzanka, we see identities as "the *products* of historically entrenched, institutional systems of domination and violence," and understanding how these intersecting aspects of identity are "organized around and coproduce social identity categories" aligns with our commitment to linking food, film, and cultural identity.[59] Although we highlight specific aspects of identity and treat these films in analytical clusters, we do so in such a way that calls attention to various intersections that complicate representations, always striving to move beyond more simplistic analyses toward more nuanced, complex ones.

Chapter 1, "Food Films and Consumption: Selling *Big Night*," focuses on restaurants as one of the key spaces in contemporary global food culture that have recently acquired increasing media visibility and relevance in the practices and imaginaries of educated consumers, allowing them to convey their identities in terms of cultural capital, connoisseurship, and cosmopolitanism. In food films restaurants also appear as places where chefs express their skills and creativity, in constant negotiations with their customers' preferences, media pressure, and business priorities. These new arenas of social and economic performances appear as suitable spaces for professionals to achieve cultural and economic citizenship through success in food business, which nevertheless requires different engagements and efforts based on class, ethnicity, and gender.

Big Night and other movies that focus on restaurants and chefs, like *Dinner Rush* (Giraldi, 2000), *Waiting* (McKittrick, 2005), *Today's Special* (Kaplan, 2009), *The Hundred-Foot Journey* (Hallström, 2014), and *Chef* (Favreau, 2014), seem to assume a critical point of view vis-à-vis mainstream U.S. food culture, revealing the tensions, contradictions, and inequalities in food business. But their distribution and self-representation through marketing reiterate the stereotypes the films appear to target. By focusing on restaurants and the chefs that command them, while playing with the gender, class, and ethnic identities of the protagonists, as well as their social status, food films help to construct notions of good taste and citizenship while defining educated consumers by appealing to their sense of cultural capital.

Whereas the protagonists discussed in the first chapter are all male, suggesting a strong connection between gender, determination, professionalism, and success in business, the second chapter, "Autonomy in the Kitchen? Food Films and Postfeminism," considers the relationship between women and food, both in professional and domestic environments. Cooking is presented as a way for women to assert themselves and their independence, while at the same time allowing unconventional negotiations of gender, class, and race with their environment. *Fried Green Tomatoes* (Avnet, 1999), *No Reservations* (Hicks, 2007) and its German predecessor *Mostly Martha* (Nettelbeck, 2001), *Waitress* (Shelly, 2007), *The Ramen Girl* (Ackerman, 2008), and *Julie & Julia* (Ephron, 2009) present the lead (white) female characters as powerful and autonomous, but the films collectively work to undermine the characters' political agency at the expense of their ability to function in the kitchen. As such, they tend to privilege a heterosexist perspective and elevate white characters over characters of color. The chapter also refers to box-office hits like *It's Complicated* (Meyers, 2009) and *Eat Pray Love* (Murphy, 2010) as a background to the discussion. Although these are not strictly food films, they highlight elements in the cultural debate about women and food that shed light on the main topic of the chapter.

Not only professional skills can lead women to cook well and achieve success. At times, magic and mysterious powers contribute as well. Because so many food films feature women, we split these films into two categories: films with and films without magical elements. These films operate in many ways on similar premises, but there are also noticeable differences. The films in chapter 3, "Magical Food, Luscious Bodies," configure the magic qualities of food as an extension of the bodies of the women—often exotic—who prepare food. In fact, these movies often embrace an approach that takes inspiration from the literary style of magic realism, where women metaphorically become food, often thrown away or in need of management because of their unruly nature. This chapter, which includes an analysis of *Simply Irresistible*, *Woman on Top*, *The Mistress of Spices* (Berges, 2004), and *Chocolat* (Hallström, 2000), illustrates how food becomes fetishized, gendered, and racialized in Hollywood films in much the same way that women's bodies have been treated by mainstream U.S. media. Food is often feminized in mainstream food media, and the configuration of food as magical, via the extension of the female—and often nonwhite—bodies that prepare it, underlines the pornographic potential of food imagery.

Just like women at times develop complicated relationships with food, so do men, especially those whose physical appearances or life situations set them apart from the mainstream. The fourth chapter, "Culinary Comfort: The Satiating Construction of Masculinity," explores unusual—and often culturally problematic—models of masculinity and their relationship to food, taking into consideration male characters as nurturers and caretakers in both the private and the public sphere. The analysis considers how these films operate in seeming opposition to films that tend to use food unobtrusively to reinforce dominant models of masculinity. Under close examination movies such as *What's Eating Gilbert Grape* (Hallström, 1993), *Heavy* (Mangold, 1995), *Eat Your Heart Out* (Adlon, 1997), and later *Spanglish* and *Sideways* (Payne, 2004) reveal that these seemingly different and innovative images reiterate mainstream forms of manhood and thus reinforce gender hierarchies. Ang Lee's *The Wedding Banquet* (1993) and *Eat Drink Man Woman*, though not from the United States, provide the necessary background to the discussion about the relationship among men, cooking, and masculinity.

These dynamics are not set once and for all but are the result of interactions, life events, and social pressures since boyhood, a time when young men find themselves negotiating between their needs and desires, on one hand, and adults' expectations, on the other. The fifth chapter, "When Weirdos Stir the Pot: Cooking Identity in Animated Movies," explores recent animated films that embrace the idea that belonging to a community does not require conformity to social expectations but rather builds on the protagonist's individuality and seeming queerness. In box-office hits like *Ratatouille* (Bird and Pinkava, 2007), *Kung Fu Panda* (Osborn and Stevenson, 2008), and *Cloudy with a Chance of Meatballs* (Lord and Miller, 2009), and in the lesser known *Bee Movie* (Hickner and Smith. 2007), *The Tale of Despereaux* (Fell and Stevenhagen, 2008), character development connects closely with food, which becomes the instrument of the heroes' redemption even when it would initially appear to be the very cause of their social isolation. This raises a question: what models of acceptable adulthood—in terms of gender, class, ethnicity, and body image—does the interaction with food present to viewers, in particular children, who are arguably among the main marketing targets of these productions? Although cooking is still often culturally framed as an element of the domestic and feminine sphere, in these films food is not domestic or related to care work, and as such it appears as more culturally acceptable for males. Even common dishes like noodles, meatballs, and vegetables allow the protagonists to assert themselves as extraordinary in very public, professional, and inherently masculine ways.

The last chapter, "Consuming the Other: Food Films as Culinary Tourism," shifts its primary focus to the analysis of food films that invite audiences to visit the homes of ethnic others as vicarious tourists. *The Joy Luck Club* (Wang, 1993), *Soul Food* (Tillman, 1997), *Tortilla Soup* (Ripoll, 2001), *What's Cooking?* (Chadha, 2000), and *My Big Fat Greek Wedding* (Zwick, 2002) operate as forms of mediated culinary tourism. Whereas the previous chapters focus predominantly on the ambivalent representations and treatment of femininity and masculinity, this chapter suggests that mainstream food films carefully appeal to the ethnic groups they represent while offering them as object of culinary tourism of mainstream white audiences through the presentation of familiar—although vaguely exotic—food. The films provide an unstable means of educating audiences about the foodways of different ethnic groups in the United States, as they reiterate stereotypes and lace ethnicity with expectations and biases, also in terms of gender and class.

The conclusion considers food films within the broader context of representations of food and points to a newer body of documentary and docufiction food films, as well as fictional films, that approach the intersection of food, cultural citizenship, and identity from significantly different vantage points. In many ways these works respond to and critique the collective body of narrative food films. Films include works as diverse as *Fast Food Nation* (Linklater, 2006), *Super Size Me* (Spurlock, 2004), *Food, Inc.* (Kenner, 2008), *Jiro Dreams of Sushi* (Gelb, 2011), and *McFarland, USA* (Caro, 2015). Unlike the other films examined throughout the book, they put food at the center of social and political debates that tend to appear in the background or are ignored in other media.

Feasting Our Eyes hopes to add to growing debates, both in academia and in civil society, about the connections among consumption, food, and media culture in the United States. Through the analysis of a genre like the food film, this book strives to illustrate that social, economic, and political circumstances determine how U.S. culture uses various strategies to demarcate identity. Through gender, race, ethnicity, sexuality, or class, and the complex combinations of these, food films position individuals and communities within ideas and practices related to citizenship and participation in public life. This positioning matters, as our seemingly innocuous consumption of food media plays a subtle, albeit important, role in helping to craft who belongs, who has voice, and who has opportunities. Our food choices and what we think of them are far from random: power does infuse what we eat and watch. And now, let's feast our eyes.

FOOD FILMS AND CONSUMPTION

Selling *Big Night*

A chef in his whites sprinkles some chopped fresh herbs on two dishes that a man, sharply dressed in suit and tie, is holding for him to inspect. Viewers soon learn they are brothers, Primo and Secondo (first and second, in Italian), and that they are not American-born. "Yes . . . go!" says the chef, Primo, while Secondo rolls his eyes, his body language revealing his impatience. The doors open and Secondo brings the food to a couple sitting in an almost empty dining room. "Thank God! I am so hungry," exclaims the woman, a cigarette in her mouth. "That looks good! You've got leaves with yours," she adds, observing the fresh basil on her companion's pasta dish. She looks inquisitively to the food Secondo is serving her (fig. 1.1). "Monsieur, is this what I ordered?" "Yes, it is risotto, a special recipe my brother and I bring from Italy," he answers, while the camera cuts to another customer who is eating alone, observing the scene with an air of detached curiosity.

"It took so long I thought you went back to Italy to get it," retorts the woman. During the waiter's canonical offer for pepper and cheese, she keeps on pushing the rice around the dish, eventually inquiring: "Excuse me, didn't you say this would be rice with seafood?" While grating cheese on the man's pasta, Secondo responds: "Yes, it is Italian Arborio rice, the best, with shrimp, and scallop." The conversation soon turns uncomfortable. "I don't see anything that looks like a shrimp or a scallop. I mean, it's just not what I expected. . . . But I do get a side

FIGURE 1.1 A core theme of *Big Night* is the clash between the culinary traditions of two Italian immigrants and the expectations of their American patrons about what Italian food should be.

order of spaghetti with this, right? I thought all main dishes come with spaghetti." "Some yes, but you see . . . risotto is a rice, so it's starch, and it doesn't go really with pasta." At this point the man intervenes: "Honey, order a side of spaghetti, that's all, and I'll eat your meatballs." "Yes, he'll have the meatballs." "Well, the spaghetti comes without meatballs," explains Secondo. As she rolls her eyes, she drops her fork and asks: "There are no meatballs with the spaghetti?" Secondo, visibly uncomfortable, comments: "No, sometimes spaghetti likes to be alone." "Then I guess we will also have a side of meatballs," she answers, clearly annoyed, while the other customer turns to look at the scene. Eventually giving up on the meatballs, she settles on a side of spaghetti. The dining room has quickly turned into a space where different culinary cultures clash.

The camera cuts back to Primo in the kitchen. "I want to know who is it for!" he declares. When Secondo tells him it is for the lady eating the risotto, he assumes an outraged expression of disbelief and disdain. "What? Why?" "I don't know, she likes starches, come on!" "Bitch!" Primo shouts. "Who are these people in America? I need to talk to her." "Please, what are you going to do? Tell the customer what she can eat? That is what she wants," states Secondo, always straddling the two worlds. "This is what the customer asks for. Make it, make the pasta." "How can she want? They both are starch. Maybe I should make mashed potatoes for on the other side." After Primo declares her to be a "criminal" and a "philistine" and insists on talking with her, Secondo pushes open the swinging door between the kitchen and the restaurant, daring him to confront the customer. Primo stands helpless in the kitchen as his almost-assimilated brother returns into the restaurant to declare that the pasta is on its way. Primo grabs a pot, just to throw it against the wall, expressing all his frustration.

The tensions between a chef's culinary expertise and his determination to assert his vision, on one hand, and the vagaries of the restaurant business, customers' preferences, and the clashes of cultural capital, on the other, loom large in this famous scene from *Big Night*, one of the first food films produced in the United States, released in the second half of the 1990s. Codirected by Stanley Tucci (who also cowrote the screenplay and stars in the film) and Campbell Scott (who makes a cameo appearance), and set on the Jersey Shore in the 1950s, *Big Night* tells the story of two Italian immigrants who struggle to realize their personal take on the American dream. Brothers Primo (Tony Shalhoub) and Secondo (Stanley Tucci) have opened an Italian restaurant called "The Paradise." Primo is a brilliant, temperamental chef who refuses to alter his cuisine to fit the American palate and cater to what he considers to be tasteless New World preferences. Secondo, on the other hand, tries desperately to function as a liaison between the customers that embody the American life to which he is acculturating, and his brother's artful cooking. The restaurant is slowly failing. Clientele wanes, while Pascal (Ian Holm), the successful, bombastic, and opportunistic entrepreneur down the street, is drawing in enormous crowds with his mediocre but flashy Italian American food.

When Pascal plants the idea into Secondo's head that Louis Prima, the famous jazz singer, would come to a "big night dinner" at the brothers' restaurant, Secondo and Primo proceed to create the meal of a lifetime, a culinary masterpiece. Prima never shows up, and Pascal is forced by his wife, Gabriella (Secondo's lover, played by Isabella Rossellini), to disclose the fact that he has manipulated the brothers into failure so that they will come to work for him. The debacle pushes the brothers to a fist fight, which ends with Primo proclaiming, "This place is eating us alive." The narrative resists closure, only subtly suggesting that the unstoppable dynamics of capitalism will devour Primo and Secondo, forcing them either to work for someone like Pascal or to return to Italy.

We have described this restaurant scene in detail because it effectively summarizes the main theme of *Big Night*, while also setting the stage for a trend that emerges in food films in the United States: the tension between adherence to one's cultural heritage, in this case of traditional Italian cuisine, and pressure to commodify it to appeal to dominant tastes and commercial priorities. We recognize these dynamics in many of the films we discuss in this book when ethnic or racially diverse chefs or food professionals—both male and female—try to assert themselves in the U.S. foodscape, where business forces, media, and consumers often feel entitled to produce their own definition of what the "authentic" foreign cuisine is supposed to be. By observing how Americans behave in a restaurant that is proposed as an authentic Old World space, *Big Night* offers a critique of consumers who display ignorance of the complexities of foreign cultures, while positioning itself as a venue through which discriminating viewers can participate in the "real" gastronomy from Italy, presented as a land that values art and refinement above business. The film also identifies the restaurant as a crucial location for customers, chefs, and staff to negotiate their cultural identity as U.S. citizens from the vantage point of class, gender, and age.

In this chapter we explore restaurants in food films. Restaurants have come to function as key spaces in contemporary food culture. Increasingly, restaurants have acquired media visibility and relevance across a range of U.S. media. We need only point to the many television shows that feature restaurants and restaurant chefs: *Diners, Drive-ins and Dives*; *Man vs. Food*; *Food Paradise*; *Eat Street*; *Unique Eats*; *Restaurant Impossible*; and so many more. Given the obvious relationship of food to restaurants, it comes as no surprise that restaurants appear as important spaces in these films. Through the lens of cultural citizenship, we seek to understand how restaurants shape relationships, experiences, and identity in these films. Frequently, the main characters in food films focused specifically on restaurants are male. How do male professionals achieve cultural and economic citizenship through success (or failure) in food businesses? Where and how do issues of gender intersect with ethnicity, race, class, and sexuality? What does the commercialization of restaurant culture say about cultural capital, connoisseurship, and cosmopolitanism? Throughout this chapter we search for the tensions, contradictions, and inequalities that emerge, often behind the scenes, in these narratives and seek to understand how this complex mixture of identity traits helps to construct notions of good taste and citizenship, while defining what it means to be an educated consumer.

BIG NIGHT AS CULTURAL CRITICISM OF FOOD AND MEDIA

Big Night establishes a clear hierarchy between traditional and seemingly authentic food prepared by an Italian chef and the American customers' culinary habits. This distinction seems to demand discernment, expertise, and good taste on the part of consumers and differentiates knowledgeable cosmopolitanism from the behavior of Primo and Secondo's uncouth table guests, who appear to prefer uninteresting and supposedly bastardized fodder. By so doing, *Big Night* implicitly fails to acknowledge Italian American cuisine as a living and rich tradition with a complex history rooted in the migrant experience and limits true authenticity to the Old World, which looms as a space of nostalgia and emotional longing throughout the narrative, as it does in so many representations of Italian foodways in the United States. At the same time, the film projects on its viewers the ability to distinguish between good and bad food, assimilating knowledgeable eaters with art-house cinemagoers. The narrative clearly positions the viewers with the brothers so that they, too, view the eaters as "philistines" who are incapable of recognizing the beauty and intricacy of the food presented to them.

As is the case in so many food films, in *Big Night* the audience is expected to develop a sense of complicity with the film in terms of both gastronomic and cinematographic good taste. The filmmakers take for granted that the viewers understand and share Secondo's barely concealed sense of dismay in front of culinary ignorance. At the same time, the scene lends itself to an ironic reading by positioning the brothers as humorous, while inviting viewers to empathize with their frustrations, pain, and awkwardness in this newfound culture. On the one hand, the story guides us to identify with the brothers' plight, despite manners and speech patterns that mark them as different. On the other hand, the film aptly assuages the painful experience of assimilation through comedy, glossing over the criticism of a social and economic system that establishes painful pathways toward assimilation. For those who understand the frustration and awkwardness of trying to make a life in a new place, the humor may function quite differently than for spectators who have not experienced the financial and emotional struggles immigrants in the United States face. Positioned as coming from a place of cosmopolitan privilege, many viewers of this—and other food films—may be able to alleviate their own anxieties about the intense pressures of living in a monocultural, bland, market-driven society without having to actually share or even acknowledge the burdens placed on immigrants by this system.

Big Night also tells a cautionary tale of corporate destruction of a small independently owned restaurant, embracing a critique of what George Ritzer calls the process of "McDonaldization, that is, the process by which the principles of the fast-food restaurant are coming to dominate more and more sectors of American society as well as the rest of the world." Much of this criticism revolves around what the sociologist describes as the "corruption of taste by commercial interests."[1] *Big Night*, as the first major U.S. food film, initially occupies a position that criticizes mass consumption—especially of ethnic otherness—and it does so from a privileged, elitist position. At the same time, the film establishes the space of the restaurant itself as crucial for the negotiation of individual and communal identities, the performance of cultural capital, and for the realization of the American dream of financial success and self-realization. Professional cooking and the restaurant industry appear as suitable choices for individuals looking to assert themselves in American society, a profound change from previous decades where all kitchen jobs were considered either domestic service or menial occupations. Restaurants constitute appealing venues for young immigrants or second-generation Americans trying to climb the social ladder. These attempts at social ascent cannot be separated from issues of class and gender. In fact, success in positions of responsibility in the food business requires professionalism, determination, strength, and ingenuity, all qualities that mainstream American culture often marks as primarily masculine.

Big Night uses food and the restaurant world to express criticism of dominant eating culture, consumption, and the socioeconomic dominance of Hollywood cinema, while exploring the process of assimilation in the United States. The film's fiscal history reveals a great deal about its positioning as an object of consumption for specific audience segments: the art-house and foreign-film crowds. Produced on $4,200,000, the film opened on September 22, 1996, and grossed $185,942 the first weekend. By mid-October it had already grossed $4 million, and as of February 1997, $11,881,000.[2] *Big Night* made the jump from art-house theaters to major movie theaters throughout the country and was heavily rented on video, demonstrating American audiences' growing interest in all things food, and in particular in chefs, restaurants, and foreign culinary traditions. This is a signal the Hollywood industry took seriously, as the many food films that follow in the wake of *Big Night* indicate.

When Roger Ebert praised *Big Night* in the *Chicago Sun Times* as "one of the great food movies," he drew a direct comparison between the film's elegant style and the delicate "perfect risotto" that chef Primo creates in the film, thus equating filmic style with food culture and culinary capital. The fact that already in the late 1990s a film critic could refer to "food movies," a genre that up to that point had been produced abroad and distributed with limited art-house releases, indicates a growing awareness of the emerging genre that reflects a sense of cosmopolitanism expressed through both familiarity with international cinema and knowledge of foreign cuisines. "Watching it," Ebert writes, "I reflected how many Hollywood movies these days seem to come with a side order of spaghetti and meatballs. And mashed potatoes."[3] The not-so-discreet subtext is that cultured and refined consumers know what risotto is and how to eat it, the same way they can discriminate between intelligent films and mainstream fodder. Already in the late 1990s, gastronomic connoisseurship was recognized as an inherent trait for the cosmopolitan and sophisticated citizen-consumer, and restaurants emerged as relevant spaces for the construction of individual and communal identities in the configuration of this dynamic.

A close look at *Big Night* unveils how consumption operates as part of food media culture and how the production and enjoyment of food and media are interwoven, helping us to understand the subtle but persuasive, impactful role that food media play in helping to define what it means to be a citizen of the United States. Within the social practices of consumption, now widely understood as a "dominant contemporary cultural force," food media have taken on a central role in constructing lifestyles and marking social positions.[4] As an ephemeral object of consumption, food receives tremendous attention by the advertising industry on television and in the cinema. Food ads and marketing constantly teach consumers that they "need" something "new" and "different," diversifying goods and introducing innovation. Food TV teaches how cuisine and lifestyle correspond to each other, determining trends and shifts in consumption and purchasing choices.

Reflecting chefs' growing presence on TV, it is not surprising that U.S. cinema turned to the topic of food professionals and their business as an appealing focus area for mainstream audiences starting in the late 1990s. In the so-called Hollywood "corporate era," *Big Night* appeared to provide a refreshing filmic contrast to ordinary commercial fare.[5] The narrative and filmic style of *Big Night*, driven by the producers' and directors' expressed desire to produce a "different" kind of cinema, disrupts many of the qualities of Hollywood's mainstream film production, the same way Primo and Secondo's effort tries to question the dominant food industry and culinary culture. The history of the film's distribution and self-representation through its marketing demonstrates, nonetheless, how firmly anchored the film was as a product of contemporary U.S. media and consumer cultures, as in many ways *Big Night* became what it attempted to deconstruct. The film's depiction of masculinity and ethnic Otherness reiterates Westernized, Eurocentric legacies that define "good taste" and "class" in distinct and limited ways.

Like many independent and semi-independent films, *Big Night* explores the tension between producing art and earning money in a marketplace that demands high returns. The sound, mise-en-scène, editing, and narrative support this thematic tension. The exposition of *Big Night*, although seemingly simple, is elegant, rich, and filled with detail. Primo naturally drifts into his native Italian tongue; Secondo conscientiously corrects him and demands that he speak English, that is, that he act "American." Indeed, the film oscillates consistently between Italian and English, often using English subtitles to translate the dialogue. The production of this filmic style—a style that was intended to and did indeed appeal to the "art house" and "foreign" film crowd in the United States—assists in staging a contrast between art-house and mainstream Hollywood film culture just as it contrasts New World individualism (associated with the United States) and Old World social structures (associated here with Italy). The film introduces a calm, naturalistic, real-time style with its minimal editing. Extremely long takes, focus on simple diegetic sound, and appreciation of subtlety and understatement contrast with the bombastic style of many Hollywood blockbusters from the same period. With its slow-paced editing, Italian neorealist-style cinematography, and deliberate rejection of Hollywood coverage techniques, *Big Night*, according to writer and director Stanley Tucci, his screenwriter cousin Joseph Tropiano, and codirector Campbell Scott, represents a different kind of cinema that draws on older, mostly European models. Tucci emphasized in an interview his desire to "make a movie in keeping with earlier filmmaking" in a style that bears a nostalgic look toward times before the influence of the Internet, when consumption and the production of art were indeed somewhat less complicated.[6] Tropiano states in an interview that a food metaphor was the natural choice: "A chef's problems were a way of exploring that theme of art and money in a way that people could access it."[7] Much of Tucci's and Tropiano's effort focused on writing a screenplay in which the characters, rather than the plot, stand at the center of the film.

Food in *The Paradise* is truly utopian. Each dish that the brothers serve is aesthetically pleasing both to the palate and the eyes, while fulfilling the emotional needs of those Americans who willingly engage with the cuisine. Tucci spent one and a half years preparing for the film in the kitchen of Le Madri in New York with head chef Gianni Scappin, with whom he and his mother later cowrote the cookbook *Cucina & Famiglia*. The meticulous attention to detail in the representation of food in *Big Night* set very high standards for food films that followed, making it necessary for actors and filmmakers to have professional chefs on set to help them pin down the right movements, the reality of the kitchen, or what dishes should look like. As a result, food stylists are often not considered sufficient any longer, as growing audience segments interested in food films have become more discriminating because of their mass exposure to visual images of food through the Internet, TV, and magazines.

The middle part of *Big Night* revolves around the meal the brothers create for Louis Prima in an effort to save their restaurant. While the film overall is highly aestheticized, the food shots of the event are particularly rich in detail. Each course of the meal is introduced through titles in white on a solid black screen, setting this part of the film off from the remainder of the narrative. With a drum roll and the words "La Zuppa," the camera opens to the sound of utensils and shots of spoons entering mouths and eyes rolling with delight. Often in close-up, we see detailed presentations of the dishes and of the dinner guests consuming them with passion. When "Il Risotto" is introduced, the film presents a high-angle shot of *risotto tricolore* in green, white, and red. As we watch a woman bite and then suck a piece of risotto that has fallen down off the side of her hand, the viewer is drawn more and more into an erotic, sensuous world of food, not just as an observer but also as an intimate participant. The exotic, mysterious food presented to the diners elevates them to a unique emotional state, revealing to them desires and sensual needs they were not even aware of having. Foreign food, and the cosmopolitan experiences that make it available, become the saving grace for Americans desensitized by consumerism and superficiality. "Il Timpano," a large cylinder of pasta shaped like a drum and filled with all sorts of ingredients, forms the dinner's centerpiece and has acquired iconic status in food films as an expression of tradition, artistry, and the chef's daring dedication to his vocation (fig. 1.2). With this attention to detail and clear linkages between food, sensuality, and sexuality, *Big Night* helps to introduce a new era of food films produced in the United States.

FIGURE 1.2 Ethnic restaurant entrepreneurs may struggle to have their skills acknowledged in the U.S. market. In *Big Night* the *timpano* becomes a symbol of the foreign chefs' attempt to commodify their culinary heritage.

RESTAURANT EXPERIENCES

Big Night deserves attention also because it constitutes the first example of the entanglement between a film and other media, objects, real-life performances, and various forms of entertainment. The food and the culinary experiences represented in the film were commodified not only through the box office but also through other modalities of consumption. Along with the video and compact disc, a novel of the same title, based on the film's screenplay and complete with "authentic" recipes, was available for purchase. The novel is not meant to stand as a product in and of its own right but rather as an extension of the film. The book, a tie-in marketing device, informs us through a red sticker on the front cover that it "includes recipes from the film":

> A lack of simplicity is one of the reasons you won't find a recipe here for *timpano*, the pasta-in-pastry dish that Primo and Secondo serve as the centerpiece of their dinner. This recipe, which comes from the Tucci family

cookbook and is specific to their village of origin in Calabria, is not only long but also somewhat complicated. It's also the subject of considerable, friendly disagreement and discussion within the family as to what amounts and types of ingredients go into it and as to the exact procedures required to make a truly "authentic" *timpano*. In short, a definitive version of the recipe is hard to pin down and I wouldn't presume to publish one. Perhaps someday the Tuccis will let the world in on their secret.[8]

In fact, when Tucci and his mother Joan Tropiano Tucci's cookbook *Cucina & Famiglia* debuted in 1999, its cover featured nothing other than a mouthwatering close-up of *timpano* and a sticker in wine red that asserts that the book "includes the recipe for *timpano* as seen in *Big Night*." The inside flap of the hard-back book version strengthens the links between the book, the film, and Italian family identity: "Captivated food lovers were spellbound by the spectacular signature *timpano* that made the movie *Big Night* famous. Now, at last, *Cucina & Famiglia* reveals the secret of this recipe, as well as more than 200 other recipes, in this wonderfully evocative cookbook that delves deep into the heart of the Italian family. . . . You will feel like a member of the family as you thumb through heirloom photographs and enjoy the heritage they represent."[9]

Almost quoting the Olive Garden restaurant chain's commercial, "When you're here, you're family," *Cucina & Famiglia* draws on mainstream rhetoric about Italian food to entice buyers to purchase this item that will somehow connect them to the Tucci family heritage and to authentic Italian cuisine. In U.S. culture, where food and identity have become highly commercialized, the greater project of *Big Night*—including the development and publication of the "family" cookbook—contrasts food as a means of connecting and preserving identity, framing the immigrant experience through the lens of food and family and food as a commodity. Tucci and Tropiano's products appeared at a time when mainstream U.S. culture regularly displayed a voracity for Italian products that were "authentic," increasingly "different," and "interesting." In the film Primo's cuisine might be, as *Newsweek* critic David Ansen writes, "years ahead of its time," but in the context of contemporary American eating culture, *Big Night*, its novelization, soundtrack, and the cookbook were all bound to be financially lucrative.[10] Artsy Italian food was already a well-known commodity in the States in the 1990s, and *Big Night* played into these desires.

What happened with this film after its release is particularly interesting in the context of food culture, media, identity, and consumption. Restaurants across the country began cooking *Big Night* meals, imitating and reproducing the "authentic" food from the film. Articles about the film began to appear in food sections. Judith Weinraub of the *Washington Post* described the film as a "'Big Night for Food Fans."[11] After briefly discussing the film, she mentions the novelization and interviews with Tropiano about the film's cuisine and includes a recipe for *caponata* and *risotto ai frutti di mare*, blurring the line between film review and cooking column. On the now defunct Geocities website a reviewer wrote that "every Monday night, Cozze's, located at 1205 S.E. Morrison Street, recreates the feast in the film, complete with Louie Prima's 'Mambo Italiano' and an optional conga line. Chef Peter Roscoe has been 'authorized' by the filmmakers and has enthusiastically perfected the culinary delights from the movie."[12] Featuring a menu of tricolored risotto, *timpano*, and roasted young pig, the film was transformed into a spectacular, supposedly authentic, eating experience, despite the narrative's efforts to critique this very relationship between consumers and food.

These performances confirm Joanne Finkelstein's observation that "the aura of the restaurant becomes integral to the pleasures of dining out. The event comes to be enjoyed as a form of entertainment and a part of the modern spectacle in which social relations are mediated through visual images and imagined atmosphere." Exploring these dynamics, Finkelstein emphasizes, "is to see how human emotions become commodified. . . . Dining out has the capacity to transform emotions into commodities which are made available to the individual as if they were consumer items."[13]

By focusing on restaurants and chefs, food films help to construct notions of good taste while defining educated consumers by appealing to their sense of cultural capital. At the same time, restaurants become places where food meets what Joseph Pine and James Gilmore defined in the late 1990s as "experience economy," indicating how the actual goals of production, business, and services in postindustrial societies shift to provide customers with experiences and the memories that accompany them.[14]

Successful food businesses like restaurants need to build their environment, design, and service flows to involve customers beyond the food served or the service itself and contribute to the customers' construction of their sense of selves and their cultural and social identities.[15] This desire to pay for memorable experiences is also behind the growth of culinary tourism, as food becomes a fundamental component of traveling.[16] Visitors not only want to get decent meals; they want to experience the new location through its products, gastronomy, and traditions. This interest in exploring different culinary realities reflects the desire for a cosmopolitan lifestyle, where individuals consider their openness to diversity and otherness as a mark of their sophistication and cultural capital. At the same time, as we will see in chapter 6, most culinary tourists prefer to access new and different cuisines from a safe and ultimately privileged position, which explains the success of films that provide viewers with a supposedly unfiltered access to the private life of migrant communities.

The shift from a product-based economy to an experience economy reflects the growing relevance of personal dietary choices in determining not only individuals' purchasing and cooking choices but also the expectation that their preferences are taken into account in public settings such as restaurants. Such behaviors, which have become relatively acceptable and common in the United States, are still unusual in other parts of the world, where cooks and chefs are in greater control of their menus and of the ways customers experience them. In this particular aspect of dining a tension has developed between the curated experiences that many high-end chefs would like their patrons to have and the patrons' desire to shape their own experience, as a reflection of their nutritional, health, or ethical choices.

It is not surprising that, from *Big Night* on, the protagonists of food films focusing on eateries and chefs are often immigrants striving to acquire full cultural citizenship in the United States. It is even less surprising that most main characters are male, marking the restaurant professional business as mainly masculine. In chapter 2 we will see how other films dialogue with this perception, focusing instead on strong women in professional kitchens. *Big Night* was the first film produced in the States that was widely involved in the increasing commercialization of food across different mainstream media, reflecting and reinforcing the visibility and prestige that restaurants and chefs have been acquiring in the practices and imaginaries of educated consumers. The film introduced audiences to restaurants as spaces for (male) chefs to assert their professional skills and their determination and for customers (and viewers) to articulate their identities and lifestyles by performing connoisseurship and sophistication. Many other films followed *Big Night*'s intuition, articulating dining establishments as new arenas for social and economic achievements where entrepreneurs, chefs, and waiters strive to achieve their goals and better their lives while negotiating their roles as men and providers for their families. In particular, *Dinner Rush* (Giraldi, 2000), *Waiting* (McKittrick, 2005), *Today's Special* (Kaplan, 2009), *Chef* (Favreau, 2014), and *The Hundred-Foot Journey* (Hallström, 2014) present elements that reflect these dynamics and engage in ongoing negotiations about cultural citizenship among both chefs and customers. These films seem to assume a critical point of view vis-à-vis mainstream U.S. food culture, although they are softened by comedic or romantic accents. Their distribution and self-representation through marketing, however, reiterate the stereotypes the films appear to target, pointing to the restaurant experience as just another commodity with a price tag.

PROFESSIONAL SUCCESS AND ETHNIC IDENTITY

The tension we noticed in *Big Night* between the new immigrants' desire to maintain their ethnic identity and their need to acquire cultural (and economic) citizenship in the United States appears in many food films from the two decades that follow the release of Tucci's seminal work. These films' narratives center on the affirmation of the chefs' professional skills and the financial success of their commercial endeavors. But it is not surprising that many of the restaurant-centered films feature relatively young males, who also find themselves responding to social expectations in terms of dominant and legitimate masculinities. In *Big Night* the culinary and business misadventures of the two Italian brothers are tightly interwoven with their romantic lives, often serving as a counterpoint for their professional problems. Their desire to date American women indicates the wish to integrate themselves in their new environment, their charm making up for their ethnic diversity and the social pigeonholing that comes with it, as their failed attempts to secure bank loans suggest. In many restaurant-focused films that followed *Big Night*, even those produced in the commercial cinema industry, we find the same anxieties regarding the commercialization of the chef's talent and authentic culinary traditions. But these elements lose some of their impact as a critique of the American business and cultural structures, absorbed and neutralized in the highly mediatized mainstream conversations about food as a leisure activity. As an increasingly visible arena in the experience economy, restaurants are places to enjoy and express lifestyles, where all unpleasantness and complication are to be avoided for the sake of the customers' enjoyment.

Bob Giraldi's *Dinner Rush* exemplifies these issues through the wrought relationship of a father and son. Udo Croppa (Edoardo Ballerini), a charming and handsome young upcoming chef in New York City, wants to bring the family establishment into the brave new world of celebrity cooking, but his father, Louis (Danny Aiello), an old-school Italian American restaurateur with dubious connections to unsavory characters, does not understand his son's creative approach to Italian food. In his view Udo's cooking does not provide nourishment but rather aims to ensure spectacle and to wow critics. "We don't make meatballs here anymore," asserts Ugo, maintaining the dismissive attitude toward Italian American traditions that we already noticed in *Big Night*. When two Italian American gangsters kill one of Louis's friends on the street, the audience realizes that the film is not only about kitchens and chefs but that it also deals with the issues of organized crime that *Big Night* had kept at the margins of its narrative.[17] Most of the story takes place on one eventful night, when Louis manages to avenge his friend and eliminate his enemies, eventually allowing his son to take control of the family business.

Udo is ambitious, skilled, creative, and media-savvy, a mix of qualities that seem increasingly relevant to ensuring a pathway to fame in contemporary fine dining. He is comfortable with his ethnic background and willing to bank on it to create his own style of cuisine, without many worries about maintaining the purity of traditions. Udo's charisma enables him to get the best out of his all-male kitchen brigade and, in particular, his troubled sous-chef, a gambling addict who owes a large sum of money to the mob. We see Udo fire a line cook because his knife is dull and because he does not know how to chop chives. Udo forces another cook to take his position, asserting his dominant role. His success with women, including female customers, adds to his image as a man successful in business and in life.

The kitchen scenes in *Dinner Rush* embrace an overall realistic approach, documenting the frantic and noisy working environment and the whirlwind of the dining room. English, Italian, and Spanish are spoken in a babel that somehow proves effective and productive, drowned in the noise of pots and pans. The film opens on a sequence in which cooks are shot in slow motion, a visual tactic that underlines the most crucial moments in the narrative. By allowing viewers to focus on the grace and coordination of the cooks' movements, the slow motion conveys the energy in cramped space and the intensity of the cooks' occupation, while disembodied voices with heavy Italian American accents discuss the prospects and challenges of the restaurant business. The contrast between images and sound highlights the difference between those who are in charge of the restaurant business and those who merely occupy a position of labor, often with little opportunity to express themselves. The old Italian immigrants have already mastered the process of assimilation and conquered their cultural and economic citizenship in the United States, while the new immigrants at the stove are still struggling to assert themselves, both as workers and as men.

In contrast, other sequences exemplify what many now refer to as "food porn," a set of visual and auditory strategies—shots, camera movements, lighting, sound, and editing—that aim to satisfy viewers excluded from the actual consumption of food represented onscreen. Graphic, acoustic, and narrative components reproduce physical experiences for spectators, often achieving comparable levels of excitement. The most interesting use of this style appears when Udo cooks for a woman, a famous food critic and a former lover, who dines in his restaurant with a female friend identified by the maître d' as an infamous "food nymph."

As soon as Ugo steps into the kitchen to cook for her, magic happens. Lobsters are dropped into a pot of boiling water, spaghetti is deep fried, champagne hisses while being reduced in a small pot over a hot flame. The audience sees the vapors and the smoke from the stove. The sounds of cooking food are distinctly audible over the loud, nondiegetic jazz soundtrack that accompanies the action. Caviar glistens, carefully handled by expert fingers. Dishes are beautifully plated and artfully drizzled with sauces that fall onto the dishes in slow motion. Knives, tongs, and ladles move with grace, turning into tools of artisanal craft and creation. The result—Udo announces—is "Montauk lobster and rock shrimp. It's in a champagne shallot sauce with vanilla beans. It's garnished with salmon caviar and *tabiko* caviar, which has a wasabi flavor. Some chives. And no butter." The verbal flourish is the perfect accompaniment for the dish, a towering composition that dominates the critic's table. The direct simplicity of Primo's dishes in *Big Night* is replaced by expert display and daring pairings, expressed in the same language film audiences have grown accustomed to through TV shows, cookbooks, magazines, and the always-expanding blogosphere on the Internet. Not only has the wording changed over the four years between *Big Night* and *Dinner Rush*; the visual representations of food are now more stereotyped, pointing to the development and solidification of a particular cinematic style in the food film genre.

In *Dinner Rush* the kitchen is a place where the chef is in control, negotiating friendships, professional relations, and hierarchies with other men. The lower tiers of the social structure are occupied by male immigrants (often spoken to in Spanish), who appear to audiences as always very intent on their tasks, with women as occasional—and not always welcome—outsiders, working in the front of the house with the staff. Sometimes the personnel includes gay men, barred from the testosterone-heavy environment of the kitchen. They operate among the customers' tables, a place for performance, both for the restaurant staff and its customers. The waiters learn and declaim the names of the dishes on the menu in Italian, which patrons seem to understand without difficulty, proving their knowledge of "authentic" Italian food. Regulars are eager to show their familiarity with the menu and to display their cultural and social capital. Critics, a crucial category of players that did not yet appear in *Big Night*, are powerful but at the same time represented as narcissistic and engrossed in power games.

Udo attempts to assert himself as a talented chef, a successful businessman in the American tradition, an integrated citizen of foreign descent, and as an alpha male, clashing with his apparently laid-back but stubborn and tradi-tional father, whose world made of violence and back-alley truces represents a completely different approach to masculinity and adherence to ethnic com-munal dynamics. In the father's world food reinforces social ties to ingratiate allies and, if necessary, bamboozle enemies. In fact, two gangsters who have set their sights on the restaurant will end up being killed in its restrooms, after an abundant free dinner on the house. Eventually, when Louis reveals to Udo that he is making him the owner of the restaurant, he acknowledges not only his son's skills as a chef but also his capacity to make his own path without following his bad example. Udo's recognition as an adult comes together with the abandonment of the old ways to embrace a more American business and cultural model.

The honesty and wholesomeness that Primo displayed in *Big Night* is gone, as is the ignorance of the patrons. Udo does not need to struggle to achieve cultural citizenship. His familiarity with the rules of the restaurant business in the United States and his burgeoning reputation allow him to build freely on the culinary traditions of his community of origin, com-modifying his cultural background to achieve popularity in the media and financial success. *Dinner Rush* situates itself within the cultural discourse of celebrity chefs and culinary prestige—already well established by the late 1990s—that considers restaurants places for both chefs and customers to display status, cosmopolitanism, and expertise.

For this reason restaurants remain crucial locations for immigrants to negotiate access to various aspects of cultural citizenship, as David Laplan's *Today's Special* reaffirms. Released in 2009, nine years after *Dinner Rush* and thirteen after *Big Night*, it immediately positioned itself in the already solidified food-film genre in terms of themes, narrative structure, and visual style. The opening titles sequence introduces a small child appar-ently looking very closely at somebody cooking food that the audience is supposed to immediately recognize as Indian: colorful spices, *paneer*, and *karanji*. The hand gestures are shot in extreme close-ups, conveying the child's point of view but also allowing the camera to linger on the cook's skills and the sensuality and texture of the food. Although the film assumes that the viewers recognize Indian cuisine, the score brings the point home with Indian swing music. In the scene a male child is learning about his

ethnic community's culinary traditions from his mother in a domestic setting, a space based on emotions rather than professionalism.

The camera cuts to adult eyes: they belong to an Indian male donning
chef's whites. He's Samir (Aasif Mandvi), a sous-chef in a Western-style
fine-dining restaurant. We immediately see him in action in a busy and
noisy kitchen, shot in camera moves that have now become stereotypical for kitchen scenes: fast movements, close-ups of preparation, midshots
to set the environment, with heightened sizzling sounds and loud order
calls. We hear Samir yell names of trendy ingredients such as arugula and
radicchio. Just like Udo, Samir is cosmopolitan, determined, and in charge.
Although he is not the executive chef, he knows how to lead a team. The
contrast between the expectation deriving from the protagonist's ethnic
background and his professional aspirations is presented from the beginning as the core of the narrative. On a date with a seemingly professional
Indian woman, he's immediately reminded of family expectations for many
children and live-in in-laws, with no regard for his culinary career.

When his executive chef does not give him the responsibility for one of
his new restaurants, explaining that he does not see enough creativity in
him, and his father (who owns and runs a traditional Indian Muslim eatery
in Queens) falls ill, Samir finds himself stuck in managing the family business, even if he dreams of interning with the great chefs of Paris. He moves
back to his parents' home, sleeping in his childhood bunk bed, a clear symbol of infantilization, emasculation, and lack of success. The kitchen in
his father's restaurant appears as a very traditional space, with disputable
hygiene, greasy food, and little organization. As Samir is not familiar with
Indian cuisine, and his first attempts end up in utter failure, he decides
to track down Akbar (Naseeruddin Shah), a taxi driver who used to be a
chef in India. Akbar's hands-on, sensual, and almost mystical approach to
cooking is a hit with customers, and the restaurant becomes so successful that Sameer is forced to do deliveries himself to keep up with orders.
When shopping for groceries, Akbar explains to Samir the role of spices in
Indian cooking, comparing each spice to a different kind of woman, metaphorically linking culinary skills with masculine prowess. This attitude is
crucial, as Akbar does not use recipes and does not measure ingredients,
thus employing a more feminine approach, where recipes and techniques

are transmitted by practice and collaboration. At first Samir does not know how to replicate Akbar's method, having learned to cook by the book, in a more systematic, rational, and supposedly professional (i.e., masculine) way. Of course, tensions develop between the two, although Akbar assumes the role of father and guide to a mysterious but fascinating culture.

In the neighborhood Samir runs into Carrie (Jess Weixler), a single mother who was the only female chef in the restaurant where he used to work. As they get closer, they repaint and clean up the restaurant together, causing his father to resent him because he feels that his son is not respectful of all he has done for years. Just as the father decides to sell to a franchise and Akbar is about to move to Ohio, the *New York Times* gives the restaurant three stars, and crowds start lining up outside the door. Samir has to take the initiative and cook, with Carrie's help. He finally gets rid of his by-the-recipe approach and lets his own talent—and to a certain extent his supposedly innate knowledge of Indian cuisine and flavors— guide food preparation and the management of his team. Eventually his father is so impressed with Samir's work that he decides not to sell the restaurant and goes into business with him. The father's acknowledgment of Samir's value in his professional capacity sanctions his status as a legitimate and respectable individual in society. Together with this newly found professional status, his blooming relationship with the Caucasian Carrie confirms both his masculinity and his ascent in the ethnic hierarchies of the United States. As with Udo in *Dinner Rush*, the father's recognition of Samir as an adult man, a woman's interest in him as a partner, and the customers' and media's admiration of him as chef affirm Samir's status and provide the film's narrative resolution. As in *Dinner Rush*, food production and consumption are constantly filtered by the media intervention through the presence of critics and the write-ups of newspapers, while ethnic identity is negotiated, hybridized, and commodified to achieve success. The restaurant, as a place that sanctions both a chef's success and the customers' value as refined and cosmopolitan citizens, provides the perfect background for the event (fig. 1.3).

The trifecta of professional accomplishment, romantic love with a Caucasian woman, and acquisition of paternal approval constitute a recurrent theme when it comes to an ethnic chef trying to make his mark.

FIGURE 1.3 In *Today's Special* a chef of Indian descent struggles to negotiate his desire to succeed in Western-style fine dining establishments while maintaining a commitment to his family's traditional ethnic restaurant.

This is also the case in Lasse Hallström's *Hundred-Foot Journey*, a film produced by Oprah Winfrey and Steven Spielberg and, as such, integrated into the Hollywood system. The success story of Hassan (Manish Dayal), a young male chef moving from India to France, works well to reassure American viewers of the value of embracing immigrant culture, at a time when xenophobic rhetoric is especially present in political and social discourse in the United States. The protagonist's journey underlines the difficulties of integration and success for migrants, while reinforcing the role of restaurants as a venue for the acquisition of cultural (and economic) citizenship also in terms of gender and class.

Hassan's family left India after their restaurant was burned down in a political riot and his mother, who taught him how to cook using his senses, died in the fire. Once again, ethnic traditions are marked as part of the female domestic sphere, quite removed from the endeavors of professional chefs. When Hassan first comes to Europe, the border officer does not seem to understand that the young man is not a kitchen porter but an actual cook, as he is apparently used to ethnic individuals only employed in menial occupations. After some traveling, Hassan's father decides to settle down and open a restaurant in St. Antonin, a small village in the French countryside, right across the street from a very famous and starred haute cuisine temple, Le Saule Pleureur, managed by the severe and rigid Madame Mallory (Helen Mirren). Hassan befriends Marguerite, a young female chef working for Mallory, who introduces him to French cuisine, a new and fascinating frontier, and to the idea of the Michelin star system (and its "restaurant Gods"). But the growing tension between the two very different establishments creates unrest in the village, where many are not happy about the arrival of immigrants, to the point that some local racist hooligans try to burn down the newcomers' place and Hassan scalds his hands. The dangers and the ugliness of racism and xenophobia could not be more clearly illustrated, positioning the film (and its viewers) as harboring a benevolent and civilized attitude toward foreigners.

Madame Mallory, who believes in the French political ideals of "liberty, equality, and fraternity," is moved by the events. After testing his newly developed hybrid French-Indian culinary skills, she asks Hassan to come work in her restaurant. His father at first staunchly refuses, but eventually he gives in to his son's desire to train in classical French cuisine. The film hits viewers hard with the notion that food can become an instrument for intercultural communication and integration among enlightened individuals. Marguerite, however, resents Hassan because she thinks he has been scheming to make it to the top, even if it means he will push her to the side. Hassan is hurt but determined to continue, slowly introducing innovation and hybridization in Madame Mallory's menu. At the same time his employer and his father get closer, building first a tentative and later a stable, if discreet, romantic relationship. When the restaurant gets its second star thanks to Hassan's work, the two celebrate together.

Hassan accepts an offer in a modern and fashionable establishment in Paris, where he is given free rein to experiment and innovate, introducing elements of molecular gastronomy in his cuisine, which nevertheless remains strongly connected with the ingredients and flavors of India. Modernist cuisine appears in the film as the international pinnacle of creativity and avant-garde, a notion that viewers may have already formed by reading about Ferran Adrià, Heston Blumenthal, and other world-renowned and highly mediated chefs. Hassan conquers the Parisian culinary scene, becoming "hot in the kitchen and very popular with the ladies," as a TV news segment declares. When a magazine defines him as a successful "boy from the gutter," his father becomes very upset, torn between pride for his son and hurt caused by the subtle racism that the media adopt to represent him. Hassan feels increasingly lonely in Paris, his longing for home and for Marguerite becoming acute when one night, after closing, he shares food with an Indian member of the restaurant staff, cooked by his wife with spices brought in from India. The day he is supposed to know about his third star he goes back to the village, where he asks Marguerite to help him cook a dish his mother used to make, using the spices she left him. Hassan and Marguerite become business partners, besides lovers, with the goal to get a third star at Le Saule Pleureur.

Once again, the narrative resolution collates professional achievements, romantic success, and paternal recognition, making the restaurant a place where men—particularly immigrant men—can claim both their masculinity and their access to cultural citizenship. Viewers can confirm their perception of the status and attractiveness of the culinary world through its commodification, operated by media, investment, and business. At the same time, by sharing Hassan's vicissitudes, the virtual access to the inner workings of restaurants, chefs, food criticism, and foreign cuisines that we enjoy as viewers can implicitly reassure us of our cultural capital and our access to the circles of experts. Patrons and audiences are not just customers: we become participant in the construction of a whole field of social interaction.

ON RESTAURANTS, MEN, AND ADULTHOOD

Dinner Rush, *Today's Special*, and *The Hundred-Foot Journey* illustrate how restaurant-related themes, narrative structures, and visual elements that first emerged in the United States with *Big Night* have become mainstays of the food-film genre, now totally embraced by Hollywood and food TV.

These films focus on restaurant life to represent coming-of-age stories and celebrations of immigrant success, seemingly opening up a broader pathway to cultural citizenship in the context of the United States: young chefs, regardless of ethnic origin and social background, can achieve a high status as men and professionals, playing into mainstream ideas of what legitimate and respectable models of masculinity are. Their stories, however, continue to privilege dominant versions of masculinity over other forms of identity. Women, gay men, and people who remain "too ethnic" do not appear to blend into this veritable melting pot.

Of course, Hollywood is eager to remind us that white males can also hit a rough patch, leveling the playing field for everybody. Jon Favreau's *Chef* stands as a warning that personal achievements and success in one's career are not to be taken for granted and that determination and inventiveness are crucial. Chefs can fail both as men—and in particular in terms of family responsibilities—and professionals, and they need to be able to reinvent themselves. The film tells the story of Carl Casper (Favreau), a renowned chef in a popular restaurant, who struggles to assert his personal style and creativity against the establishment's owner (Dustin Hoffman), who is only interested in the bottom line and wants to play to his customers' and critics' expectations. When Carl receives a terrible review from a famous blogger (Oliver Platt) for the menu that the owner insisted on, accusing Carl of lacking imagination, he learns from his young son, Percy (Emjay Anthony), how to tweet and writes a venomous message to the reviewer, which goes viral. Carl tries to rethink the whole menu but the restaurant owner fires him, causing him to go on a verbal rampage against the critic, achieving unwanted Internet fame. Jobless, he reluctantly accepts the idea from his former wife, Inez (Sofia Vergara), to launch a food truck, a clear step down from his previous position. He decides to start from Miami, where he first began cooking, creating a Cuban-inspired menu and going on the road with his son and his Hispanic sous-chef Martin (John Leguizamo). Thanks to Percy's ability to use social networks, their trip on the truck from Miami back to Los Angeles becomes an Internet sensation. In the end the blogger who had destroyed Carl's reputation is so impressed by his food that he asks him to become the chef in his new restaurant, leaving him complete creative freedom. The last scene takes place in the new restaurant, while the celebration for Carl and Inez's second wedding is taking place.

Chef opens with a now classic—and stereotypical—sequence showing Carl in the kitchen, moving fast but with grace and determination. Close-ups of ingredients, hand movements, camera pans, and medium shots of the chef allow viewers to experience Carl's skills directly. We see him butchering a whole pig and shopping at the farmers' market, which shows his familiarity with the "farm to fork" style of cooking and attention to local, fresh ingredients, now considered key elements for a modern chef's success. The film uses a similar visual approach when he cooks for his lover (Scarlett Johansson), who watches him with an expression of both lust and appetite as he experiments on a new menu or makes a grilled cheese sandwich for his son. His rough demeanor and his portly body do not make him less sexually attractive for the young woman. Food porn camera shots showcase the chef's skills and creativity, as is often the case in the genre, but also illustrate his fascinating masculinity and his affectionate—although at times clueless—attempts at mature fatherhood.

The most original element in the narrative is the relationship between Carl and his son, Percy, which had taken a backseat when Carl worked at the restaurant. The road trip allows father and son to get to know each other better, using food as a means of communication, something that Percy had desired all along but that Carl did not know how to handle. Sous-chef Martin encourages spontaneity in the interaction among them. He brings an atmosphere of fun and teamwork during the trip, enjoying being a man among other men, without the responsibilities of fatherhood. His presence keeps the relationship between father and son from becoming too schmaltzy. The truck becomes a place of male bonding, with an abundance of sexual jokes about balls and penises, and rough language that Percy does not always fully understand but appreciates as a window into the world of adult males. This rugged masculinity pairs with a professional ethos based on the love for one's trade, commitment, and determination. At first Percy does not want to clean the kitchen, and he shocks his father when he wants to let people eat a slightly burned sandwich. As they work together on the line, the boy learns to enjoy hard work and collaboration with the adults, to the point that, after singeing a finger on a hot surface, he tells his proud father that he wants to go on.

Like so many mainstream films, and consistent with Laura Mulvey's reading of classic Hollywood cinema, the whole narrative is built around Carl regaining his lost prestige, together with his male pride.[18] He experiences the loss of the restaurant job and feud with the critic as forms of castration, worsened by his need to ask his ex-wife for help. "You robbed me of my pride, my career, my dignity," he says to the critic. By reconquering his pride and fame as a chef, having his skills and creativity recognized by the critic, regaining his son's and ex-wife's love, Carl finds peace in a respectable and traditional masculinity. Interestingly, he rebuilds his "street cred" through the appropriation of an ethnic food tradition that is not his own, Cuban sandwiches, which he nevertheless embraces as his professional culinary roots. Martin, who is Hispanic, generously shares his knowledge and does not resent Carl, to whom he shows respect and dedication, for using his insights. Without fully embracing it head-on, the film hints at the thorny theme of cultural appropriation of an ethnic culinary tradition, a discussion that is inherent to many forms of American hybrid cuisines and more recent trends about fusion.

Chef was conceived, produced, and released in the atmosphere following the 2009 financial crisis, when many U.S. workers found themselves out of work and had to scramble to make a living. Of course, the protagonist of the film is in a completely different position, as he can count on his experience, family ties, and celebrity to start over. He manages to get back on his feet without tapping into his previous professional network, expressing a desire for a clean break and a new life. Unlike in the other films we have discussed, the place for his human and professional redemption is not a restaurant, which the film represents as a space with little possibility for creativity because of the necessities of business and the pressure from the media. Carl chooses to start a food truck, the new frontier of culinary creativity and democratization of high-end cuisine. Although this new outlet continues the old tradition of street food, stalls, and carts in the United States, its clients are usually young, looking for novelty, and reflecting a hip attitude toward gourmet food.[19] Food trucks have become such important fixtures in urban U.S. foodscapes and landscapes that they appear routinely on TV food shows and even in the feature-length cartoon *Turbo* (Soren, 2013), which presents a snail that dreams of becoming a racing champion and turns into a speedster in the Indy 500 by accident, trained by a young Hispanic cook who runs a taco truck. They, however, position themselves in a different sphere from the usual street vendors who hawk food from stalls and carts, usually immigrants with little access to cultural and financial capital and without media savvy.[20]

Roy Choy's Kogi Korean BBQ food truck, launched in 2008 right when the real estate market was plummeting in the States, is often indicated as one of the initiators of the food truck movement. Young chefs have chosen this form of business because it requires relatively low investment, strong concepts, and social media skills. It also represents creative autonomy, as well as freedom from excessive economic and financial preoccupations. As illustrated in *Chef*, trucks often announce their location and menus through Twitter, Instagram, and other apps, establishing faithful followers who are intrigued by being in the know and stay on top of what's new and hot. In the film it is Carl's young son who understands the power of these new means of communication (as opposed to a blog, represented instead as an expression of the media establishment) both to drum up business and to create his father's new public persona. Incidentally, the boy also uses his social media skills to express his admiration and affection for his father through images and videos. Carl's story illustrates the symbiotic relationship between food and media (including the film narrating the story), as an inevitable aspect of the business, and the consumers' willing complicity in these dynamics.

Chef's narrative, although it culminates in success, develops against the constant possibility of fiascos in the food business, presented also as a failure from the personal point of view. A ruthless market constantly threatens Carl's professional success, conflated and identified with his masculinity and his social standing. We close this section with Rob McKittrick's comedy *Waiting*, which brings the losers and slackers of the restaurant world to the front, focusing on waiters, line cooks, and managers who do not consider their occupation as a path to success or as a way to express their inventiveness but as an inevitable grind that is necessary to survive. The film, a member of a line of deliberately offensive comedies like Paul and

Chris Weitz's *American Pie* (1999), dispels any romantic notion about the restaurant world. We are not in the realm of fine dining: the action takes place at Shenaniganz, a fictional establishment that represents all casual dining franchises, a step up from fast food but not a place where customers come to find creative and stimulating cuisine. As a matter of fact, patrons are a pitiful assortment of mean, ignorant, and overall unpleasant people. Food is spat on, used for sexual innuendos, and disrespected in all possible ways. It is a commodity without any emotional or cultural meaning.

The only glue that keeps the restaurant together is an uninterrupted performance of inane masculinity. The all-male kitchen staff plays a game where the goal is to show one's genitals to unwitting coworkers, who win the chance to kick them and call them "faggots." The men in the story have nowhere to go, socially or emotionally, and are stumped in their growth as adults, professionals, and males. The only exception is the protagonist, Dean (Justin Long), who, after receiving the offer to become an assistant manager in the restaurant, realizes that there would be no exit from that world for him and eventually quits. The women, who all work the front of the house, seem to express greater awareness of their unsatisfactory work and love life; nevertheless, they do not seem to do much to get out of it. *Waiting*, as disturbing as it aims to be, offers an intriguing counterpoint to the idealized visions of the restaurant world offered by most food films.

But the other food films we have explored in this chapter also feature losers—cooks, waiters, and other restaurant employees—who allow the male protagonists to shine in their success. These dynamics are often exemplified through tensions and interactions between alpha and beta males, between older and younger individuals, and between the creative and determined chefs and the rest of the staff. When the protagonists experience setbacks that could jeopardize their professional careers and their role as providers and family men, they eventually push through as winners, a necessary outcome in the Hollywood ethos (unlike *Big Night*, an independent film, that leaves its conclusion open to interpretation). As their narratives build around the personal growth of the (male) protagonists, even when they represent temporary defeat or struggle for acceptance, thus offering a mild critique of American society and consumerism, the films we have discussed reinforce mainstream perceptions of success and acceptable social ascent. Women are often absent from the kitchen or on the sides of the narrative. Interestingly, *Today's Special* and *The Hundred-Foot Journey*, in which the protagonists are ethnic chefs, allow for stronger women to play a more important role, tending toward a less-than-decisive model of masculinity among the immigrants. From their inception food films have marked restaurants as places where cultural identity—in terms of ethnicity, gender, age, and class—is constantly negotiated around food and its preparation.

Women who take the driving position in the kitchen risk upsetting the rules of the game. How can female chefs find a balance between professional success and determination—usually coded in Hollywood films as masculine traits—and the roles of domestic cooks and caregivers, traditionally attributed to them? As we will see, mainstream food films deal with these tensions by sapping much of the potential subversion of accepted gender roles out of them.

AUTONOMY IN THE KITCHEN?

Food Films and Postfeminism

One of the key characteristics of mainstream food films in the United States is what has been described as the "utopian" depiction of food.[1] In many of them the complications surrounding the production and consumption of food slip into the background and enable cooking and eating to emerge as celebratory elements that unite and connect the characters. The negotiations about labor, power, and exploitation manifest themselves only obliquely in an absence of direct political statements, while the films create happy endings based on beautiful, enticing food. As we discussed in the introduction to this book, U.S. food films tend to glorify the domain of eating and intertwine food with gender and sexuality in ways that gloss over the social dynamics that hold in place divides based on the intersecting influences of gender, sexuality, social class, ethnicity, and other markers of identity, enabling some individuals to experience privileges others may never know. In this chapter we explore the negotiations surrounding women when they become engaged as professionals in the world of food, and we examine the extent to which they may be able to have voice and exercise power toward full citizenship in U.S. culture. Given the important connections among bodies, sexuality, and gender in media, food films provide particularly rich grounds for seeking to understand women's power and participation as full citizens.

It comes as no surprise that a great many of the food films produced in the United States focus on women as their central characters. After all, these films are frequently romantic comedies, a genre that grew out of the tradition of the romance novel and the woman's film.[2] Furthermore, the numerous representations of women and food reflect their historical roles as caretakers and nurturers.[3] As food studies sociologist Marjorie DeVault pointed out more than three decades ago in her analysis of American families and cooking, "feeding work has become one of the primary ways that women 'do' gender."[4] U.S. media across time—including and beyond food films—have provided representations of women's social roles in their connections to kitchens and cooking, from the iconic 1950s depiction of mother June Cleaver in the television show *Leave It to Beaver* to Joan Crawford's edgy portrayal of the eponymous restaurant executive in *Mildred Pierce* (Curtiz, 1945) to 1980s sitcoms featuring characters like Roseanne Barr. Of course, these representations have morphed over time, both influencing and being influenced by changes in women's social position.

This chapter and chapter 3 both focus on these women. We have divided the analysis of lead female characters into two chapters for analytical purposes. Here, we turn our attention to a series of films that feature women with professional lives connected to food: *No Reservations* (Hicks, 2007), *Julie & Julia* (Ephron, 2009), *It's Complicated* (Meyers, 2009), and *Waitress* (Shelly, 2007). We consider these films in the context of other influential films, the Danish film *Babette's Feast* (Axel, 1987) and one of the earliest major U.S. films to explore the interconnection of food, sexuality, and gender, *Fried Green Tomatoes* (Axel, 1989). What is important to note up front about these films is that they all feature white women, primarily and quite visibly from privileged middle-class or upper-middle-class backgrounds, with the exception of *Waitress*, which highlights the experience of a working-class woman. Thus, our primary lens throughout this chapter is on the intersection of femininity, whiteness, and social class. Chapter 3 explores a group of films that link food, women's bodies, and magic, and these magical films tend to focus on women of color. We note this divide because the treatment of gender in each of these groups produces a different discourse about femininity and its intersection with race, ethnicity, class, and sexuality. Indeed, when the films feature white women as food professionals (chefs, bakers, writers), they tend to deemphasize the relationship between women's bodies and food that the magical food films often exaggerate and even exploit.

As we elaborate in chapter 3, women of color tend to be equated with food and represented *as food*, and both the food and these women's bodies are highly sexualized. The intersectionality of whiteness, sexuality, and femininity frequently grants the characters a different kind of power that is not linked as directly to their bodies. Both chapters 2 and 3 address issues of power and autonomy, but the discourses diverge enough to warrant two separate discussions that examine these dynamics respectively in greater depth.

Drawing on a long history of women and food in media, women represented as professional chefs in these films fail at femininity if they prioritize their role as experts over their role as nurturers. Almost assuaging the anxieties provoked by these shifts, recent shows hosted on food television by women—many of whom are expert chefs—have centered around facilitating culinary experiences for others by hosting tours (Tori Ritchie's *Ultimate Kitchens*), highlighting others' accomplishments (Sarah Pinkney's *Food Finds*), giving advice about home hospitality (Martha Stewart), sharing recipes (Sara Moulton), illustrating easy-to-prepare everyday meals (Rachael Ray), and promoting healthy, low-fat/low-calorie recipes (Ellie Krieger's *Healthy Appetite*). In contrast, male star chefs, who have abounded on television from *The Galloping Gourmet*, which began airing with Graham Kerr in 1969, to *Yan Can Cook*, which introduced star chef Martin Yan in 1982, appeared from the beginning as expert masters of cuisine. The professional male chef became more visible with the emergence of a significant group of television stars featured on the Food Network in the 1990s, such as Emeril Lagasse, Bobby Flay, Mario Batali, and Ming Tsai. This group has evolved to include current TV chefs ranging from the over-the-top rock-and-roll hypermasculine Guy Fieri to the quirky science-nerd style of Alton Brown, along with many others. Emeril Lagasse was one of the first male TV chefs to exemplify dominant cultural associations in the United States between masculinity and food and took both to a performative extreme, a tradition that chefs like Guy Fieri have advanced. Lagasse's boastful, expressive, loud, and—above all—active style reinforced mainstream perceptions of heterosexual masculinity, underlined by often boisterous, male live audiences. Appearing unconcerned with his massive use of high-calorie ingredients or alcohol in his dishes, Lagasse's style reinforces the idea that dieting and body image are feminine concerns.

Male star chefs in professional kitchens are likely to stand in the limelight in front of live public audiences, displaying their technical skills and their culinary creativity. Mainstream media can represent men at the stove as long they embody masculine traits, such as action, dedication to one's craft, and professionalism. Cooking and food preparation in the domestic environment, instead, have traditionally been coded as feminine. Julia Child herself, often considered one of the modernizers of American cuisine, did not work as a professional chef but rather made French cuisine, until then considered too technical and complicated, approachable to the average American home cook—at the time, quite likely mostly women. Celebrities like Long Island socialite Ina Garten, musician Trisha Yearwood, and Pioneer Woman Ree Drummond tend to provide advice for domestic cooking. Media present us with images that strengthen the connection of women to the domestic sphere, even when they are skilled experts.

Even more disturbing is the way that mainstream media have tended to represent women eating. Susan Bordo stresses that women in film can enjoy food when it enhances their erotic attractiveness to men, as is the case in films like *Pretty Woman* (Marshall, 1990), *When Harry Met Sally* (Reiner, 1989), *Flashdance* (Lyne, 1983), and many others. As she writes, "When women are positively depicted as sensuously voracious about food (almost never in commercials and only very rarely in movies and novels), their hunger for food is employed solely as a metaphor for their sexual appetite."[5] Other socially acceptable options for women to eat and enjoy food are lean: when they are pregnant, suffering from an eating disorder, or are simply overweight/obese to begin with (in which case the images tend to be punishing ones).[6] Moreover, many films depict food binging as a way to overcome emotional stress or romantic disappointments. Scenes in which women devour ice cream or chocolate after a fight with a loved one or after a breakup are a staple in romantic films, which is particularly puzzling as these works are meant for females as their main audience.

Very few films feature women simply enjoying food. *Eat Pray Love* (Murphy, 2010) presents itself as a liberating and uplifting narrative about a white, middle-class woman who learns to appreciate food as a step on the path toward self-reliance and self-awareness. After a painful divorce and an apparently intense but in reality meaningless relationship with a much younger man, Liz (Julia Roberts) decides to go on a yearlong trip to find herself. Her first destination is Rome, where she is exposed to a different way of relating to food and enjoyment. Interacting with her new local friends around meals, she realizes that Americans know entertainment but do not know pleasure, lured by commercials to eat and consume. Italians seem experts in "*dolce far niente*," doing nothing and then resting while eating copious quantities of amazingly simple but sexy food. This is one of the many stereotypes that the films build on to mark the protagonist's evolution. Italians are also represented as loud and expressing themselves through dramatic gestures; they live in eternal mayhem, including at the counter of a bar to order coffee; men catcall, whistle, and touch the butts of women, crowding the bar to get an espresso.

Liz overcomes her guilt about letting herself go and learns to eat as much as she likes. First we see her attack with increasing relish a simple dish of spaghetti with tomato sauce and fresh basil. Then she goes to a restaurant with friends and orders fried artichokes, prosciutto and melon, and eggplant parmigiana, just for starters. The visual representations of these dishes are borrowed both from commercials (close-ups of Julia Roberts eating and sensually savoring food) and TV "food porn" (close-ups of dishes, pans on the stove, fingers preparing food). The word that she chooses to encapsulate Rome is *sex*: at this point in her journey food is replacement and sublimation for sexual desire. "I am in love; I am having an affair with my pizza," she states. During an outing to Naples to explore the local pizza, a Swedish female friend hesitates to partake, admitting she is worried because she has gained weight. Liz, who has instead decided that she would eat whatever she likes, convinces her friend that men will like her just the same, and that the following day they will just go and buy larger size clothes. She hates having to think about "every single calorie I ate" and "how much self-loathing I take into the shower." "I'm going for it," she asserts. "I have no interest in being obese. I'm just through with the guilt." Of course, the clothes that they buy are ones that only very slender women can wear, as their weight gain is insignificant, leaving them both still extremely slim. As they try on jeans, the camera cuts back and forth to a scene with a group of Italian men intently following a soccer match on television. As Liz lies on the floor, her friend successfully buttons the pants and yells "I did it!" The camera immediately cuts back to the room of men, cheering, the humorously intentioned use of crosscutting suggesting that they are saluting the women for buying new pants. The decision to allow oneself to gain weight appears as an act of rebellion, when in truth Liz can still fit into a pair of very skinny jeans.

Liz starts cooking for herself and then for others; viewers never saw her in a kitchen in her previous American life. She is represented as a woman who, after a whole life spent with men or breaking up with men, decides to focus on herself. The film seems to suggest a feminist moment of budding autonomy, which the protagonist's financial security, her upper-middle-class position, and all the explicit and implicit privileges that automatically come with being white and from the United States allow. Her encounters with women of other ethnicities in her travels suggest this trend as well. The premise seems to support women's independence, but the narrative actually builds around a romantic theme: at the end of the movie the main female character achieves true happiness and self-understanding when she finds the right man, in this case a sensitive, passionate, and cooking foreigner, who incidentally happens to own a jewel business. While the film gives a nod to supporting women to move beyond the social norms that dictate thin bodies as the only appropriate ones, in the end it reinforces thinness as normative and desirable—at least for white women—and reaffirms Liz's role as a romantic partner to a wealthy man.

While Julia Roberts's character appears to celebrate women's power and agency, she does not do much to subvert the social rules that govern when, what, or how much women can eat onscreen. Like the other films in this chapter, *Eat Pray Love* embodies a postfeminist perspective that seems to suggest that the goals of feminism have been achieved. Yet the films undermine women's social power. We recognize that the term *postfeminism* has multiple meanings. Here, we maintain that these films tend to embrace a version of postfeminism that functions as a reaction to second-wave feminism. As feminist scholar Susan Faludi argued, a backlash against the feminist movement in the 1980s was mobilized through consumer culture to distort and undermine key feminist concepts and women's power. In this commodified version of women's power—which we refer to here as postfeminism—the reaction against women and the women's movement perverted women's genuine quest for economic and social independence into a narcissistic, consumption-oriented aim for self-improvement that undermined their actual social power.[7] Similarly, feminist cultural studies scholar Angela McRobbie uses the term *postfeminism* to describe a movement that assumes the work of feminism has been accomplished and women can now turn their attention to other issues. McRobbie recognizes postfeminist trends in media in her examination of films like *Bridget Jones's Diary* (Maguire, 2001) and television shows like *What Not to Wear* as neoliberal sites of feminist backlash that seductively invite women to assume they are occupying positions of power when they are not.[8] The co-optation and commercialization of the feminist movement ultimately undermine women's real power and sell them, instead, an individualized choice that detracts from the aim of advancing equitable political, social, and economic power for women. As we see these trends playing themselves out in food films, we draw on the concept of postfeminism to frame our analysis. In short, these films reassure audiences that, although women have obtained more power than they have had in the past, they are still under control and not a threat to the dominant social order. As citizens, women's power appears manageable, and the preparation and consumption of food help to keep women in a not-too-threatening place.

The films discussed in this chapter form sites of contention: they oscillate between reinforcing postfeminist, dominant standards of femininity and questioning the very tenets on which this construct is based. This tension mirrors and reproduces dynamics around femininity and power in the contemporary United States, and it channels these through the lens of food and cooking. Depending on their particular production contexts, the films are more or less successful in their ability to take on dominant gender, class, and race norms and question their validity, while others capitulate to dominant discourses and reinforce existing social arrangements. Collectively, we see this group of films as appearing to question social arrangements that undercut women's power but also as undermining women's political agency if that entails renouncing their ability to function—as proper women—in home kitchens outside of the public domain. Furthermore, these films tend to privilege a heterosexist perspective, and they focus primarily on white middle- to upper-middle-class women. Women of color do not exist in the narrative worlds of *No Reservations, It's Complicated, Julie & Julia,* and *Waitress.*

FOOD-FILM LEGACIES

Before we examine the films that emerged in the early 2000s, we turn our focus briefly to important predecessor films that provide background for our discussion of women, food, and power. The now renowned Danish film *Babette's Feast* focuses on a dinner prepared by Babette, a famous French chef who survived the aftermath of the 1870 Paris Commune and lives incognito in a small Protestant fundamentalist community on the coast of Denmark, working as a cook for the two daughters of the community founder. Fourteen years after her arrival, Babette wants to thank her employers by cooking a French meal, for which we learn she will spend a great sum of money won in a lottery. With much hesitation the frugal and pious elderly sisters agree to this undertaking but are horrified as the food arrives: a live tortoise; cages of live quails; and boxes of wine, fruit, and cheese. The sisters and their deceased father's followers, a group of elderly townspeople, agree to partake of the meal but neither to enjoy it nor talk about it. In the end the dinner overcomes the diffidence of the villagers, who consider any physical pleasure an entryway to eternal damnation. The sensuality that the food gently brings to them helps them shed their pettiness and limitations, and eventually brings them closer to their founder's ideals of mutual love (fig. 2.1). *Babette's Feast* received tremendous acclaim from American media and won numerous awards, including the Oscar for Best Foreign Film in 1988. When critics in newspapers and journals discuss the genre of the "food film," *Babette's Feast* is often one of their primary examples and has also become one of the food narratives "cited" by recent food films.[9]

Babette's Feast presents its protagonist as "a maestro, a Rubinstein of cuisine. The kitchen is her orchestra, the spoon her baton."[10] Babette possesses a level of seriousness typically reserved for male chefs. Unlike many of her predecessors in film and on TV, she never poses for the camera as a sexual object. She appears engrossed in the task at hand and approaches food and

FIGURE 2.1 The members of a severe Protestant sect in nineteenth-century rural Denmark find joy and reconciliation through a shared meal and the pleasures of the table in *Babette's Feast*, a seminal work in the emergence of the food-film genre.

cooking with great dexterity and skill. We see her working in silence, the only sound the crackling of fire in the stove and the clinking of pots and cooking utensils, unlike food films that revolve around female characters and rely on nondiegetic music to create a sensuous, feminine environment.

We position this film in contrast to dominant representations of women and food, which frequently have offered images of women as victims of food. As food studies feminist scholar Carole Counihan argues, "For U.S. women the permeability of their bodies represents their weak sense of autonomy and power, and that as a result the acts of eating, copulation, or birth—which cross the physical barriers of the body—can constitute terrifying threats to the psychological integrity of the self."[11] Compared to the way that U.S. media tend to represent women as disempowered by food, in *Babette's Feast* food functions as a meaningful expression of self and identity. *Babette's Feast* serves as an important marker, given the stark contrast most other food films provide.

Let us briefly consider one of the first U.S. films to bring food-related themes to the fore, the 1989 *Fried Green Tomatoes*, which nevertheless does not yet present the visual, textual, and narrative elements that will later come to characterize food films. Based on a novel that represents two of its main characters—Idgie and Ruth—as a lesbian couple, the film implies this relationship without directly naming it as such, a move that—at the time that the film was produced—helped it to resonate with straight, mainstream audiences, while carefully negotiating its relationship with GLBT spectators. *Fried Green Tomatoes* seems to offer a feminist utopian possibility to rethink food and femininity, but it reduces its own power by privileging whiteness, emphasizing dominant notions of beauty, and poking fun at fat women. The film cuts back and forth between a contemporary friendship between the overweight character Evelyn and her friendship with the elderly woman Ninny and the story of Idgie and Ruth in the 1920s. Idgie saves Ruth from a violent marriage, and the two women run the Whistle Stop Café, a space that subverts traditional hierarchies: here, women and people of color run the show, which angers the Ku Klux Klan in the small Alabama town. In one of the film's key scenes we learn that Idgie and Ruth have murdered Ruth's abusive spouse and are serving his body as BBQ to a local policeman. In their roles as professional cooks and restaurant owners, Idgie and Ruth transform food, eating, and cooking into realms of upheaval, where women can bond in safety, roll around on the floor covered in flour in a quasi-erotic embrace, and provide food to impoverished, starving people in dust bowl settlement camps (fig. 2.2).

Although the café appears to be an idealized arena of female power (always under threat by white men), the film undoes its seemingly progressive narrative by relegating black characters to secondary roles, conforming to mainstream Hollywood definitions of beauty, and poking fun at Evelyn's compulsive eating disorder. The film recreates dichotomous thinking that aligns "good" eating with thinness and "bad" eating with fatness, lack of control, and hysteria. Nonetheless, *Fried Green Tomatoes* stands out in its depiction of women enjoying food without having to have follow-up sex with men. Furthermore, it places the two women as owners of a food establishment who can exercise control in a world that, otherwise, undermines their power. Food offers the possibility of empowerment and refuge and is connected to economic and social autonomy.

Fried Green Tomatoes and *Babette's Feast* serve as important entry points into a discussion of the food films about professional women that emerge

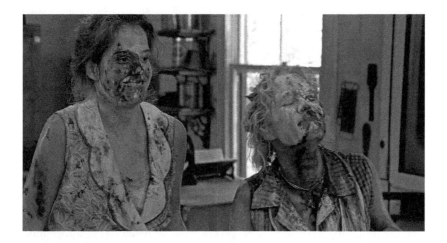

FIGURE 2.2 In *Fried Green Tomatoes* a commercial kitchen becomes a safe space for two women to explore their feelings for each other through the sensual exploration of food.

in the early 2000s. Across all of them, some common themes surface: kitchens as a site of struggle for autonomy, power, and liberation (sometimes, but not always, sexual liberation); issues of control; complexity surrounding the divide between domestic and public spheres; and female bonding and women's empowerment as a strategy for combatting domestic violence. The food films that follow in the wake of *Babette's Feast* adhere to a pattern of quasi liberation in cooking, a phenomenon that Elspeth Probyn describes as a "new sphere": "beyond the now tattered dream of liberation in the bedroom, and freed from the obligations of cooking, the kitchen is now sold to women as the new sphere of sensual liberation."[12] In the following sections we explore how these themes emerge and consider what they can tell us about women, power, and citizenship.

NO RESERVATIONS? CONTROL AND PASSION IN THE PROFESSIONAL KITCHEN

Framed in the cold blue light of a medium close-up that features her standing in the room of the upscale New York City restaurant for which she works as executive chef, reserved and icy Kate (Catherine Zeta-Jones) processes her anger over the gradual loss of control of her kitchen. Kate, the protagonist of *No Reservations*, experiences a jolt to her controlled life as a professional chef when her sister dies in a car accident, leaving Kate's nine-year-old niece, Zoe (Abigail Breslin), to live with her. In therapy for her control issues, Kate must adjust to significant changes in her life, including the responsibility (and joy) of having a child, sharing her restaurant kitchen with rising chef star Nick (Aaron Eckhart), and dealing with her boss, Paula (Patricia Clarkson), who is unwilling to indulge Kate's obsessive-compulsive nature. As the title suggests, Kate must learn to give up being reserved to live a fulfilled life, renouncing her status as a star chef and downgrading her professional position to co-owner of a comfort-food café. Temperamental, demanding, and opinionated, Kate initially defies traditional female roles in her refusal to kowtow to others and submit herself to the wills of ignorant restaurant goers. Much like Babette, she prides herself on her culinary competence, at least in the first half of the film. What is missing is any shred of warmth, and the repeated images of Kate escaping to the restaurant's cooler emphasize her social and emotional coldness. Ironically, Kate is able to express her bottled-up emotions only in the mise-en-scène of the restaurant's cooler, a claustrophobic, frigid bluish space where she finds solace and refuge when she can no longer cope.

An insipid remake of the thoughtful, touching German original, *Mostly Martha* (Nettelbeck, 2001), *No Reservations* grapples with women's power and ability to find a place in society as professionals. Although an experienced, established culinary expert with an excellent reputation as a chef, Kate is unable to enter into full adult life until she falls in love with Nick, a soft, gentle male who fears leading a kitchen of his own. He would prefer to share a kitchen with Kate and presents himself as a nonthreatening beta male. As Roger Ebert aptly writes about the film, "and they cooked happily ever after."[13] Kate appears to be a woman who is just too much to handle, a threat to a dominant order that privileges heterosexual relationships and prefers that women in kitchens play more comforting roles. Kate, however, is anything but comforting, at least until the film places her in an appropriate gender position in a respectively appropriate kitchen. She is cold, rude, and inaccessible throughout much of the film.

Only a gentle, nurturing, nondominant man can handle her and help her find her way back to proper femininity. Even Kate's therapist, whom she feeds in analysis sessions rather than having to talk with him, throws up his hands at her inability to connect.

The film makes an effort to show us that it takes professional women seriously. When a condescending patron complains that Kate's *foie gras* is overcooked, Kate looks at him aghast. "It's nothing to be ashamed of, honey," he states; "even the best stumble over *foie gras*." Irate, Kate seizes the plate and describes that the *foie gras* has been prepared *comme il faut*—as it should be—and calls him "honey," her hand defiantly placed on her hip. A fight ensues, and the customers leave in anger. The film asks us to empathize with Kate when this ignorant customer talks down to her, assuming that she, as a woman chef, is not among the best and lacks experience. Reaffirming her excellent training and knowledge, the film invites us to see her as an expert.

It is, however, this expertise that keeps her from having a full adult life. Her sister and one of her neighbors quip on her extreme focus and her unwillingness to give up rules. "So what's the problem with having rules?" Kate states defensively to her therapist. "It's not as if I'm controlling or anything. I just prefer for things to be done exactly right. That's why I wind up doing things myself. Do you have any idea how difficult it is to coordinate forty dishes at once?" The therapist, slowly reaching his wits end with Kate's need to control everything in her environment, slices into a scallop she has prepared for him as he feebly attempts to offer help: "I thought we agreed you weren't going to cook for me anymore." Kate's ability to cook and feed, although based on tremendous expertise and experience, are represented as control mechanisms, rather than tools to express nurturing and emotional connections.

Kate's expertise is bathed in a negative light as it becomes an obstacle to establishing meaningful relationships. After the death of her sister she cannot get Zoe to eat anything. We see a shot of the sister's interment at the graveyard, and the camera then brings us to Kate's apartment. Zoe is seated at the table, and we assume her point of view, as Kate slides a plate toward us that contains a whole cooked fish. The dead fish head stares back at Zoe—and us—and the child refuses once again to eat. Kate's insensitivity toward her niece's grieving (and her own lack of grieving) converge in the act of serving a perfectly prepared but emotionally cold meal that makes Zoe feel more alienated and sad than before. The film suggests that women cannot have it all and must choose between expertise and emotion.

It is only through direct conflict surrounding Zoe's problems at school and Nick's consistent willingness to defer to Kate's power that she is able to let herself open up. Melting Kate's hard core also requires some sexually suggestive scenes, including one in which she is blindfolded and Nick makes her taste a sauce and detect the ingredients. Nick reverses the relationship so that she is subject to his control. Kate sheds her coldness only when she steps down from running a kitchen in a top-notch restaurant to prepare comfort food in a bistro that she, he, and the kid run together as a family affair.

Throughout the film we see gorgeously plated but emotionally sterile food prepared by Kate (fig. 2.3). We rarely see her eat; her obsession with preparing perfect food and her need to control her environment make her appear as emotionally anorectic. Nick's food, in contrast, is inventive, responsive, and engaged. Zoe has refused to eat since the death of her mother,

FIGURE 2.3 The limitations that Kate, the female chef protagonist of *No Reservations*, experiences in her emotional life hint at the difficulties women face when working in restaurant kitchens while trying to balance personal and professional lives.

until Nick hands her a plate of pasta to hold for him. The camera cuts to an image of this sad, lost orphan girl gaining connection and beginning to recover through the plate of pasta, which she eats with great vigor. Kate is astounded at this response, as her relationship to food is complex and conflicted. Although the film does not equate her with food in the same way that many of the magical food films we will examine in chapter 3 do, she and her food appear in parallel. Tender, frail, and vulnerable like the quails and *foie gras* she prepares, Kate requires careful handling.

Unlike in the original *Mostly Martha*, where the lead character, Martha, achieves happiness through a warm and happy-go-lucky foreign man (the Italian Mario) and a trip to his homeland of Italy, Kate does not experience redemption through a connection with ethnic difference but rather via the handsome blond, white, laid-back Nick.[14] The film references the Italian context of its predecessor when Kate reenters her kitchen for the first time since her sister's death, Verdi's "Celeste" from *Aida* blaring and Nick as new chef in the kitchen. We see him turn up the music even louder, as he sings and dances around, energizing the kitchen staff. Kate is horrified as he directs the staff to sing along, holding an uncooked quail in his left hand and a basting brush in his right.

While the German original questions traditional Teutonic stolidity, the American version simply reasserts a traditional heterosexual gender pattern that involves a harsh woman being saved by a kindhearted man. Leaving her professional life as a notable chef in a highly ranked New York restaurant to continue her life in middle-class family bliss tells a subtle but important story about women, power, and food: Kate can never experience happiness just by having a professional career. In fact, her career is killing her emotional life because her expertise alienates her rather than connecting her with others. She fails at being female until she accepts her role as nurturer rather than expert. Unlike Babette, Kate cannot own her professional identity without having the parameters of a family to surround her and an appropriate career in a comfort-food café that moves her away from the public domain into a more private—and also feminine—sphere.

Women's development and success in a professional kitchen is represented as even more conflicted in *The Ramen Girl* (Ackerman, 2008), the story of Abby (Brittany Murphy), a white American young woman who relocates to Japan to be with her boyfriend. When he breaks up with her, she decides that learning how to make ramen noodles from Maezumi (Toshiyuki Nishida), the owner of the shop next door to her apartment, would give sense to her life. Maezumi's specialty (which apparently has the almost magical power to make people feel better) and its preparation are shot in the best "food-porn" style, highlighting the gestures and skills of the master, represented as a repository of Japanese culinary tradition and philosophical wisdom. These representations are quite different from those offered in Japanese movies, such as *Tampopo* and the more recent *Udon* (Motohiro, 2006), which focused on the impact of media on traditional Japanese food artisans. The fetishization of the East as hard to understand, but brimming with a sapience that the West needs to find as a stable way of life, is embodied in the relationship between the noodle master and Abby and reiterates orientalizing, Eurocentric tropes and a narrative framework similar to films such as *The Karate Kid* (Avildsen, 1984): rote repetition of apparently senseless actions to learn discipline and, eventually, an art.[15] At the same time, this trope affirms Abby's whiteness and highlights her ability to take on Japanese culture without ever having to give up her privileged place of white femininity. The hard-drinking, always-yelling, rough, but deep-down-sensitive ramen maker, who does not speak a word of English, is quite confused by this young blond, who cannot communicate in Japanese herself but seems determined to stick with him.

At first, she does not even know how to wash pots and pans, showing up for her first day of training in a cute black dress and high heeled shoes. Over time, she demonstrates a very rational, how-to, step-by-step perspective to cooking that clashes with the more instinctual and spiritual approach of the noodle maker. This contrast echoes the connection between ethnic, nonwhite traditions with sensory-based skills and instinctual cooking, rather than with rational techniques and discipline, which we observed in the films focused on ethnic professional chefs discussed in chapter 1. Abby becomes the master's official apprentice, taking the place of the male child who went to Paris to study French cooking but creating waves in the all-male community of the noodle masters. Even when the grand master of all noodle masters does not give her his blessing, stating she is good but needs more time and restraint, her teacher still declares her his successor. Eventually she goes back to New York, where she opens her own ramen shop and starts a new life with a Japanese man she had met in Tokyo, who has quit his company to follow his heart and be with her.

In the film it falls to a white woman to bring change to a conservative and sexist professional community, reinforcing the trope of Westerners as bringers of modernization and progress.[16] From the point of view of gender, however, Abby does not cook from a place of expertise but rather is coached to cook from the heart, silencing all her inner turmoil. The film's insistence on labeling her a "girl" in its title reaffirms her subservience and lack of power. Abby, as a girl, has to learn love to put love in the food she makes, which necessitates that she establish a solid and stable romantic life. When Abby cries over a pot of stock, her clients also become sad, remembering all their pains and losses (in chapter 3 we will see this magical property of food becomes a common theme when the female cooks are ethnic or exotic). Although we never see men crying into cooking pots and spreading their feelings through their tears, this trope has become commonplace in many food films with female protagonists. Although *The Ramen Girl* tries to package this message as emanating from Japanese culture—in this case from the chef's old mother—it reiterates common perceptions of how we are supposed to understand women's relationship to cooking. Abby's success as ramen chef is only complete when a man comes across half the globe to be with her. Whereas *No Reservations* punishes its lead character for having an excess of expertise and not enough heart, *The Ramen Girl* enables its leading woman to become accomplished through her heart. Her mind is simply not enough, whereas Kate's is too much. The tension between romantic love as true call for women and their ability to become professionals and business owners persists, echoing cultural themes that have long held powerful, historical force.

WOMEN CHEFS CAUGHT IN THE PUBLIC-PRIVATE DIVIDE

In nineteenth-century British and U.S. cultures the idea of a "cult of true womanhood" arose. Perhaps best exemplified in the poem *The Angel in the*

House, by Coventry Patmore, published initially in 1854, this cultural ideology affirmed a long-standing value system that aligned women with the four cardinal virtues of submissiveness, piety, purity, and—unsurprisingly—domesticity.[17] A century and a half later, cookbook author and television star Nigella Lawson urges women to reclaim their inner "domestic goddess" and turn to domesticity as a form of healing. We quote a passage from her website at length because it illustrates a turn to the domestic born out of the cultural ideology of true womanhood that reemerges in postfeminist discourse and in food films:

> I do think that many of us have become alienated from the domestic sphere, and that it can actually make us feel better to claim back some of that space, make it comforting rather than frightening.
>
> . . . Baking stands both as a useful metaphor for the familial warmth of the kitchen we fondly imagine used to exist, and as a way of reclaiming our lost Eden. . . .
>
> The trouble with much modern cooking is not that the food it produces isn't good, but that the mood it induces in the cook is one of skin-of-the-teeth efficiency, all briskness and little pleasure. Sometimes that's the best we can manage, but at other times we don't want to feel like a post-modern, post-feminist, overstretched woman but, rather, a domestic goddess, trailing nutmeggy fumes of baking pie in our languorous wake.
>
> So what I'm talking about is not being a domestic goddess exactly, but feeling like one. One of the reasons making cakes is satisfying is that the effort required is so much less than the gratitude conferred . . . and the returns are high: you feel disproportionately good about yourself afterwards.
>
> This is what baking . . . is about: feeling good, wafting along in the warm, sweet-smelling air, unwinding, no longer being entirely an office creature. . . . Part of it too is about a fond, if ironic, dream: the unexpressed "I" that is a cross between Sophia Loren and Debbie Reynolds in pink cashmere cardigan and fetching gingham pinny, a weekend alter-ego winning adoring glances and endless approbation from anyone who has the good fortune to eat in her kitchen.
>
> The good thing is, we don't have to get ourselves up in Little Lady drag and we don't have to renounce the world and enter into a life of domestic

drudgery. But we can bake a little—and a cake is just a cake, far easier than getting the timing right for even the most artlessly casual of midweek dinner parties.[18]

The mythology of the domestic goddess, a long-standing trope in British and U.S. cultures, reemerges in a number of food films. In particular, it emerges in films featuring professional women who move back into the domestic sphere, where they find greater fulfillment and happiness. In keeping with this tradition these food-film characters inhabit professional lives that situate them in domestic contexts, a confusing move that simultaneously invites women to achieve greater happiness by returning to professions associated with the home. *Julie & Julia* and *It's Complicated* present a careful realignment of power structures that repositions a woman's place as being in the home, cooking beautiful food and embracing this as her ideal role, echoing the tradition of the angel in the home and the domestic goddess.

Julie & Julia follows two parallel narratives, which the film reminds us are "two true stories." We open to the scene of a bright blue sky and the sound of traditional French accordion music to meet Julia Child (Meryl Streep) enjoying a meal with her husband Paul (Stanley Tucci). Nostalgic imagery of Paris situates us in the world of the historically distant sublime. "Butter," Julia sighs, as the camera cuts to an image of perfectly prepared *sole meunière* sizzling in a pan. Shot in close-up, the waiter debones a fish so beautiful that we can almost smell and taste it. "Oh my goodness," Julia chuckles, as we see her lift a piece with a fork to her mouth, her plaid jacket, pearl earrings, necklace, and beige hat providing a highly stylized image of the famous chef. "You have to taste this," she says as she leans toward her husband and places the fork in his mouth. In a state of utter speechlessness, he pats her gently as she regains her composure after this encounter with perfection. "I know, I know," he murmurs gently. Perfect food frames the film's beginning in this transmediated story that began as Julie Powell's blog (http://juliepowell.blogspot.com/), which formed the basis for a book, *Julie & Julia: 365 Days, 524 Recipes, 1 Tiny Apartment Kitchen*, transformed then into the film itself.

The film cuts to Queens, New York, in the year 2002 to the story of Julie Powell (Amy Adams), a twenty-nine-year-old white woman who works for an insurance company that is dealing with post-9/11 insurance claims. Julie and her husband, Eric, are moving from their tiny Brooklyn apartment to a larger place in Queens. We see her packing, as the camera frames her copy of *The Art of French Cooking* as Julie places it in a moving box. The robust sound of packing tape being ripped as it covers the box seals the connection between Julia and Julie. Once placed in the car, the box with the word *Cookbooks* written in large print on it serves as a visual harbinger of things to come. From the outset the two women appear in parallel, and the film crosscuts between their lives to remind us both of similarities and differences between them. Julia's apartment in Paris represents an elegant, idealized, romantic vision of France, while Julie lives in an unglamorous, crowded flat. While Julia travels throughout Europe, Julie is trapped in her small claustrophobic cubicle, wedged between other skyscrapers in now traumatized Manhattan.

The film depicts Julia Child as Julie wants to see her. Even the film's title echoes this in listing Julie first, then Julia. Positioned in the past, Julia Child can eat food with abandon, much like the characters of Idgie and Ruth can in *Fried Green Tomatoes*. Unlike Liz in *Eat Pray Love*, Julia Child is allowed to be a bit plump yet never struggles to squeeze into clothes. Julia eats, celebrates sex, and couldn't care less about gaining weight. She becomes an ideal, after whom Julie begins to pattern herself. In stylized retro clothing, often sipping a martini, Julie imagines a connection to Julia Child that helps her to find her way in post-9/11 New York and a world that has become too competitive and disconnected. The film offers a return to domesticity as the solution to an injured, confused world but only a return for women. Julie even sees Julia as a kind of imaginary friend: "I would like to be a bridesmaid in her wedding in 1947." Julie's Julia is a romanticized blur of the past, not an actual individual contemporary woman. Julia Child, as we learn later in the film when Julie undertakes a pilgrimage to Child's reconstructed kitchen in the Smithsonian Museum, does not return this connection. "Julia hates me!" Julie cries with despair when she learns of Child's response to her blog, as the camera cuts to Julia echoing the sentiment, "They hate us!" with regard to Houghton Mifflin's assessment of her manuscript. The crosscutting provides a constant comparison and contrast between the two women and differentiates the worlds in which they live(d).

Although Julie brushes off Julia Child's attitude about her blog, Child's editor, Judith Jones, later clarified how Child felt about the project before her death:

> [Mastering the Art of French Cooking's] excellent introduction to French cuisine notwithstanding, Jones says Child did not approve of Powell's cook-every-recipe-in-one-year project. The editor and author read Powell's blog together (Julie and Julia was published a year after Child's 2004 death). Julia said, "I don't think she's a serious cook." Jones thinks there was a generational difference between Powell and Child. "Flinging around four-letter words when cooking isn't attractive, to me or Julia. She didn't want to endorse it. What came through on the blog was somebody who was doing it almost for the sake of a stunt. She would never really describe the end results, how delicious it was, and what she learned. Julia didn't like what she called 'the flimsies.' She didn't suffer fools, if you know what I mean."[19]

Just as Jones describes the generational distance, the film utilizes the historical distance between Julie and Julia: placing images of women enjoying food without repercussions in the past carefully packages them as distant yet accessible enough for contemporary women to enjoy.

Food becomes a refuge from a harsh world for Julie. After an awful day of handling one terrible phone call after another in the office, Julie heads home. She passes a store window featuring a large Scharffen Berger chocolate add, the window reflecting Julie as she peers into the display. "Chocolate cream pie," she states. "You know what I love about cooking? I love that after a day when nothing is sure, I mean nothing, nothing, you can come home and absolutely know that if you add egg yolks to chocolate and sugar and milk, it will get thick. It's such a comfort." Dressed in a cute little blouse with a red pin, Julie speaks as we see her mixing a luxurious batter in her small, utilitarian kitchen. Her husband approaches the bowl. "Bad day?" he asks, as he dips his finger in the chocolate mixture and sighs with pleasure. He hands her a martini, which she sips, as he continues to lick the mixture from the spoon. While work is hell, home provides safe refuge and the potential for happiness. Food is depicted here as comfort and nurture, but this nurturing food is prepared in a home, by a woman, rather than in a restaurant.

Food represents both comfort and distress in this context: it connects Julie with Julia, but it also creates a divide between Julie and her husband (with whom she refuses to have sex until the *New York Times* writes about her blog), her mother, and her friends, who see her commitment to cooking in the domestic sphere as a means of avoiding life. Manhattan and its fast-paced culture loom constantly in the background, and Julie finds herself unable to connect with women she thought her friends. Julie's professional companions appear as self-aggrandizing narcissists who follow pounding professional schedules, care only about money and fashion, and are missing out on life's more meaningful aspects. At their "ritual cobb salad lunch," which she is "dreading, dreading, dreading," Julie feels as alienated from these women as she does from her work. The only reasonable option she recognizes is to head home and find comfort in domesticity. Sumptuous images of raspberry Bavarian cream, chicken with mushrooms in cream sauce, and poached eggs provide moments of connection and refuge from a cruel, exterior world.

The emotionally anorectic lunch with her pseudo-friends triggers a new desire in Julie. She steps into the dining room with a large knife, dressed in yet another cute white blouse with an apron, and complains to her husband that her friend Annabelle is writing a blog, a vapid, insipid blog. "I could write a blog. I have thoughts," she exclaims, pointing the knife toward her husband to emphasize her frustration. "Writing a blog," she explains, would be an equalizing force, "in the way that cooking is a way that I get away from what I do all day." Cooking represents flight from an awful work world to a safe home environment, where there are pretty flowers on a vase on a small 1950s style dining room table. "I could just cook my way through Julia Child's cookbook, I could blog about that." She reminisces about her mother cooking Julia's *bœuf bourguignon*. It was "like Julia was there in the room, like some great big, good fairy. And everything was going to be all right." The nostalgic memory amid the experience of feeling of alienation propels her into *The Julie/Julia Project*.

Throughout the film Julia moves more and more into the public sphere while Julie retreats to cooking in her home, a move that she utilizes to reenter the public sphere as a kind of born-again domestic goddess who can cook her food and eat it too (fig. 2.4). The return to the public sphere is one that happens on postfeminist terms: Julie becomes public—and happy—through her renewed investment in traditional femininity, expressed publicly and shared with a growing number of readers through her blog. While Julia Child's life is clearly colored by overt politics (her husband is asked by a McCarthy era panel whether he is a homosexual, and they are moved out of Paris to remote places like Oslo), Julie's life remains devoid of clear political references. Julia's life explicitly defies political pressures. As she describes to her sister with early feminist era sounding but jovial defiance, their dad "wanted us to stay in Pasadena, marry Republicans, and breed like rabbits." Julia's commitment to cooking is a political one, in which she challenges traditional gender expectations. She describes her male classmates at the French cooking school: "You should have seen the way those men looked at me. As if I was some frivolous housewife wanting to kill time!" In food Julia finds her calling: "I've been looking for a career all my life, and I've found it." Julie, however, wallows in self-pity. In one scene we

FIGURE 2.4 *Julie & Julia* exposes the rift between the reality of daily cooking toil and the ideal of culinary artistry, as well as the impact of food media on home cooks.

see her sitting on the floor crying as she attempts to restuff raw poultry that has slipped and fallen. In an expressly unfeminist moment in the film Julie describes herself as a "bitch" and complains that she's "gotten fat." The film oscillates between the stories of these two women, and in doing so, it reminds us of the opportunities that women have (had) while also reassuring us that happiness can be found in the public sphere only through a return to the domestic. Once the *New York Times* writes about Julie's blog, her life turns around: she reunites with her husband and leaves a stick of butter below Julia's picture in the Smithsonian to thank her for what she's done for her life. "I love you, Julia," Julie states, after which the Smithsonian kitchen transforms into Julia's real kitchen, with Julia alive, well, and cooking. Past and present blend, and the film ends with a freeze-frame of Julia at her sink.

Julie & Julia complicates the understanding of women's role in public and private space by positioning Julie as happiest in her home and defining her engagement with the public sphere via the Internet. Certainly, the blog is public, yet it keeps her comfortably in her home. While Julie appears to move into the public, we ultimately see her in the domestic setting, and the film reinforces how awful the external world is and how much happier she is cooking at home. At the same time, the film reminds us that Julia tried out domesticity and was utterly bored with it: "Wives don't do anything," she affirms, whereas Julie finds refuge in the domestic sphere, which offers refuge from awful work and mean friends. Certainly, Julie's blog becomes a safe pathway toward reentering the public sphere, but it happens distinctly through the private sphere and, more specifically, through food. It's about cooking in the home. In constant tension between public and private spheres, the film utilizes food and women's relationship to it to redefine domesticity as the new public sphere, a move that we see as deeply regressive. Escapism into the past winds up as a renewed alignment of femininity with domesticity.

To be sure, other films follow a pattern of women returning to the domestic sphere—carefully coded as quasi-public spheres—in ways that seem to grant them power and autonomy but that ultimately limit their capacity to participate as full-fledged political, economic, and cultural citizens. White female middle-class citizenship emerges as a carefully negotiated space that is not too public and therefore not too powerful. Films like *It's Complicated* (again starring Meryl Streep as the lead character, this time Jane) iterate a similar pattern. In *It's Complicated* Jane is a successful bakery owner in Santa Barbara who winds up in a torrid affair with her ex-husband of ten years, Jake (Alec Baldwin) at the same time as she is falling in love with architect Adam (Steve Martin), who is redoing her kitchen. After a decade of abstinence following an ugly divorce that occurred because Jake had an affair with a much younger woman, Jane finds herself having (and enjoying) sex as her ex-husband's other woman. As *Washington Post* reviewer Michael O'Sullivan writes, the film provides "Food Network porn, hot, middle-age sex and a happy, if slightly bittersweet, ending. For a particular audience—but not just for that audience—what's not to love?"[20] The film tells a tale of middle-aged, white women and sexuality and aims to strike an appeal with audience members of the same ethnicity, age, and gender as Jane. "I love it when you smell like butter," Jake says to her, likening her to the wondrous pastries her bakery produces. Although an independent business owner who has clearly done just fine on her own financially (she is finally getting the kitchen at home she has always wanted in her gorgeous California house), Jane rarely appears in her public persona; rather, her sphere is her home kitchen, where she cooks food for her family and love interests. When we do see her in her bakery—a flourishing business—it is after hours with love interest Adam, as they make and eat a batch of chocolate after getting stoned at a party. As O'Sullivan observes, director "[Nancy] Meyers sets as many scenes as possible within its homey confines."[21] We actually never see Jane engaged in work at her business—we see her there after hours or popping in during work hours briefly. Like Julie, Jane appears almost exclusively in the domestic realm. The film thus exemplifies a deep sense of ambiguity, like the other films we explore here, about working women involved in the production of food.

These films seem to suggest that women can indeed find happiness, to revisit Nigella Lawson's words, as "domestic goddess, trailing nutmeggy fumes of baking pie in our languorous wake." The film seems to suggest that a woman's place is—mostly—in the home, cooking for loved ones and dressing nicely. While these films are indeed a far cry from the original image of *The Angel in the House*, where Patmore wrote that

"Man must be pleased; but him to please is woman's pleasure," we find remnants of this discourse emerging as a form of unconscious politics that affirms (heterosexual, white) women's alignment with domesticity and food as a powerful force that assures professional women cooks a place in the public sphere through their alignment with homes, families, and domestic cooking. Women can have their cake and eat it too under the following conditions: they do not rely too heavily on knowledge and expertise, they cook mostly in the home, and if they cook in professional settings, they rely on their hearts to guide them.

WAITRESS: WORKING-CLASS WOMEN CAN HAVE THEIR PIE AND EAT IT, TOO

A refreshing deviation from the conservative discourses in the films we have explored, the independent film *Waitress* undertakes a more focused attempt to talk back to idealized images of women and domesticity. Directed by Adrienne Shelly, the film focuses on the life of Jenna (Keri Russell), who works as a waitress in Joe's Pie Diner somewhere in the southern United States. Jenna lives with her abusive, ignorant husband, Earl (Jeremy Sisto), whose name calls forth memories of a song made famous by the Dixie Chicks in 2000, "Goodbye Earl," in which best friends Mary Anne and Wanda murder Wanda's abusive husband, Earl, with poisoned black-eyed peas. Reminiscent, as well, of *Fried Green Tomatoes*, which is also set in the South and features an abusive husband (who is murdered and eaten in the film), *Waitress* taps into a contemporary narrative tradition of disempowered southern working-class women taking back their lives through ownership of restaurants and food businesses. In the song "Goodbye Earl," characters Mary Anne and Wanda, as the lyrics go, "bought some land and a roadside stand out on Highway 109. They sell Tennessee ham and strawberry jam, and they don't lose any sleep at night, 'cause Earl had to die, goodbye Earl." Like Mary Anne and Wanda and Idgie and Ruth, Jenna moves from the domestic horror of being beaten, humiliated, and controlled, living in constant fear, to the status of independent restaurant/business owner. Like the other women of the South listed above whose narrative develops along a similar line, Jenna comes from a blue-collar, working-class southern background, with no educational training and familial empowerment to take a stand, and yet she does. In all three cases this transformation emerges through food. In Jenna's case this food is pie.

A talented pie maker, Jenna creates recipes with titles inspired by her life, a talent she has learned from her mother. Throughout the film we see her dream up and bake dozens of pies. From Pregnant-Miserable-Self-Pitying-Loser Pie to Marshmallow-Mermaid Pie to I-Don't-Want-Earl's-Baby Pie to Bad-Baby Pie, Jenna uses food to talk back against the life she has inherited. Ultimately, it is her pies that gain her access to power, success, and freedom. First, however, she must endure an initially unwanted pregnancy, go through a torrid affair with her gynecologist, Jim Pomatter (Nathan Fillion), and put up with Joe (Andy Griffith), the owner of the diner who all waitresses fear to serve because of his curmudgeonly attitude. Ultimately supported by Joe, who leaves almost $300,000 to her on his death, and bolstered by her own self-confidence, Jenna becomes the new owner of the diner (now called Lulu's Pies, named after her daughter), wins a big pie contest, and walks hand-in-hand with daughter Lulu as the film concludes. We learn that Jenna has gained her pie-baking skills from her mother, who taught her when she was young. This suggests that women can empower and support each other, even if it does so through a tale of pies, a food that, like so many sweets, has traditionally been associated with women and femininity.[22]

Unlike the previous films we have explored in this chapter, *Waitress* tells a story of women supporting women toward autonomy, success, and a fulfilling life. Feminist undertones run throughout the film. Jenna battles continuously with herself over her pregnancy and questions whether she should remain pregnant. She even fantasizes about selling the baby, stating, "Not everybody wants to be a mama." "I feel nothing like affection," Jenna utters in the thoughtful and honest process of grappling with the realities of entering into motherhood. "Nobody ever tells you before how ridiculously hard it's gonna be," she says. Jenna is honest about her feelings in a way that defies dominant narratives about women, power, and motherhood: "I'm not a happy woman, Dr. Pomatter, and I don't want you to save me. I don't want to be saved." Domesticity is a trap in *Waitress*, and Jenna's continued efforts to escape are undermined by her violent spouse until her baby is born, when she discovers a deep sense of love and a voice of authority that empowers her to leave Earl. The film is willing to engage the notion that motherhood is not a magical dream where women live happily ever after, and it emphasizes that women can and should have a choice about pregnancy and their bodies.

The women in the film support each other, looking to each other for advice about relationships, work, and life. Jenna, in writing a journal to her baby—which really is a journal to herself—discovers a sense of autonomy and power. Pies appear hear as a feminine source of empowerment. Jenna sings the song her mother sang to Lulu: "Baby don't you cry, gonna make a pie, gonna make a pie with a heart in the middle." When Joe tells her that her Strawberry-Chocolate-Oasis Pie "could solve all the problems of the world," he genuinely seems to be describing the power that Jenna possesses, which, at that point in the film, is still unknown to her. Rather than simply a power to cook and make men happy, Jenna develops the power to convene, bridge, and connect.

Certainly this alignment of women with food runs the risk of positioning women *as food* and thus as objects of desire. We dig into this phenomenon in the next chapter, where women's existential essence is magically imparted into the food they produce, usually in a sexual manner. In *Waitress*, food is the only domain to which Jenna, as a white working-class woman, has access, and she channels her power consciously through it. The film never sexualizes her or reduces her to an object of men's desire but rather consistently calls attention to the predicament in which she finds herself. Rather than looking down on her, the film asks us to walk with her and experience her humiliation and rise to power, all in a rather lighthearted manner that also avoids demonizing men. Indeed, kind men like Joe (disguised as an old curmudgeon) help her to establish autonomy but then go away and let her inhabit center screen with her daughter. While the film's focus on pie as Jenna's arena of expertise is problematic, as is its exclusive focus on white women and their empowerment, we see this film talking back to many representations of women and food. Certainly, the food invites questions about social class, domestic power, the right to choose what happens with one's body, and the ability of women to live independent lives.

DIGESTING THE CAKE WE ARE SERVED . . .

The films we have explored in this chapter demonstrate different approaches to women and femininity. Most of them reestablish white, privileged women's (postfeminist) place as in the home, while trying to find ways to reaffirm women's power and authority. *Waitress* is the only one that does not fundamentally capitulate and move women back into middle-class domestic bliss. What the films fail to do is just as interesting. All of these characters are white, able-bodied women, and the only one who does not come from the (upper) middle class is Jenna in *Waitress*. The other films seem to suggest that women don't need to fight any longer and that they can comfortably withdraw into a (female) domestic space. Furthermore, all of these films privilege heterosexual relationships, even *Fried Green Tomatoes*, which is based on a novel that makes explicit the lesbian relationship between Idgie and Ruth. The film carefully avoids becoming too explicit about this relationship, a move that may express something about the time when the film was made. In all of these films women of color are mostly absent. This discourse excludes their voices from the conversation. When women of color appear as professionals in the world of cooking, they head down a different pathway altogether, one that is paved with magic and that turns them into objects of consumption like the food they prepare. The only other exception to this is the eldest daughter in the film *Tortilla Soup*, which we explore in chapter 6.

Scholars like Nancy Fraser have long argued that women are excluded from the public realm.[23] Seyla Benhabib troubles the notion that there is a neat divide between the private and public spheres, however, proposing that what happens in the realm of the private is part and parcel of what the public experiences. As she writes, "All struggles against oppression in the modern world begin by redefining what had previously been considered private, nonpublic, and nonpolitical issues as matters of public concern, as issues of justice, as sites of power that need discursive legitimation."[24]

Indeed, there is no neat divide, yet the emphasis on returning to the domestic sphere to find satisfaction and to lead a fulfilled life leaves us with a troublingly bitter taste in our mouths. Considering that our analysis has focused on how food films contribute to shaping who gets to participate in which ways as a citizen through the lens of culture, these films are especially troubling. They suggest that women should go back to a previous time in which they held less power. Disconnecting women from expertise in the realm of food, in particular, marks an especially regressive moment, given how women have been historically conceptualized as tied to hearth and home. Women can make food but not as experts and certainly not at the expense of heterosexual relationships. While constraints about body size may have been relaxed somewhat, the women in these films are consistently thin and adhere to dominant standards of beauty. Having our cake and eating it, too, is a complicated batter. We can eat it, but not too much, and it had better emerge from a place of love and not exclusively from women's knowledge.

MAGICAL FOOD, LUSCIOUS BODIES

Contemporary images of food in media tend to convey striking degrees of an erotic aura. As we discussed in our introduction, a specific visual style, often referred to as "food porn," has emerged out of food films and all food-related media. Food magazine covers feature close-up shots of glistening dishes, while Food TV voyeuristically depicts images of perfect meals on designer plates. Tumblr and Instagram are full of pictures of dishes and whole meals, made as appealing and desirable as possible with undertones of erotic enticement. The sexualization and eroticization of food in mainstream U.S. media has become pervasive, situating food itself as an object of desire that can stand on its own without human intervention. Yes, food can be sexy and erotic in and of its own right, without a sexualized body having to be placed on display in conjunction with it.

Websites like epicfoodporn.com and foodporn.com take this trend to a new level and self-consciously poke fun at the idea that they are turning visual representations of food into objects of desire in the way that women have often stood in that role. The subtitle of foodporn.com boasts that its purpose is "Redirecting Perverts to the Refrigerator Since 1999." The website mimics traditional pornography genres, even assuming its viewer to be male and allowing visitors to choose from the categories of *Amateur*, *Asian*, *Barley Legal* (a play on the word *barely*), *Celebrities*, *Hardcore*, *Self-pleasing*, and *Table Dance*. Instead of naked, glistening bodies, this participatory sight features users' images and descriptions of gloriously plated food, shot in close-up. Although these particular websites do not explicitly feature people, this does not mean the human element is completely absent: across a variety of visual media food is made sensual and suggestive by its connection with luscious bodies. In many of these occurrences food tends to be linked to female bodies. It becomes feminized, and frequently these images endow food with magic powers, rooted in the expression of exotic and mysterious cultures. How do these eroticized images of food and their connection with female bodies work in terms of determining who belongs and has voice in U.S. culture? What do they tell us about how women's power and social roles are framed, inside and outside the kitchen?

In the previous chapter we considered films that depict white women of privileged social class backgrounds as professionals in the world of food and how their roles as dedicated and creative professionals clashed with social expectations that see them as nurturers and caregivers. In the U.S. mainstream mediascape it is not just skills, determination, and creativity that lead women to cook well and achieve success. Sometimes, magic and mysterious powers contribute as well, taking away from women's hard-earned merits and dedication to their trade. We turn our attention to the strategies through which food and women's bodies are represented with magical overtones in contemporary U.S. food films. In *Simply Irresistible* (Tarlov, 1999), *Woman on Top* (Torres, 2000), *The Mistress of Spices* (Berges, 2004), and *Chocolat* (Hallström, 2000) food is not only magical but also fetishized, gendered, and racialized. Whereas the films we explored earlier focus exclusively on white (mostly middle-class and upper-middle-class) women, these magical films tend to focus on women of color. The intersectionality of gender, race, ethnicity, sexuality, and social class has resulted in the production of different cultural discourses that manifest themselves in this group of films. They also bear thematic and visual similarity to the Mexican film *Like Water for Chocolate* (Axel, 1989), widely considered seminal in the development of the global food-film genre. Unlike in *Like Water for Chocolate*, the U.S. films that link women, food, and magic tend to objectify female sensuality and sexuality for the viewer's enjoyment rather than embracing them as instruments for women to assert themselves.

It is not unusual for mainstream U.S. films to take up topics and themes explored in films from other countries. Indeed, it is a core process of how we communicate with other cultures, filtering and adapting content that would otherwise be out of place in the U.S. context. Besides these specific intercultural aspects, scholars of literature and media highlight intertextuality, the general process of using one text to shape another text.[1] Far from a simple issue of style in which one novel, poem, or film resembles elements of another text, intertextuality can be intentional or unconscious. As Julia Kristeva writes, "any text is constructed as a mosaic of quotations; any text is the absorption and transformation of another."[2] From this point of view we can understand films—like any other form of communication—as part of complex networks of texts and authors that generate meaning by interacting with each other.[3] *Like Water for Chocolate* may not ever be directly cited by the U.S. films we discuss in this chapter, and the screenwriters and directors may not even have been conscious that they were referencing *Like Water for Chocolate*, but we see and hear its legacy and influence through this body of magical food films.

In the transposition of visual imagery and narratives of *Like Water for Chocolate* into the U.S. context, the relationship among food, media, gender, and sexuality experiences a significant shift. In these U.S. films women's liberation becomes equated with ultimately disempowering notions that reduce rather than amplify women's power. Beauty and sex become the vehicles through which women access "power," an equation that actually serves to further demean women. In fact, we argue that in mainstream U.S. films, visual images of food are set up like the standardized Hollywood visuals of women—as objects of the viewers' gaze. Feminist film scholar Laura Mulvey developed highly compelling insights into the language of film and how it reproduces gender and sexuality in her famous 1975 essay "Visual Pleasure and Narrative Cinema." Although scholars have provided important updates and contestations of Mulvey's original argument, there are tenets from the reflection she developed about women, looking, and cinema that are important to revisit here. In particular, Mulvey gives us a language to consider how images of food are represented in a similar way to the images of women's bodies in mainstream cinema.

Mulvey writes, "In their traditional exhibitionist role women are simultaneously looked at and displayed, with their appearance coded for strong visual and erotic impact so that they can be said to connote *to-be-looked-at-ness*."[4] In other words women appear onscreen just to be looked at rather than as autonomous agents, and this position as object of the gaze undermines women's power. Rooted in a tradition of psychoanalytic inquiry that investigates the relationship between viewers and screens, Mulvey's argument, applied to contemporary images of food, helps us to identify similarities in how food and women are visually displayed and in the narrative approaches surrounding them. In short, we argue that food is frequently treated as "feminine" and serves as a disembodied extension of female bodies on film. Mulvey's article assumed that spectators—whether men or women—are positioned as male in how they are invited to gaze at images on the screen. For Mulvey, as for many film scholars, spectatorship implies a hypothetical relationship between a viewer and the images on the screen. These contemporary food films are particularly interesting in terms of spectatorship, as they take the form of the romantic comedy, an approach that mostly assumes female viewers and thus troubles the idea of the ideal spectator as male.

Although we realize that scholars have critiqued Mulvey's ideas, we are tantalized by her notion that women are displayed as if their inherent nature were *to-be-looked-at*. How does this phenomenon operate in food films, particularly in magical food films? Are these stories the expression of women's fantasies in which they become more appealing to men thanks to their relationship with food, in reality often experienced as work and toil? Is the presence of magic just wishful thinking on the part of dissatisfied women, or is it rather a way for the story to free men from responsibility in relationships? Does the magic invite actual viewers (women, in particular) to free themselves from the legacy of the feminist movement and find comfort in more traditional, politically regressive models of femininity? Or are these images a parody to critique politically regressive models of womanhood?

The four U.S. films we consider in this chapter, along with *Like Water for Chocolate*, foreground eroticism and sexuality in much the same manner as the contemporary romance novel, a genre specifically designed for heterosexual female readers. This is not to say that the films we discuss do not attempt to or succeed in striking appeal with male audiences or lesbian spectators. These films, like any media product, open themselves to a variety of readings, a key point to understanding their intertextuality and spectatorship. But the scripts and the marketing of the films indicate ideal spectators similar to the audience of romance novels.[5] Because so much of this chapter is rooted in the concept of spectatorship, it is important to emphasize that we focus on hypothetical spectators who do not read the films "against the grain" but rather consume these films in alignment with the films' preferred readings, as embedded in the narrative and in the visual material themselves.[6] We start with a brief analysis of *Like Water for Chocolate* to provide a background for how this key text approaches women, power, magic, and food.

SENSUALITY AND MAGIC IN TITA'S KITCHEN

Like Water for Chocolate, which received tremendous acclaim in the U.S., is in itself an intriguing example of intertexuality, as it is based on the homonymous novel by Laura Esquivel, who was married to the film's director, Alfonso Arau, when the film was produced. Both the novel and the film tell the story of a disenfranchised woman's relationship to food, of the power of food and the power women can gain through food, which has the capacity to engender feelings of love and connection between people (fig 3.1). Looking at how food interacts with bodies, sexuality, and gender in media provides a fruitful position from which to examine issues of women's power and their participation in social and cultural life as full citizens.

Like Water for Chocolate makes clear that strong connections exist between the erotic and the culinary. Critic James Berardinelli describes the film as having "an almost ethereal, undeniably erotic quality."[7] Every single reviewer mentions the film's depiction of food and sensuality, as well as their relationship with the body. The wide resonance of these themes is clear, as *Like Water for Chocolate* is one of the most successful Spanish-language films ever released in the United States. Within only seven months the film had grossed more than $20 million, and the novel on which the film is based was among the top ten best sellers in the States. *Like Water for Chocolate*, distributed by Miramax, appealed primarily to the American art-house crowd.[8] As Dianna Niebylski observed, the film was able to speak to mass audiences both in Mexico and abroad.[9]

FIGURE 3.1 The complex connection among food, the senses, and sexuality provides the narrative core for *Like Water for Chocolate*, a film that explores women's lives in Mexico at the turn of the twentieth century.

The story, which takes place in Mexico at the turn of the twentieth century and is narrated by the grandniece of Tita, the main character, is embedded in a larger framework of women's storytelling through food and cooking. Tita's story continues to live through her grandniece, who reads from Tita's recipe book in the opening and closing scenes of the film. As the youngest daughter of a well-to-do family who owns its own rancho, Tita (Lumi Cavazos) has inherited the role of caretaker for her mother and is, therefore, not allowed to marry. Her mother treats her cruelly and insensitively to eradicate her desire to be with young Pedro (Marco Leonardi) rather than to take care of her mother forever. When Pedro marries her sister Rosaura to be close to Tita, Tita finds an alternative realm for her passion in the kitchen, where she is raised and taught to cook by the Indian cook Nacha. She soon discovers that she can do strange things with her cooking. The food she prepares takes on supernatural qualities, always linked back to her body and her desires. After Tita's mother and sister have died and years have passed, Tita and Pedro are finally able to unite. In a final scene of passionate lovemaking their hut goes up in flames, and the fire consumes them.

Tita's story emphasizes relationships that women develop through food and cooking, both positive and negative. For her the kitchen becomes a space of empowerment and self-expression, where women can connect with each other, heal each other, share joys and sorrows, and articulate their individual and collective identities. The film celebrates the kitchen rather than relegating it to an inferior realm. Shot in beautiful sepia tones, the ranch's kitchen is a warm, inviting, comforting space with large sunny windows that provides Tita refuge from the bitterness surrounding her. Preparing and serving food becomes a means of expressing identity and power through the collective act of cooking. Unlike cooking venues in the U.S. films examined in this chapter, Tita's kitchen provides women with a space to rebel against tradition. But the film also illustrates more conflicted relationships that women can entertain with food and cooking. Tita's sister Rosaura does not enjoy cooking and eating, while the other sister, although an avid eater, prefers to have others cook for her (including her revolutionary husband). For Tita's mother, cooking is a chore and a responsibility that comes with the rancho.

Like Water for Chocolate is an erotic film. Tita's sexual and emotional desire for Pedro and his longing for her stand at the center of the film's narrative. Food becomes a venue through which Tita expresses her desire and passion, both consciously and unconsciously. When her tears fall in the batter for her sister's wedding cake, all the guests ingesting it are suddenly caught by great sadness about their lost loves and end up being sick. Images of food itself in the film are, at times, highly eroticized. The sequence in which Pedro gives Tita fresh roses serves as a good example to illustrate the connection between food and sensuality that the film develops. Forced by her mother to throw the roses away, Tita opts instead to use them, at the suggestion of Nacha's ghost, to make quail in rose sauce. As she holds the roses up to inhale their scent, the thorns scratch her chest and cause her to bleed; the blood-filled food in turn causes a remarkable effect on the people who eat the meal prepared with the roses.

While the quails are consumed, the table appears brightly lit, almost magical. The voice of the narrator tells us that "a strange alchemical phenomenon seemed to have occurred. Not only Tita's blood, but her whole being had dissolved into the rose sauce, into the quails, and into every aroma of the meal." A soft yellow light with a magical quality now outlines all the faces. "That's how she invaded Pedro's body—voluptuously, ardently fragrant, and utterly sensual," the narrator continues as Tita's sister Gertrudis breathes heavily at the table and her mother struggles to contain herself. "They had discovered a new way of communicating. Tita was the sender, and Pedro the recipient." The scene builds to ecstasy as we see Gertrudis opening her blouse. The camera, in close-up, tilts down as she exposes her breasts, and we hear the narrator's voice: "Gertrudis was the lucky one within whom this sexual encounter was synthesized through the meal." In the following shots we see Gertrudis running to the shower outside, her skin letting off steam as she attempts to cool down, the camera caressing her body. Completely nude, the heat of her body causes the shower hut to erupt in flames. She exits the burning structure only to meet with a soldier, one of the Federales, who swoops her up onto his horse. The two ride away in a state of sexual delirium.

Tita literally becomes food, and food takes on Tita's spirit. When she first meets Pedro, we learn that she "understood exactly how raw dough must feel when it comes into contact with boiling oil." Food consistently serves as a metaphor to express Tita's state. But *Like Water for Chocolate* does not essentialize the connection between Tita's body and food by reducing her to the level of an object to be consumed; rather, it establishes this correlation as a form of empowerment. The film's use of magical realism suggests that there is power in nature that can be tapped into—possibilities, richness, and depth that can be explored—should one choose to make use of these opportunities. From this point of view *Like Water for Chocolate* reflects the same inspiration and a similar use of magic realism that we can notice in Jorge Amado's novel *Dona Flor and Her Two Husbands*, which Bruno Barreto turned into a successful—and in many ways groundbreaking—film in 1976. Flor's connection with food as a cook and a culinary instructor helps her overcome the suffering caused by her first husband, a gambler and a womanizer, and allows her to find a world of sensual satisfaction during her second marriage, with a trustworthy but boring pharmacist. The worlds of the living and the dead, like for Tita, collide around food, contributing to its magical powers.

While food exudes erotic potential, *Like Water for Chocolate* treats sexual imagery differently than mainstream Hollywood films do. Tita's and

Gertrudis's bodies appear nude onscreen, but the camera does not fixate on their bodies as objects for the viewer's gaze but rather retains a polite distance. The film differentiates women's roles as sexual beings and explores a variety of meanings for women's bodies and their sexuality. Tita exerts a great deal of agency, as it is through her eyes and her narrative that we watch events unfold.

Although *Like Water for Chocolate* produces a strong, clear connection between the erotic and the edible, it does so in a manner that differs substantially from the U.S. films that draw on it as their narrative source. The success of this film sparked a number of U.S. "remakes"—like *Woman on Top*, which fixates on the Latina as a "hot" number—that lack the Mexican film's differentiation of sexuality and the erotic but that pick up on precisely this closeness between the female body and food. In this process of Americanization the narratives are stripped of their richness and depth.

SIMPLY RIDICULOUS? FAIRY-TALE ROMANCE AND FOOD IN *SIMPLY IRRESISTIBLE*

We meet Amanda Shelton (Sarah Michelle Gellar), the protagonist of *Simply Irresistible*, in the first scene of the film as she goes to a farmer's market to purchase items for her restaurant, The Southern Cross. Dressed in a skimpy gold lamé top, she tosses her teenybopper-styled reddish hair over her shoulder as she wanders into the market. A far cry from the likes of Babette or Tita, the naive chef, a young white woman who has taken over her deceased mother's restaurant, first learns from one of the market people that the business is on the brink of closing. Safely ensconced in her childlike world, Amanda does not realize how poorly the restaurant is doing. Suddenly a magical man (whom we assume to be an angel) appears with a bucket of crabs for Amanda. "I wouldn't know what to do with a crab," she responds, as the soundtrack plinks out magical tones reminiscent of the 1960s television show *I Dream of Jeannie*. As Amanda proceeds to chase one of the crabs through the market, she bumps into Tom Bartlett (Sean Patrick Flanery), a wealthy department store manager.

Things start changing at the restaurant: one of the crabs she bought is magical and gives her the power to make good food out of thin air. Suddenly, beautiful and seductive entrees appear on plates, and Amanda is stunned at her own capability. Her desire for a romantic relationship with Tom has had a tremendous impact on her cooking. Instead of serving their old standard comfort food, the restaurant now boasts trendy, sexy items such as sautéed *foie gras*, inside-out sashimi salad, and crab bisque. We quickly learn that Amanda has been given the ability to put her feelings into her food. When Tom visits her restaurant with his date, Chris, within seconds of biting into their dishes, they both are overcome by a state of drunken stupor. Out of jealousy Chris proceeds to smash plates through the restaurant, and Tom is in a state of orgasmic euphoria. Tom breaks up with Chris and starts dating Amanda, until he realizes she may be a witch casting spells on him. But when the chef who is supposed to open the restaurant in the department store that Tom manages quits, his company hires Amanda over Tom's objections. The new place is a smashing hit, and eventually Tom gives in to Amanda when he realizes that her real power is to make him get in touch with his emotions.

Simply Irresistible draws directly on *Like Water for Chocolate* in a variety of ways, as critics were quick to notice. Roger Ebert quipped, "It's *Like Water for Chocolate* meets *Everyone Says I Love You*."[10] The *San Francisco Chronicle* reported, "Not so bad, but as far as food and sensuality go, 'Like Water for Chocolate' still has the edge."[11] Magic, in this film that is marketed as a "bewitching romance," as the film poster asserts, is not a power that emanates from Amanda as a means of asserting herself. Rather, it is a random sort of "blessing" from a magical crab that sits on the shelf of her restaurant throughout the film, waving his magic claw every time she cooks. We see the layers of food added to the plate in one quick shot after another, but we never see Amanda actually placing it there. The food simply appears in front of the camera. The magical power of cooking that allows Amanda to connect sentimentally and sexually with Tom is reduced to a simplistically romantic context that presents women as passive, hypersexualized, and dependent on men. This represents a long-standing trend of positioning women as helpless and weak.[12]

Both Amanda's body and the food she prepares are strongly fetishized and turned into objects of desire and consumption. In glistening close-ups the camera focuses on her body and on the food she produces as "beautified" objects of desire. The association of food and the female body becomes especially clear in a scene in which Amanda prepares a vanilla sauce with fresh vanilla orchid petals, a trope the film takes from the bloodied rose petals in *Like Water for Chocolate*. A thick white fog develops in the pot and spreads throughout the kitchen and dining area of the restaurant, where Tom kisses her, declaring she tastes "sweet and a little spice[y]." The camera remains focused on Amanda the entire time, clearly positioning her as the visual object of desire who also *tastes* good. Eventually the couple submerges into the vanilla fog.

Simply Irresistible quotes *Like Water for Chocolate* to the extent that it recreates, albeit in a different context, the wedding cake scene in which Tita's tears in the cake batter cause the guests to recall their long-lost loves. Whereas Tita's tears signify the deep sense of sorrow and loss of self that she is experiencing, Amanda's tears emanate from her insecurity as a chef. As she takes over the kitchen at Tom's department store for the grand-opening meal, she looks to the magical crab for help: "Hey little man—stay close—I need all the help I can get." As she cries, one of her tears of insecurity falls into the sauce. Where Tita is active, determined, and driven by self-respect, Amanda is whimpering, hesitant, hysterical, and irrational, reiterating the many stereotypes about women that feminists have fought to overcome for so long.[13] When the guests have finished the blissful, magical meal that has them eating in a silent, ridiculously mesmerized state, Amanda leaves the restaurant, distressed, only to be saved by Tom, who provides her with a pink dress, diamond headband, and new shoes. In another vanilla fog that envelops the restaurant guests, Amanda and Tom dance together, as Tom tells her, after only one date with her, "I love you."

Amanda's ability to arouse feelings through the meals she prepares supports patriarchal myths that women are able to seduce men through their bodies and their cooking. That the food passively appears on plates assures the viewer that Amanda is not consciously in charge of what she is doing and that she is not a professional. Amanda's body and the food she happens to create become equated with each other, both through the narrative treatment, cinematography, and editing. This close association positions Amanda, like food, as a body with very little agency and choice. Despite her ownership of the restaurant, her participation in social life and food business does not take place as a form of autonomy but rather through the interest and appreciation of her male counterpart, a successful professional who is fully aware of the dangers of magic. The romantic resolution of the plot, however, tries to resolve these tensions by way of abandonment to passion.

WOMAN ON TOP AND THE RED-HOT LATINA BODY

Woman on Top handles the transposition of *Like Water for Chocolate* to the U.S. film industry in as problematic a manner as *Simply Irresistible*. A key difference is that ethnicity enters into the conversation about women, magic, and food. A lighthearted comedy, *Woman on Top* depicts the life of Isabella (Penelope Cruz), a talented Brazilian chef with terrible motion sickness. Isabella leaves Toninho (Murilo Benício), her adulterous husband, who feels emasculated by the fact that Isabella, to avoid feeling ill, has to be in control while dancing, driving the car, and being "on top" during sex. She ventures off to San Francisco to stay with her transsexual childhood friend Monica (Harold Perrineau). After giving classes in a cooking school and achieving immediate success, she befriends Cliff (Mark Feuerstein), a television producer who helps her become the star of her own cooking show. Toninho realizes his loss and travels to America to find Isabella. Eventually, after proving to her that he truly loves her and has become a "real man," she accepts him back into her life. Together they open up a successful restaurant, and Cliff and Monica become a happy couple.

Like *Simply Irresistible*, *Woman on Top* draws on *Like Water for Chocolate* in a variety of ways, and the film's critics noticed. Roger Ebert wrote that Isabella "owes something to Tita, the heroine of *Like Water for Chocolate*."[14] *Woman on Top* does consider the connections among food, sex, and women. Like Tita, Isabella is raised in the kitchen, where food quickly becomes her gateway to socialization and her primary form of expression.

We see Isabella as a child beating a sauce in a bowl, surrounded by plates of beautiful vegetables and caught in the friendly, warm light of a space that is in many ways visually similar to Tita's childhood kitchen. We learn that Yemanja, the goddess of the sea, has blessed this motion-sick child with both extraordinary beauty and a gift for cooking.

Whereas *Like Water for Chocolate* emphasizes the relationship between Tita and the Indian servant Nacha, who guards Tita even from the after-life, *Woman on Top* literally pushes the family cook into the background. We hear the narrator, Monica's voice, describe Isabella's development as a chef as the film displays a montage sequence that cuts from the image of a child's hands to that of adult Isabella skillfully slicing vegetables. The black cook stands in the background in the right corner of the screen, her back to the camera, while the film visually and acoustically foregrounds Isabella. Unlike Nacha, this cook remains nameless, and she never appears again in the film. The family cook serves simply as backdrop to Isabella's character rather than as an integral part of her development. It comes as no surprise that this woman is black; the black figures in the film serve as exotic backdrop and caring support systems to the lighter-skinned Brazilian characters. Racial hierarchy asserts itself in the film's visual coding.

Isabella's cooking is sexualized early in the film, turning into a sort of coy foreplay. "She blossomed into a shy but dazzling girl who could melt the palates and hearts of men," the narrator tells us during the childhood sequence. In fact, U.S. consumers learned that Isabella was a sexual icon long before the film even starts. The various movie posters depicted images of Penelope Cruz's face in close-up, with her reddened lips in the center of the frame. Below her lips, Cruz held a glistening red chili pepper whose shape graphically matched that of Cruz's lips. On the lower left side of the poster, the title *Woman on Top* was displayed, with two chili peppers put together to look like a woman's lips next to them. The text on one of the posters read, "Spice up your life," a reference both to the spiciness of the dishes Isabella prepares in the film and to her spicy, overtly sexualized nature as a Latina. The TV spots, trailers, and previews produced a similar narrative and visual coding, promising a strong and titillating correlation between sexuality, exotic food, and Cruz's body.

One of the most problematic issues in this film's illustration of femininity and food is the representation of Isabella as a "hot pepper," a correlation that is simultaneously highly gendered and racialized through the film's narrative, cinematography, and mise-en-scène. Toninho tells her, "Your hair held the scent of cinnamon. And when you kissed me, your lips burned with chili pepper." Isabella is food, and food is Isabella. We learn early on that peppers have a special meaning for Isabella; they remind her of her husband, Toninho, and the memories she has of him are always sexualized. Her cooking is "laced with fiery chilies." As she sniffs one of the *malagueta* peppers ("my passion," as she describes them) she is using in her general public cooking class at the culinary institute, the viewer is sent back into her life with Toninho in Brazil. Soft sexy music plays as the shot of Isabella in the cooking school dissolves into a close-up of her and Toninho making love. The camera tracks upward, and we see him tracing her lips with a red hot pepper (fig. 3.2). Isabella's eyes are closed, and we hear the distinct sound of a heartbeat pounding as the tension builds. As Toninho kisses

FIGURE 3.2 The body of a female chef from Brazil becomes visual fodder for U.S. male TV viewers in *Woman on Top*. Her culinary skills and the typical foods from her land are steeped in a magic aura that renders men defenseless.

her "hot" lips, the camera swoops down to a shot of her cleavage and the picture dissolves, once again, into a close-up of Isabella in the cooking class with a tear running down her face.

Food and the Latina body—a hot, red chili pepper—become interchangeable as objects of desire. Colonialist representations of people of color as particularly animalistic, write Ella Shohat and Robert Stam, tend to "associate Latin America, and especially Latin American women, with verbal epithets evoking tropical heat, violence, passion, and spice."[15] The film continually repositions Isabella in this manner, situating her in a long line of Latinas on the silver screen, including Lupe Velez, "the Mexican Spitfire"; Olga San Juan, the "Puerto Rican pepperpot"; and Carmen Miranda, "the Brazilian bombshell," whose style and character *Woman on Top* references through its portrayal of both Isabella and Monica, who appears garbed in flamboyant Bahian dress. As Angharad Valdivia writes, "In contrast to the rosary-praying maids or devoted mothers, we get the sexually out of control and utterly colorful spitfire, an image quite specific to Latinas."[16]

Both the food she prepares and she herself are consistently represented as "hot" and "spicy," conflated in the perspective of northerners, who wear more clothing and live in colder climates than her region of the world, "where it's hotter than the rest of the planet and where the natives are stereotypically wilder, sexier, and more naked than other people."[17] Northern consumer culture seems to neatly package "diversity through digestion," appealing to desires for supposed "authenticity." As many scholars have pointed out, cultural difference sells.[18] In fact, Isabella's exotic charms and her command of a different and exciting culinary culture allow her to take advantage of the U.S. media industry, creating a space for herself as a local TV celebrity. Although not fully aware of how her foreign origin is exploited by the producers, she is nevertheless given a position of power, which she displays by choosing the staging and the lighting for the show. She knows how to play the exotic card to have her professional skills recognized, paving the pathway to cultural citizenship and professional success.

Just like Tita, Isabella uses food as a realm of self-expression and as an arena to assert herself in the world. Unlike her predecessor, however, Isabella's ability is directly connected to her being sexy and beautiful.

We see her teaching culinary classes, where students are attracted more to her charm and passion than to her technical skills. Despite her work in a restaurant kitchen, Isabella's cooking is not learned in a professional way but rather through woman-to-woman transmission, which somehow leaves her within the sphere of domesticity. In fact, in her restaurant in Bahia her husband runs the front of the house and enjoys the accolades for the food, while she is relegated to the back, at the stove.

Isabella's touch and body fluids, like Tita's, have a magical effect. When a bead of Isabella's sweat drops onto a rose she is wearing, the rosebud suddenly blossoms into a magnificent flower. Apparently, Isabella's scent has a similar effect, and the food she makes creates an intoxicating aroma that appears only to affect heterosexual men. An analysis of one of the scenes clarifies this point. Isabella, having rid herself of her love for Toninho through a religious ritual to the goddess Yemanja, suddenly blossoms the following day into the exquisite beauty she was before he betrayed her. In medium close-up we see her preparing coffee in Monica's small kitchen. The camera captures her as she adds sugar, coffee, and cinnamon to a pot. The nondiegetic soundtrack, which otherwise consistently plays Brazilian music, now builds tension with the sound of a piano and synthesizer, as Isabella, dressed in a sea-blue silk robe, pours the coffee into a strainer. The music gradually gets faster, and we see the aroma travel from the coffee out the window. The music has now developed into a full-fledged bossa nova, and the smell travels across the street and through the open window of television producer Cliff, who falls off his treadmill in a state of shock when it reaches his nose.

The film cuts to a shot of Isabella, now garbed in a short, tight-fitting red dress with spaghetti straps, as she exits the apartment building walking to soft, sexy bossa nova music. The film crosscuts between this image and a long shot of the group of men that has started to form behind her, chasing her down the street with gleeful smiles on their faces. The camera continues to focus on different body parts from the male group's point of view: her hair and back, her legs. In an attempt to render humorous this magical effect that Isabella has, a group of wilted tulips stand up at attention when Isabella passes by them, a not-so-oblique reference to Isabella's ability to make limp penises erect and restore masculinity. We continue to follow her through the point of view of the pack of men as she enters the cooking school where she teaches. Like animals that need to be tamed, the employees of the cooking school manage to fight off the group of men, but a few slip through. Masculinity is coded here both as hypersexual and highly vulnerable to the sexual power and prowess that women can exert at will over men. Men cannot control themselves in the presence of a sexy woman like Isabella.

Isabella, like Tita, is able to invade bodies through her cooking, but it appears that she only has this effect on heterosexual men. Despite some feeble attempts at political correctness, especially through its representation of the male-to-female transsexual Monica, the film ultimately asserts heterosexuality as the dominant form of sexuality. The kitchen itself becomes a site of heterosexual foreplay, and Isabella is allowed a certain degree of rebelliousness but only insofar as her spiciness represents a form of sexuality that serves the interest of straight men. She is depicted as a fantasy female, whose spiciness proves too hot for some.

The same connection between exotic spicy food, luscious female bodies, and magic appears in Paul Mayeda Berges's *The Mistress of Spice* (2005), based on the homonymous novel published in 1997 by Chitra Banerjee Divakaruni. Since childhood the protagonist, Tilo (Aishwarya Rai), is aware of her powers as a seer. Kidnapped, she escapes and ends up on a beach where an old woman, the First Mother, raises and educates little girls to become mistresses of spices, witches trained to use spices for the benefit of others. Strict rules govern their activities: for their magic to be effective, they cannot leave their place of ministry, touch the people they try to help, or use the spices to satisfy their own wishes.

When Tilo grows older, she is sent to develop her call in a spice store in San Francisco. When biker Doug (Dylan McDermott) has an accident near the store and she unintentionally touches him while tending to his injuries, she falls in love with him. She soon has to pay for her act, losing her power to heal through spices and seeing her relationship with the clients she used to help deteriorate. When she loses her powers, her plants of chilies wither, and her almonds teem with worms. She prays to the spices to give her just a night with Doug, after which she will dedicate herself completely to them. After a night of love, she goes back to the store and tries to burn herself with the spices to go back to the First Mother. Having demonstrated with her sacrifice that she is ready to give up everything for the spices, the spices eventually allow her to keep her powers and her love for Doug.

In Tilo's story the theme of immigration and cultural citizenship is more prominent than in *Woman on Top*. Tilo is confused by America and by Americans, including Doug, and she maintains her status of outsider all along. We hear her inner muse: "America, a land no older than a heartbeat. There is so little that I know about you." She uses spices to help immigrants, Indians and non-Indians, forget their sorrows and bad memories and overcome their struggles to find a place in this new land and become fully adjusted members of their host societies. Tilo's art consists of recognizing which spice will work for whom, as each has different purposes and effects. She gives recipes to her clients and prepares spice mixtures, but we never actually see her cook, a narrative choice that highlights the magical aspect of her skills. She cannot really communicate her own feelings but only listen to others. Much of her dialogue is internal, in an ongoing conversation with the spices. She facilitates conversations between immigrant parents and their children, who strive to build their own cultural identities by distinguishing themselves from their family origins. India remains in the background as a place of authenticity, tradition, and wisdom, attributes that are so foreign to the United States that they are perceived as myth and magic.

Because of the rules governing her art, the mistress of spices can never leave the store where she operates, so she is forced to be a lifelong shopkeeper, an activity in the United States frequently carried out by Indian immigrants. In a sense the mistress, destined to a life of service hinging on the preparation and the ministration of food, cannot participate in the upward mobility that the other immigrants are so keen on achieving. Tilo's store has very Old World looks, with wooden shelves and containers, defining a space of difference, quite distinct from the typical American grocery store.

From a visual point of view Tilo is often shot behind the spices, which appear blurred in the foreground. The opening sequence is composed of extreme close-ups of spices, frying in oil or in their raw state, and of the fingers of the cook, mixed with shots of Tilo's getting dressed and the hands lighting candles. But during the opening sequence we see only her hands or other parts of her body, while her full body appears only when the camera zooms out to shoot Tilo opening her store. She even turns to spices as her way of flirting with Doug. When she is trying to fight her feelings for him, her desire generates a vision of the two of them in various degrees of undress, lying over a bed of red chili peppers. Like we saw in *Woman on Top*, the spices become the substance of their passion, and the camera identifies her and her sexuality with them. When she decides she is ready to have sex with Doug, she massages herself in spices and wears a red dress, appearing against a background of red chilies. After an earthquake, Doug finds her half covered in chilies, and in the last shot we see both of them again in what seems postcoital bliss on a bed of red chilies (fig. 3.3).

Unlike Isabella in *Woman on Top*, Tilo is very demure and shy. We could never imagine her flaunting herself for a TV show. In different scenes, however, we see her body, often in close-up and detailed shots that underline its materiality and, in a way, her similarity with the spices. The two women share the same magic connection with food, deriving from their

FIGURE 3.3 Ethnic ingredients and dishes often appear in food films as commodities ready for the U.S. consumer, as much as the people who prepare and sell them. In *The Mistress of Spices* an Indian sorceress is bound to service her clients in a grocery store.

origins and their connections with an exotic culture that appears mysterious and not fully understandable to most Americans. She is as sensual as Isabella, and her sexual fantasies about Doug remind us of Isabella's, but her magic does not have the same arousing effect on men. She is destined to service and caregiving. In this sense Tilo is much more traditional than Isabella, and her rebellion—although punished severely—is much more limited. The two are also different in their integration to the host society: while Isabella takes advantage of opportunities like cooking schools and media to assert herself professionally in the public sphere, Tilo remains tied to her little store, at first unable to ever pass its door.

DO WOMEN REALLY NEED CHOCOLAT?

A food store, aside from functioning as a place to commercialize exotic products and dreams of faraway locations, becomes a fortress to stake a claim to citizenship for Vianne (Juliette Binoche), the protagonist of *Chocolat*. This film provides another significant variation of the magical connection between women's bodies and food, using chocolate as a vehicle for the expression of female desires and needs and for challenging patriarchal structures of domination. While the film makes a more conscious effort than either *Woman on Top* or *Simply Irresistible* to comment on and challenge misogynist hierarchies, it ends up undermining its own attempts. *Chocolat* draws heavily on foreign food film predecessors such as *Like Water for Chocolate* and *Babette's Feast* and on the U.S. blockbuster *Fried Green Tomatoes*. Reviewers of the film also pointed out its similarities to *Woman on Top*. Jeffrey Anderson writes, "In *Chocolat*, a woman breezes into town and changes everyone's lives because her cooking is so good. Isn't this the same movie as *Woman on Top*, but with a more prestigious cast and crew?"[19] Roger Ebert writes, "Vianne's chocolates contain magic ingredients like the foods in 'Like Water for Chocolate,' and soon her shop is a local healing center."[20]

Chocolat follows the events that transpire in 1959 in a small, conservative French town, Lansquenet, when Vianne and her young daughter, Anouk, arrive to open a new shop, "Chocolaterie Maya," right at the beginning of Lent. The chocolate shop causes a grand stir in this small, quiet nest, and the Comte de Reynaud (Alfred Molina), the town's mayor and moral leader, takes it upon himself to ruin Vianne's business and run her out of town because he is angry that she has the audacity to open her shop during a period dedicated to religious fasting. It is clear from the outset that Vianne will bring significant change to the remote village. Throughout the course of the film her chocolates—which have magical qualities connected to Vianne's exotic ancestors—help to unite an elderly woman with her grandson and daughter; create sexual desire in a marriage grown old; bring together an elderly widower with an elderly widow; and save a woman from her abusive husband. When a group of "river rats," gypsies who live on houseboats, arrive in Lansquenet, Vianne falls in love with one of them, Roux (Johnny Depp), and fights to have the group accepted by the townspeople. After the gypsies' houseboats are burned down, Vianne feels the north wind that has carried her from town to town pressuring her to leave, a pressure that she ultimately resists. The film ends with the townspeople embracing Vianne and her chocolaterie, the return of Roux to Vianne, and the town in a happy, much improved condition.

Chocolat is a tale of liberation, in particular of a town's liberation from old, entrenched patriarchal and Catholic rule, and of individual women's emancipation from repressive sexuality and domesticity. Drawing on themes we identified in *Babette's Feast*, these expectations center on adhering to restrictive customs proposed by the town's church and enforced by its domineering, controlling mayor. Like Babette, Vianne is a visitor from afar, a character whose presence disrupts the individual, social, political, and economic lives of those who come into contact with her. Like Babette, Vianne is self-assured, confident, assertive, and focused, often engrossed in her cooking. Vianne also becomes a defender of the disenfranchised, empowering a kleptomaniac to leave her abusive spouse and offering the gypsies support and refuge from the angry townspeople. In its representation of Vianne and her desire to disrupt the status quo, the film draws decidedly on feminist tropes through a variety of means. The film associates Vianne with sexual freedom and choice. Many of those who come in contact with her and her chocolate experience a personal sexual renaissance. Furthermore, the fact that Vianne owns her own business, and thus has control over capital and mode of production, is key to her construction as a feminist.

Much like Babette, Vianne and her food become identified as religious threats; she is perceived as a witch of sorts. The priest, under the influence of the Comte de Renaud, is forced to deliver a sermon that affirms how "Satan wears many guises . . . at times the maker of sweet things . . . for what could seem more harmless, more innocent than chocolate?" In the very next scene we see Anouk, who has heard the word about town, "Are you Satan's helper?" Vianne's rebelliousness through her culinary art must, according to the villagers, have satanic roots. Chocolate is indeed a drug that allows her to see her social class position as oppressed woman.

Whereas magical realism in *Woman on Top* and *Simply Irresistible* provides Isabella and Amanda with the power to seduce men, magic in *Chocolat* is more reminiscent of Tita's powers in *Like Water for Chocolate* and Tilo's in *The Mistress of Spices*. Vianne has the ability to read people's desires and see their problems. Vianne's chocolate also has magical powers that affect people in a variety of ways, most of which are related to sexuality. Like the other female chefs discussed in this chapter, Vianne has the ability to transform people's lives magically through the food she creates. Her chocolate brings out a sense of yearning, wildness, and rebelliousness in people; it opens them up to tell their own stories. Vianne's chocolate, like her presence, also has a healing power, and the chocolaterie becomes a hangout space for the morally rebellious and a sort of confessional, where people tell Vianne their hidden desires, fears, and problems.

Vianne's abilities, we learn, are passed down from her Mayan mother to her (hence the centrality of chocolate, originally domesticated in Meso-america). Vianne's magical chocolate and cooking, coded as utopian, have functioned as a catalyst to produce tolerance and understanding. She consciously uses her powers to assist people and to change their lives. Chocolate is indeed seductive, devilish, alluring, and passionate. Glistening in gorgeous packaging and beautiful shapes in Vianne's window, illuminated by white light that delineates its contours and depths, chocolate is visually displayed in the manner in which we are accustomed to viewing female bodies in Hollywood cinema. Chocolate is coded as sensual and other from its entrance into the narrative and onto the screen. We see Vianne grinding and pounding cocoa beans with a traditional Mexican/Mayan metate as children look through the cracks of paper covering her window. Our first gaze at chocolate is a secretive, voyeuristic one. This sexualized element of chocolate is pronounced throughout the film to the extent that it becomes sexier than the women's bodies in the film.

Unlike *Woman on Top* and *Simply Irresistible*, women's bodies and food do not necessarily become represented as sexual objects of consumption in conjunction with and alongside each other. But the sexualization of chocolate is still gendered. Chocolate is coded as female, and the "sexual" acts we see in the film take place between people and chocolate, the most obvious being the final scene with the Comte de Renaud, chocolate functioning as a sort of stand-in for the female bodies we otherwise voyeuristically consume. Having deprived himself of food, pleasure, and enjoyment throughout the Lenten feast, the Comte takes it upon himself to destroy Vianne by smashing her Easter festival chocolate with a large knife. In the shop's window he proceeds to decapitate the nude chocolate figure in the center of the display and to cut her arm off. In his siege against the chocolate (and thus against Vianne's willful disregard for his austere brand of Catholicism), he gets a tiny bit of chocolate on his lip. Licking it, he gasps. Losing control of himself, he begins to eat, sighing and gasping in a state of rapture, panting as he devours figurines and truffles, chocolate smeared all over his body and face. The scene appears orgasmic, a one-man-sex-show in which the Comte lies in the window laughing and then sobbing to himself. The scene fades to black, and we find him the following morning blissfully asleep in the storefront window, delirious from his night of over-indulgence. Vianne kindly offers him an Alka-Seltzer. The sexualization of chocolate is a fetishized displacement of the female body onto food.

Vianne hangs her sign "Chocolaterie Maya" in the window as she is setting up shop, an undeniable exhibition of the foreignness and otherness of the products in which her shop specializes. In this dull, tranquil village the Mayan sign and glamorous storefront stand out. Vianne's shop is warm, inviting, chic, and upbeat. It resembles the design of contemporary coffee shops, with its trendy Latin American color scheme, hand-painted images on the wall, gorgeously tiled floor, and pseudo-exotic artifacts. Mysterious music chimes as Vianne spins an ancient Mayan plate and asks customers (as if looking like a fortuneteller at a crystal ball), "What does it look like? What do you see in it?" to read their personalities and desires. Chocolate itself is always on magical display, and the film links its magical powers and abilities to a Mayan mythology.

Chocolate is positioned as other, reinforcing the mystical, native roots that the film establishes. In a segment in the middle of the film Vianne tells the story of "grandmère and grandpère" to Anouk. Her father was traveling in Central America when he first saw Vianne's mother, Chitza, a native woman who dispensed traditional remedies from village to village. During this narration, we see images of the Central American region that George visits, where long-haired native women are grinding cocoa beans, the sound of the roller echoing mysteriously. Shot in low-key lighting with a mysterious bluish tone, flames flicker from offscreen, and Chitza is fiery, sexy, exotic, and desirable, as is the chocolate she makes. She is sexualized in a similar manner to Isabella in *Woman on Top*, her spicy Latin Americanness the cause of George's abandonment of his Catholic values. This is the legacy that Vianne is spreading through her sexy, wild chocolate, linked to her mother's body through the film. The tropes of nativeness in this film reiterate Eurocentric patterns of thinking that position otherness as the spice that makes whiteness more interesting.

Chocolat, like the other films in this chapter, echoes shifts in contemporary eating culture in their representation of exotic foods and exotic women. Alexander Cockburn writes, "The impact of foods and styles of cooking from annexed, former colonial and neo-colonial geo-political areas on culinary tastes in the former imperial countries does indeed seem to have promoted . . . an 'orgy of gastroglobal eclecticism.'"[21] The representations of food visited here can be described as pornographic. In her book *At Home with Pornography: Women, Sex, and Everyday Life*, Jane Juffer discusses the role that pornography plays in women's everyday life. While Juffer's argument focuses on women's relationships to and uses of pornographic material (for example, Victoria's Secret catalogues), we situate food films in the context of pornography and the everyday, which she outlines "across a number of sites at which these texts and artifacts are produced . . . the texts' attempts to reconcile the erotic with the everyday, to infuse sexual representations and products with elements of the mundane, yet to retain enough distance between the mundane and the profane so as to preserve a potential realm of fantasy, to avoid drowning in the details that need to be acknowledged and yet threaten to overwhelm the excesses of sex."[22]

The food films we have examined in this chapter parallel Juffer's definition of "domesticated pornography." Pornography, she argues, does not simply consist of "texts that continually represent taboos but rather texts that help [women] reconcile the world of fantasy with their everyday lives."[23] Films such as *Woman on Top* and *Chocolat* begin with the formulaic "Once upon a time" trope that signifies entry into a fairy-tale, mythical world. The combination of sexual fantasy, visual alignment through cinematography and editing of women's (especially women of color) bodies with food, and eroticization of food images situate these films within a field of texts that constitute everyday, domesticated pornography.

WOMEN, MAGIC, AND FOOD: A BITTER PILL TO SWALLOW

The glistening, beautiful food is portrayed with the kind of *to-be-looked-at-ness* that Laura Mulvey ascribed to the representation of women in mainstream Hollywood cinema. We see this depiction of food on a regular basis in food magazines, on television, and in cinema, and it parallels how we are often, and unconsciously, asked to look at women's bodies. Food itself becomes feminized and fetishized, usually through the intervention of magic, a mysterious power from which men cannot protect themselves. We emphasize that the bodies of all the women in these films are beautiful and thin, in alignment with dominant U.S. values. Women's bodies are put on display for consumption, fetishized to take away the threat that women and women's bodies, women's sexuality, and women's power pose for men. Food images serve a similar function here, displacing anxiety and diffusing the perceived threat to the gender and ethnic identities of so many U.S. citizens. Food films that adapt *Like Water for Chocolate* for U.S. audiences clothe themselves in a seemingly progressive cloak, but ultimately they remain quite conservative, depicting food as female and reducing women to bodies. A veneer of sexual self-assertiveness repackages the old batter of women to be as consumable as food itself.

Returning to the core question of this book, we consider how gender interacts with the concept of cultural citizenship. As Anh Hua writes, citizenship is "a deeply gendered concept."[24] These films provide women characters with little opportunity of real political or economic influence. In the previous chapter we looked at white, middle-class to upper-middle-class women with professional careers related to food, and we determined that most narratives tend to push women back into the domestic sphere. In the magical food films, professional women—often of humble origin—are eroticized and sexualized, with especially disturbing, destructive images of women of color. Hua writes, "Culture is an important site for political contestation for it can be the expression of resistance to oppression and exploitation."[25] These films embrace an underlying politics of citizenship that aligns women (especially women of color) with food as objects of consumption and objects of the gaze, squeezing them into passive rather than active roles. The concept of citizenship, however, implies the right to active participation and engagement. Certainly, these films express fantasies about food, sex, and relationships, but we maintain that they do so in a politically, socially, and culturally regressive fashion. The use of magic in these films does not serve to free women but rather to repackage servitude (especially sexual servitude toward men) as attractive and compelling. We do not exclude the notion that some viewers might view these films as parodic and therefore critical of the spaces women are invited to inhabit, but we maintain that the films do not aim specifically to engender such a response. As in chapter 2, we argue again here that these films reflect and support a postfeminist ideology that suggests women have reached their potential and no longer need to seek cultural, economic, and political equity. Perhaps a return to nostalgic images of sexy, magical women evokes comfort in some viewers, as long as they are either relegated to the controlled environment of the home or to performing their culinary skills to take care of the needs of others. But what of men who embody similar roles as nurturers and caregivers, both in domestic and professional environments? In chapter 1 we discussed the restaurant as a place where male chefs express models of masculinity rooted in values such as expertise, success, determination, and creativity. In the next chapter we turn our attention to food films about men who embody different forms of masculinities and the struggles they seem doomed to face.

CULINARY COMFORT

The Satiating Construction of Masculinity

Images of handsome men with nude upper bodies nurturing small babies started appearing in advertisements and on posters in the late 1980s. One of the best-selling posters of all time, Spencer Rowell's 1987 picture "L'enfant," displays a bare-chested twentysomething man dressed only in jeans looking down at a small baby in his arms.[1] Similarly, Marty Evans's "Man with Baby" presents a strikingly attractive man hugging a small, naked baby up against his nude chest, as light falls through venetian blinds, emphasizing a large gold wedding band on his hand. These images depict sensitive, caring men playing nurturing roles usually reserved for women, yet their muscularity, demeanor, and strength reassure us of their dominance and power in paternity, increasingly disputed by a wide variety of views and practices.[2]

Images of sensitive men as nurturers begin to appear in international and U.S. films around the same time, often highlighting the role of men as caretakers of their families. These representations involve food-related activities that are usually carried out in the domestic sphere and that, as such, are still often perceived as feminine and potentially emasculating in mainstream culture. As they are not connected to the public domains of business and the marketplace, these activities enjoy a different level of prestige compared to professional engagement in restaurant cuisines, as also reflected in the rising appeal of male star chefs in media. Even in the food business, as we discussed in chapter 1, issues of class, ethnicity, and age can mark certain occupations as demeaning: a busboy or a prep cook in a restaurant does not embody the same kind of alpha-male masculinity that executive chefs do.

Despite the continuing identification of food preparation with women and low social status, from the early 1990s U.S. comedy films such as *Kindergarten Cop* (Reitman, 1990) and *Mrs. Doubtfire* (Columbus, 1993) started portraying masculinity and men's interactions around food and eating in situations where they found themselves forced into caregiving responsibilities. These comedies highlighted the inadequacies of men as nurturers, while defusing the embarrassment related to symbolic emasculation through laughter and ultimately confirming traditional gender roles. By making fun of men's ridiculous lack of skills in cooking and feeding others, in particular small children, these comedies reinforced the judgment that domestic roles are inherently extraneous to masculinity. At the same time, the final success of the protagonists suggested that if men really put their heart into it, they could become as good as women, if not better, at care work.

As the food-film genre developed, it was inevitable that it would explore the relationship between men and the more domestic dimensions of cooking. In contrast with the restaurant-centered films we discussed in chapter 1, which focus on professional kitchens and chefs as successful, creative, and motivated males, despite the differences connected to ethnic origin and class, the films we explore in this chapter feature men negotiating situations that seem to question mainstream gender roles. Ang Lee's *Eat Drink Man Woman* (1994), coproduced by the filmmaker's own company with Taiwan's Central Motion Pictures and the U.S. independent film production and distribution company Good Machine, provides early examples of this approach to food as a way for nondominant masculinities—in terms of race, gender, and age—to assert themselves. The same tensions emerge in *What's Eating Gilbert Grape* (Hallström, 1993), *Heavy* (Mangold, 1995), *Eat Your Heart Out* (Adlon, 1997), and later *Spanglish* (Brooks, 2004) and *Sideways* (Payne 2004).

These films range from low-budget art-house films to Hollywood productions. By presenting their lead male characters as struggling with their roles as nurturers—chosen or imposed—the films appear to question traditional tropes of masculinity, while in fact they cautiously and subtly reassert them. It is precisely the explication of the tension between the expectations in the public sphere and the demands of domesticity that is the focus of this chapter. In considering how these films negotiate ideal forms of male cultural citizenship, it is compelling that food becomes a vehicle for personal growth and for the development of emotional understanding. As viewers we are invited to empathize and identify with the protagonists and their stories. We stand in their shoes and see the world through their eyes. In the end, however, the films ensure that men's dominance is reestablished. This often happens at the expense of key women in their lives: wives, daughters, girlfriends, colleagues, and especially mothers. We focus on the interplay of masculinity and femininity to uncover these dynamics from the visual and narrative points of view. We also call attention to how men and women characters negotiate power and difference in terms of ethnicity and class, and we consider how these interwoven discourses help to promote particular concepts of cultural citizenship.

Representations of masculinity from the 1980s to the early 2000s were complex and varying, as a wide range of images and narratives circulated simultaneously in film, on television, and in other media. Many Reagan era films, for example, worked to bury the Vietnam syndrome and reassert a form of masculinity that converged with U.S. nationalism, as media and gender studies scholar Susan Jeffords has argued.[3] Screens were filled with rampaging angry white males embodied in the star images of Bruce Willis, Arnold Schwarzenegger, Mel Gibson, and Sylvester Stallone. Television and film witnessed a reassertion of strong masculinity dedicated to law and order in shows like *NYPD Blue* and *ER* and in films like *Se7en* (Fincher, 1995) and *Fight Club* (Fincher, 1999). Fred Pfeil points to a series of "yuppie redemption films," in which middle-class, mostly white, professional men discover that family is more important than professional success.[4] In an essay on Tom Hanks, Pfeil noted how a new alternative profile of man was emerging in American cinema. This new man, as empowered and mainstream as ever, displays three main features: "First, there is his *boyishness*, and the particular form of homosociality that accompanies it; second, his *sexual passivity*, or *mutedness*; and third, the extent to which he quite literally *plays out* his various roles as a distinctly happy and creative worker within the *professional-managerial class.*"[5] At the same time, this era also saw the emergence of androgynous characters in award-winning and highly rated TV shows like *Dawson's Creek* and *Buffy the Vampire Slayer*. While these media targeted different audiences, the coexistence of such diverse imagery suggests that mainstream media functions as a core site where ideas about masculinity, gender, and the role of men in U.S. society are continually debated.

These dynamics play themselves out in the food films we analyze in this chapter, but they also reflect changes in other food-related media where cooking was and is often associated with careers, entrepreneurship, and artisanal craft rather than with the purposes of subsistence and care work, often perceived as feminine domains. The predominance of media representations on television that feature men as highly trained, specialized chefs and women as caretakers, nurturers, and facilitators corresponds to sociological findings in Marjorie DeVault's analysis in *Feeding the Family*, where caring in the form of feeding consistently occurs across socioeconomic class and ethnic lines as "women's work." DeVault's findings indicated that the work of cooking and caretaking remains highly gendered in the contemporary United States.[6] When men do cook, it tends to be around a special event, and certain cooking rituals in U.S. culture are generally reserved for men (barbecuing, turkey carving, special weekend breakfasts, etc.), meant to highlight masculine skills, even when women do much of the prepping, serving, and cleanup work. Television and mainstream film representations have tended to mirror this tendency. Yet perceptions and practices in terms of gender roles are also changing when it comes to the daily toil of food procurement and preparation, as well as feeding family and children, especially in a domestic setting.[7] The subset of food films that we address in this chapter offers a contrast to the still prevalent images of men cooking, as do some of the more recent cooking shows on TV like Jamie Oliver's *Jamie at Home*. In them we experience men in homes, folding underwear, cooking everyday meals, and dealing with family conflicts. These men get to be caretakers *and* experts.

EXPERT NURTURERS

As we discussed in chapter 2, women depicted as professional chefs in food films typically fail at femininity if they prioritize their role as experts over their role as nurturers. For men the reverse holds true: to function effectively as men, they must maintain their expert role and negotiate their positions as nurturers. In this section we look at Ang Lee's seminal and influential films *Eat Drink Man Woman* and *The Wedding Banquet* to explore how male characters straddle the private-public divide, mirroring and contributing to the changing cultural understandings of masculinity, power, and privilege, as this is critical to how cultural citizenship operates. While the first film only presents Asian characters from a similar social background, the second examines how issues of ethnicity and class intersect with perceptions and practices of masculinity, specifically in the United States.

Directed by American-educated Taiwanese director Ang Lee, *Eat Drink Man Woman* tells the story of a Taiwanese father in Taipei who is left to raise his three daughters after the premature death of his wife. The film was very influential and served as the basis for the U.S. remake *Tortilla Soup*, which we discuss in chapter 6. We note that *Eat Drink Man Woman*, although made in Taiwan and spoken in Chinese, was produced for and marketed toward a transnational audience. Ang Lee is a Taiwanese-born director who has worked extensively in the United States and has made films in English for the international market. *Eat Drink Man Woman* is very important for the development of U.S. food films as it introduced themes and narratives that found extensive resonance in the genre, while establishing a specific aesthetic and visual language in the way food and cooking are represented. Given that our focus here is on U.S. cultural citizenship, our reading of this film accounts for how it invites U.S. viewers to view it, rather than exploring its meanings within a Taiwanese context.

Chu (Lung Sihung) is a master chef, famous among his peers for his culinary artistry (fig. 4.1). Although he has lost his sense of taste, Chu manages to prepare elaborate meals in his home simply from memory, with the goal of keeping his family together. His three daughters, however, all leave home during the course of the film, causing a renegotiation of

FIGURE 4.1 In *Eat Drink Man Woman* a retired male chef negotiates his worth and his masculinity through his culinary talents, both in his domestic environment and in professional kitchens.

relationships and emotional ties. In fact, Chu is a better chef than a nurturer, and by the film's conclusion, he announces his decision to marry and settle down with his eldest daughter's best friend and her young daughter, who is able to bring out the gentler and more comforting aspects of Chu's personality. Although he is not able to express his affection for the young child through words and physical proximity, he cooks delicious lunches for her every day, unbeknownst to her mother, who cannot cook. Once order is restored at the end of the film, with Chu reclaiming his patriarchal status by marrying a young and visibly pregnant woman, he regains his sense of taste and of life. The film's conclusion releases him from this double burden as masculinized star chef and feminized nurturer, establishing a new equilibrium. The fact that the new wife is not a good cook does not seem to relegate him to a caregiving position but rather to underline his all-around superiority, despite the age difference.

We first encounter Chu in the quiet and solitude of his own home, where he is engrossed in cooking. During the film's opening titles, the camera frames him as he prepares an abundant and elaborate banquet, dissecting hot red peppers with a skillfully wielded large cleaver, frying, steaming, and braising various fish, frogs, and cuts of meat. His technique and well-honed movements in the traditional kitchen are underscored by the framing, the lighting, and even the amplified sizzling and simmering sounds from the stove. Backed up by a three-rowed wall of approximately forty to fifty knives, Chu's home kitchen represents power, even when he is cooking for his daughters. Later, we see him untangling bras, panties, and nylons as he works through piles of laundry, cleans dishes, and wakes his daughters. Cooking advice delivered by phone to a female friend situates him in the traditional sphere of women. We learn why Chu is the sole caretaker of his three daughters when we see a picture of his long-deceased wife. Chu has grown frustrated with this imbalanced life. In a line that reiterates the film's title, he expresses discontent. "Ah! Eat, drink, man, woman—nourishment and sex—the basics. There's no avoiding them. My life, every day, that's all I've done. It pisses me off. Is that all there is to life?"

Although we experience him primarily in the domestic sphere, the film firmly establishes Chu's professional expertise. In his home Chu prepares grandiose, restaurant-style meals that always bear the mark of technical skill and artistry. At the end of the first meal we see him share with his daughters, which becomes an occasion for family tensions to emerge and expose the cracks in the domestic life into which he has been forced. Chu is called by former colleagues to save a fine-dining banquet at the Taipei Grand Hotel from culinary disaster. The camera tracks Chu with high-energy in a Steadicam style that marks a distinct departure from his representation at home. With a clear, aggressive sense of direction, Chu marches through this loud, busy space in his street clothes to be greeted by the manager, who holds up a white chef's uniform for him as he enters and sighs with relief, "Thank goodness you're here!" To the thunderous roar of cooking oil, Chu says, "Menu," like an emergency room doctor, as if he were asking instead for a scalpel. In no time he saves the meal and maintains the restaurant's reputation.

From the beginning the film presents Chu's skills, determination, and focus as he immerses himself in his work, dispelling at the same time any doubt about his masculinity. Gender lines are clearly differentiated:

although Chu appears tolerant and supportive of his daughters' roles in the public world, we learn that he "couldn't stomach a woman being a chef" and forced his oldest daughter Jia-Chien (Wu Chien-Lien) out of the kitchen so that she would find a different career. In the end the film depicts her preparing the family Sunday dinner, offering a nod toward a newer role for contemporary women within the public sphere and inviting us as viewers to see some aspects of gender as flexible. Women may be able to gain some power but never at the expense of men. Keeping this balance is important to maintaining Chu's sense of masculinity and offsetting his fragility, which the film must resolve to create a happy ending. *Eat Drink Man Woman* never actually disavows mainstream masculinity by having its characters step out of traditional gender binaries; rather, it uses this conflict between male and female roles to provoke a happy ending in which traditional gender order prevails through a new marriage.

Ang Lee has never shied away from treating onscreen such issues as homophobia and gender socialization. His previous film, *The Wedding Banquet*, features a homosexual interracial couple (Wai-tung, a Taiwanese man, and Simon, his Caucasian partner) living in the United States and trying to protect their relationship from Wai-tung's traditionally minded parents, still living in Taiwan. Similar to *Eat Drink Man Woman* in the use of food as both an expression of care and an instrument for oppression, *The Wedding Banquet* questions but does not fundamentally undermine an established gender order. Wei-Wei, an immigrant woman in pursuit of a green card, agrees to pose as Wai-tung's girlfriend when his parents visit, essentially forcing him to have sex with her. She is not able to cook, and Simon—the more nurturing figure in the gay couple and the one in charge in the kitchen—has to teach her the basics, apparently blurring the traits usually perceived as masculine and feminine. Furthermore, Simon is a physical therapist, an occupation not as prestigious and lucrative as his partner's employment in high finance. Food becomes the arena where dominant heterosexual family arrangements clash with new gender dynamics, both in the domestic and in the public spheres, culminating in a luxurious traditional Chinese wedding banquet, full of sexual double entendre and hints at reproduction. Eventually, Wai-tung's father embraces Simon as the person who loves his son and cares for him, although he cannot talk about it with his wife, who is also aware of the situation. Certain things are meant to be kept quiet.

THINKING ABOUT MASCULINITY AND MEN

The male characters in Ang Lee's *Eat Drink Man Woman* and *The Wedding Banquet* and their relationship with food, care work, and nurturing address questions about men and masculinity, that the feminist movement helped to provoke. Some scholars point to a crisis in masculinity that emerged in the 1980s regarding the meaning of manhood, often citing backlash against the feminist movement of the 1970s. Masculinity studies scholar Michael S. Kimmel argues that this crisis has "structural origins in changing global geo-political and economic relations, and in the changing dynamics and complexion of the workplace."[8] Barbara Ehrenreich insists that this crisis in the "breadwinner ethic" has been in a gradual state of collapse for the past fifty years independent of the feminist movement.[9] The impact of the women's movement, the gay and lesbian rights movement, and the civil rights movement provided further challenges to the way masculinity has traditionally been positioned in the United States. Furthermore, the disappearance of lifelong careers for men, the expansion of service-oriented industries that do not necessarily require male employees, and changes in the legislations concerning family, inheritance, and even sexual behaviors also seemed to cause growing disapproval of traditional masculinist behaviors at the cultural, social, and political levels.[10] Shifting gender dynamics interplayed with new debates about race, ethnicity, and class that questioned the traditional dominant status of the white middle-class male. This state of affairs was interpreted as a "legitimation crisis" more than an actual crisis of patriarchy and masculinity, the ideology that sustains it; men can refuse any change in the situation, acknowledge the structural inequalities without doing anything at the personal level, or alternatively suffer from an "acute gender identity crisis" without abandoning their gender commitments.[11]

Together with these social changes and the cultural debates they engendered, a new but quickly expanding body of scholarly research and reflection sought to evaluate men's lives as part of social arrangements and understand the dynamics that emerge as a result of gender-power relationships. While feminist writings challenged traditional conceptions of "woman," breaking them down through the lenses of race, class, ethnicity, and other markers of identity, in the 1980s masculinity studies began to examine men's lives through the perspective of masculinities in the plural, to indicate the presence of different and competing models of male values and behaviors, just as the feminist movement had challenged a fixed concept of womanhood and femininity.[12]

Masculine identities came to be explored in terms of power, that is to say in their political and social effects in multiple arenas, such as sexuality, family, the state, and capitalist work, where changes were possible as the result of the interplay between structures and praxis, between expectations and actual behaviors. Inspired by the work of Italian political theorist Antonio Gramsci on cultural and political hegemony, the concept of "hegemonic masculinity" was introduced to explain power dynamics not only toward women but also among men.[13] In the fulgurating definition given by Michael Kimmel, "the hegemonic definition of manhood is a man in power, a man with power, and a man of power."[14] In this approach, sexual and biological differences, and the body in general, do not constitute the basis for masculinity but rather function as objects of cultural and social practices, taking on different meanings in different contexts.

The idea that a determined type of masculinity might be dominant for a particular time within a culturally and historically specific pattern of gender relations and institutional power presupposes two main elements. First of all there can be multiple masculinities operating at the same time, defined by many factors such as age, class, race, ethnicity, religion, and geography, just to mention a few. This, in turn, implies that different masculinities coexist in relationships of competition, dominance, and subordination. These are often complicit, partaking of the benefits derived from patriarchy and befalling all men. Sometimes, particular types of masculinity are marginalized as the result of the attempt to deprive certain categories (homosexuals and ethnic minorities, for example) of these benefits.[15] The second element is that these masculinities do not constitute a fixed typology of static characters but are rather the result of shifting relationships and contexts.

Therefore, like femininity, they require a dynamic analysis because they are culturally and historically contingent.

From the late 1980s, postmodern and poststructuralist theories influenced the debate on masculinity, which scholars increasingly understood as resulting from discourse, or more of "a diversity of discourses among which there is no necessary relations but a constant movement of overdetermination and displacement." In this framework masculinity was only one among the multiple subject positions constituting the individuals, as generated by the constitutive tension between subjection to power and resistance or agency.[16] It was also viewed as an effect of performance and "identity work" in the form of self-regulation and self-discipline aimed at receiving validation from dominant power structures and ideologies.[17] As we have mentioned, starting in the 1990s, the United States witnessed a multiplication of models of masculinity, partly as a response to the slow shift of gay culture into the mainstream and to efforts by marketers and media to create new segments of male consumers ready to buy products that before would not have been deemed masculine.[18] What Mark Simpson defined as the "metrosexual man" in an article on Salon.com formed the epitome of this trend. The piece's subtitle was particularly telling in this regard: "He's well dressed, narcissistic and obsessed with butts. But don't call him gay."[19]

Building on these reflections, we want to clarify that we consider masculinity a gendered performance rather than a fixed position related to an individual's biological sex. From this perspective women can perform and embody masculinity, and men can perform and embody femininity. Gendered performances are never in a fixed state but are rather defined by "configurations of practice generated in particular situations in a changing structure of relationships."[20] As masculinity studies scholar William Pollack writes, men and boys may learn that they need to become dominant and powerful, to "wear the mask of coolness, to act as though everything is going all right, as though everything is under control, even if it isn't."[21] Inevitably, changes that challenge the established understanding of fundamental categories of difference, like gender, find expression in culture, from media to art and literature, while affecting social and economic dynamics. The films we discuss in this chapter indicate how media both reflect and participate in determining shared notions of gender and sexuality. As Adam Beissel, Michael Giardina, and Joshua Newman argue about social class, masculinity, and cultural citizenship, we, too, "see citizenship as tied to processes of self-making and being-made by power relations and structures of the broader collective citizenry" that is fundamentally tied to culture.[22] The dynamics we explore in these films can help to shed light on how culture supports or undermines certain power dynamics according to gender.

VARIATIONS ON A THEME: THE SEXY NEW-AGE MALE

As cultural and scholarly debates indicate, in the 1990s the tensions within men's roles between public professionalism and private domesticity, between self-affirmation and the necessity of caring for others acquired growing relevance and visibility in media, including cinema. The small-budget U.S.-German film *Eat Your Heart Out* (Adlon, 1997) provides an interesting twist on the motif of the sensitive, nurturing man struggling with his public persona as a successful professional. The story, which revolves around a charming, handsome young television chef whose seductive body is portrayed as an object of desire, targets a female (and perhaps also gay male) audience. The film seems to interrogate dominant notions of masculinity.

The lighthearted food comedy/romance film features Daniel (Christian Oliver) as a young chef who works in a kitchen supply shop, where he gives cooking lessons—an occupation that does not rank too highly in the culinary world in terms of prestige. Daniel shares a large, loft-like downtown L.A. apartment with his tomboy female housemate, Sam, and Peter, a tough guy who works as a butcher, traditionally a very masculine occupation. Daniel, who aspires to create his own cookbook, prepares elaborate meals for his friends and seduces women with food. During one of his cooking demonstrations, television producer Katherine offers Daniel the opportunity to start his own cooking show, *Cooking for Two*, on a major network. Unlike ethnically ambiguous Isabella in *Woman on Top*, after some initial trepidation Daniel cooks in his chef's whites, comfortable with his technical skills and the privilege that comes with being a professional white male. Women viewers call the network to express how much they love Daniel, who nurtures the female viewers with words of wisdom about cooking and love. Daniel abandons his friends and enters a relationship with a friend of Katherine's, a manipulative woman named Jacqueline, but grows unhappy that he no longer cooks for people, only for the show. When Daniel's father, with whom he has a tense relationship, lies dying in the hospital, roommate Sam attempts to alert Daniel of his father's illness. Jacqueline and Katherine keep the news from him, and Daniel's father dies before he can make it to San Francisco. Angrily, Daniel abandons the show and leaves Jacqueline. Eventually, he and Sam become a pair. In the end Daniel has opened up a restaurant called "Eat Your Heart Out" in L.A., where he and all of his thirtysomething friends live happily ever after.

In this film we recognize a developing tendency that gender studies scholar Susan Bordo described as a societal shift that has "discovered and begun to develop the untapped resources of the male body."[23] While it is currently unsurprising to see sexualized images of men's bodies across a wide range of media in the United States, at the time that *Eat Your Heart Out* appeared, these images were still relatively unusual, and male bodies (especially white ones) were just beginning to turn into explicitly sexualized objects for the public gaze.[24] Gentle yet virile, Daniel's body appears on display alongside the food he cooks, as objectified as his dishes. But unlike Amanda in *Simply Irresistible* and the other women in the films we discussed in the previous chapter, his success does not derive from magic but from his actual skills and his professional training. Throughout the film we see repeated shots of the elaborate meals that he creates, interspersed with shots of him romancing various women. Like a series of films from the 1990s that explored the insecurities of male identity, often depicting handsome gay men as a best friend to a central female character (e.g., *My Best Friend's Wedding* [Hogan, 1997]), *Eat Your Heart Out* explores the softer side of men. Yet the film consistently underscores Daniel's masculinity and attractiveness, carefully ensuring that he never becomes a passive object of the gaze in the way that women do. Daniel's well-trained body and mastery of cooking articulate a construction of the masculine that parallels how popular images of the male body changed throughout the Reagan and Bush presidencies. As masculinities studies scholar Susan Jeffords writes, "In the broadest terms, whereas the Reagan years offered the image of a 'hard body' to contrast directly to the 'soft bodies' of the Carter years, the late 1980s and early 1990s saw a reevaluation of that hard body, not for a return to the Carter soft body but for a rearticulation of masculine strength and power through internal, personal, and family-oriented values."[25] Daniel's ability to charm women and the film's constant reinforcement of his heterosexuality assure the viewer of his validity as a "real" man, despite his seemingly soft appearance. Real men can bake quiche and eat it, too.

Like *Eat Drink Man Woman*, *Eat Your Heart Out* challenges mainstream models of masculinity in a number of ways. Daniel nurtures people with food, and his desire to cook for others is more important to him than fame and fortune. The film positions Daniel as a contrast to his roommate Peter, a butcher who drives a jacked-up truck, talks about women's bodies, eats like a slob, and neglects his girlfriend's feelings. The juxtaposition of a chef, who creates something out of an array of diverse ingredients, and a butcher, who dismembers animals for a living, could not be clearer. But the film manages to undo some of its power to critique dominant masculinity by demonizing two female characters: Katherine is referred to as a "witch" and Jacqueline as the "sorcerer's apprentice." This treatment of the female characters mirrors what Fred Pfeil noticed about a series of early 1990s films like *Regarding Henry* (Nichols, 1991) and *The Doctor* (Haines, 1991), which depict "sensitive" white men: "in these films, for all their differences, [there is] a similar operation on the field of gender: one in which the female is simultaneously vindicated and doomed or thrust aside, while the male is simultaneously feminized and re-empowered."[26]

Daniel seems to understand women. One viewer on his TV show, concerned with how eating olive oil might make her fat, asks Daniel for advice. "You look beautiful," Daniel retorts in a gently calming voice. The camera cuts to show us a group of women smiling and pleased with his response. At the end of the scene the woman slips Daniel her phone number. This scene plays on the obsession many American women have about food and their bodies: that eating will lead to obesity and render women unattractive to men. Daniel's soft-spoken European voice assuages this anxiety, highlighting the inherent beauty of a broad range of body types.

In many ways *Eat Your Heart Out* assumes straight women as its primary audience, while never fully alienating potential gay male spectators. In its Chippendale-like display of Daniel's body, and in particular his bare, muscular chest, the film is careful to underline his heterosexuality, presenting his body as a sexualized object of desire, opening up more explicit avenues for other spectator positions. Sam's new gay Native American housemate is also placed on display. Posing nude on the couch for Sam as she sketches him, his body is completely exposed with the exception of his genitals. When the doorbell rings, he stands up to go to the door. The camera follows closely behind, focusing on his buttocks. With overt focus on beautiful nude bodies, both white and nonwhite, *Eat Your Heart Out* positions itself as a contemporary women's film, while inviting gay male viewers as well. As males in various degrees of nudity became increasingly more visible in media, from cable TV to cinema (the film was released at the same time as the first season of the HBO series *OZ*, which features frequent and often frontal male nudity), it is possible that by showing the protagonist *en dishabille*, the film was already responding to always shifting arrangements in audience segmentation.[27]

Unlike Chu in *Eat Drink Man Woman*, Daniel operates in the public sphere, although his work makes him miserable. He would much rather cook for friends and intimates than be on public display. The theme of the successful chef who is overwhelmed by the pressures of his public persona and longs for a more domestic lifestyle emerges again in *Spanglish*, starring Adam Sandler as John Clasky, a sensitive and loving chef struggling with his own success. The protagonist finds consolation in food when his personal life and the complicated relationship with his wife overwhelm him. He uses cooking as an expression for his emotions and his desire to create strong and warm relationships. When his restaurant is given four stars in a national newspaper, he does not hesitate to give 20 percent of his business to his sous chef, so he can spend more time with his family. John struggles with the idea that people will try to get reservations from all over the country and that his restaurant will not be able to accept walk-ins and maintain its local character.

Interestingly, he never cooks for his narcissistic wife, who is obsessed with maintaining her tight physique and tries to impose a slim body image on her slightly overweight daughter. In fact, she is interested in her husband's restaurant as a successful business rather than as a place to build community. Once again, a woman functions as a cause, or at least as catalyst, for a sensitive man's troubles. Only the chef's daughter, who has a difficult relationship with food *because* of her mother, understands her father's efforts. The family dynamics change for the better after Flor, a Mexican maid, moves in with the family, injecting a good dose of sanity into the domestic dysfunction. Although she does not cook, unlike John's (white) wife she has a healthy and sensual connection with food that does not seem to have any effect on her sexy body. As we will see in chapter 6, *Spanglish* reiterates the trope of the exotic woman who becomes a savior for the white characters who seem to have lost touch with what really counts in life.

Interestingly, both Daniel in *Eat Your Heart Out* and John in *Spanglish* unintentionally take advantage of their positions as middle-class white men, having the opportunity to question their satisfaction with their occupations without worrying too much about their own and their family's financial stability. Somehow, they operate on the assumption that they will be able to make it, and that their emotions are as worthy of attention as their professional lives. Moreover, women seem to be both the cause and the solution to their problems.

BLAMING WOMEN

Not all chefs onscreen are interested in finding a balance between their professional success, their affirmation as males worthy of respect, and their family lives. Reflecting ongoing social shifts and cultural negotiations about masculinity, a number of food films depict men cooking in domestic or domesticated settings that force them to sacrifice their presence in the public sphere. In this section we explore two films, *Heavy* and *What's Eating Gilbert Grape*, which focus on men who are symbolically emasculated by an imbalance of gender power that expresses itself through food. In these films women function as both the root cause of men's suffering (especially domineering mothers) and as an antidote to help men recover from their disempowerment (in this case, beautiful young women and girls).

James Mangold's *Heavy* shows us the struggles of a sad, lonely character named Victor (Pruitt Taylor Vince), who is oppressed and infantilized by his overcontrolling mother to the point of forfeiting his adult masculinity and sexuality. The film's title reflects Victor's complex relationship with his body image and with the unbearable emotional weight of his life. Set in a small upstate New York town, the film focuses on Victor, who, while aspiring to be a trained chef, finds himself making pizza at his family's roadside diner, Pete & Dolly's, named after his mother and deceased father. Victor is a recluse, and his eyes dart about like a trapped animal's. He is, as the film's title suggests, significantly overweight, and the cause for his heaviness is his oppressive world, including an inability to separate from Dolly (Shelley Winters), his controlling mother, and stand up to the violent, aggressive dominance of other men in his life. When Dolly hires beautiful young Callie (Liv Tyler) to wait tables, tension grows between her, Victor, and Delores (Deborah Harry), a worndown waitress who has worked at the diner for fifteen years. Rather than pointing to the cultural context that supports a gender hierarchy that blames women for men's suffering, *Heavy* reiterates the very privilege that it seeks to eradicate by vilifying the female characters and by turning women into victims of each other. When Callie enters Victor's world, the possibility of a middle-class life (through a formal education at a culinary institute) and healthy male sexuality emerge. For Victor, Callie comes to stand for adulthood and independent life, which nevertheless remains out of his reach.

When Victor finally asserts himself, he reverts to dominant masculine behavior by exploding with violence. After Dolly's death, Victor, unable to cope, denies her passing until forced to acknowledge reality. Outraged and confused, he devours an entire pizza and, turning his anger outward, proceeds to break bottles and glasses. Spent, he sinks to the floor and finally, for the first time, begins to weep. We later see that his hands are bleeding. Instead of internalizing his anger by overeating—a mode of dealing with anger that is traditionally coded as female—Victor is able to gain some sense of resolution, closure, and balance only after his violent outburst.

The film hints that a productive, creative life could be available to Victor outside the depressing, hopeless one he currently leads. Victor's circumstances force him to operate in a poorly defined social space between the domestic sphere and the public establishment his mother runs. Both spaces are emotionally controlled by women, barring him from expressing his creativity, skills, and entrepreneurship, the traits usually attributed to successful male chefs. He feeds the dog, prepares breakfast, makes all the food at the restaurant, goes grocery shopping, washes dishes at home, empties trash in the pouring rain, and does whatever his mother demands of him. Denied the pursuit of an artistic and self-actualizing food vocation, in the diner Victor is forced to cook simple diner food. He only acquires glimpses of a successful cooking career in the public sphere, as illustrated in an oneiric scene where he longingly views the Culinary Institute of America from afar. Bathed in beautiful white light, the institute, with its professional chefs in white jackets and toques, represents Victor's utopia, his realization of manhood, and the potential to escape from his infantilizing mother. The diner, which Delores sarcastically refers to as a "bone orchard," appears in contrast as a private space of entrapment. Victor's forced role as caretaker emphasizes his gentle nature but also takes a toll on his emotional and physical health. Contrasted with the other male characters of his age in the film, who listen to rock music, Victor follows talk radio shows of women complaining about their sad lives.

Food is Victor's only solace, and he overeats as a way to compensate for his lack of power. He suffers as a result of his body size, which makes him feel vulnerability toward food, an emotion typically associated with women's experiences. As we saw in chapter 2, cultural critics have observed how lack of control over one's appetite has been considered a threatening, but common, female characteristic throughout history.[28] In *Heavy* these visual tropes are transferred onto a man. We see Victor struggling to unzip his uncomfortably tight pants, overeating, and struggling with food. Director/writer James Mangold wanted to unpack fat prejudice: "I was driven to make a movie about someone who was very big, but very unseen. . . . Fat is a kind of ugliness that we're blamed for. It's a dramatically potent place to be."[29]

Heavy critiques mainstream models of masculinity, often imposed on men, and articulates the pain that people with nonnormative bodies experience. It does so by asking us to identify and empathize with Victor, an unusual move for a film about an obese person, also inviting us to rethink how we conceptualize masculinity.[30] Although the film could, depending on how the viewer reads the narrative, actually work to reinforce stereotypes of the "fat man" as weak, a loser, or as having no self-control, we argue that the film attempts to deconstruct this image by forcing the viewer to identify with Victor rather than allowing us to stand back and laugh at him. *Heavy* does not allow us to remain at a distance from Victor's experience or to occupy a position of moral superiority. Victor is never the butt of the joke; rather, we watch him with compassion. His suffering stems from his social setting rather than from a fatal character flaw.

This approach distances *Heavy* from other films about "fat" men. Even the 1980 *Fatso* (Bancroft), which asks for a great deal of empathy from the audience for the main character's suffering, consistently holds Dominic DeNapoli (Dom DeLuise) up as an object of laughter alongside sympathy. Later in the 1990s, the grotesque images of characters like Fat Bastard in *Austin Powers: The Spy Who Shagged Me* (Roach, 1999) and Professor Klump in *The Nutty Professor* (Shadyac, 1996) provided excellent examples of the condescending way overweight men are ridiculed in mainstream cinema, regardless of their ethnicity or social status. Tony Perkins in Walt Disney's *Heavyweight* (Brill, 1995) and White Goodman in *Dodgeball* (Thurber, 2004), both played by comedian Ben Stiller, offer a comical but sometimes cruel look into the personalities of men who have lost weight as a way to acquire a sense of self-worth and affection from others. Both characters overcompensate by becoming exercise freaks and obsessing about their body image, trying to force their priorities on others and compromising human relationships to attain their physical goals.

Heavy embraces the notion that men suffer from body-image and eating disorders and dispels stereotypes that mainstream media perpetuate about overweight people. In the United States excessive body mass is often interpreted as a sign of lack of will and determination and as an external manifestation of emotional shortcomings and lack of self-control, both for men and women.[31] As a consequence, body images play a fundamental role in defining what socially acceptable individuals should look like, both males and females. Yet it strikes us that there is a lack of comparable images that focus on women in such insightful, compassionate ways, as the literature on weight prejudice and fatness suggests. In *Fat History* Peter Stearns explores the social meanings of fat in the modern Western world and illuminates how obsession with fat arose in conjunction with a significant increase in consumer culture, women's rights, and changes in women's sexual and maternal roles.[32] Of course, distinctions are visible in terms of class, race, and ethnicity, as more voluptuous bodies may be acceptable in nonwhite, non-middle-class communities.[33] In fact, it would seem that in the contemporary United States a fit body is increasingly read as a reflection of healthy eating, cultural capital, and refinement, a perception that intersects with judgment on social status and, often implicitly, with race and ethnicity.

Feeling too closely identified with the suffering of an obese female character may pose a greater risk for mainstream audiences than identifying with a similarly overweight man. The few films about obese women that attempt to engender empathy often simultaneously provoke laughter, keeping viewers at a comfortable distance. *Fried Green Tomatoes*, which we discussed in chapter 2, asks us to empathize with the overweight character Evelyn (Kathy Bates), who in the film is the present-day listener for events that happened decades ago at a roadside restaurant in the South (fig. 4.2). As the story develops and she becomes fascinated with the fearless and convention-breaking female characters she hears about, she tries to take control of her eating habits, her body image, and her sexuality, all while asserting herself as an autonomous individual, especially against her husband. At the same time, the narrative and her own perception of herself position her as "hysterical." "I can't stop eating," she cries. "Every day I try and try, and every day I go off. I hide candy bars all over the house." Evelyn is told that her eating disorder is related to menopause and hormonal imbalance, blaming her female anatomy and aging process for what feminist eating disorder specialists view as an effect of socially reinforced gender patterns that make women believe they are sick if they like to eat.[34]

The camera pans alongside her as she devours candy, carefully situating us in her counterpart's position, an older and frail woman, so that we look at her from a thin person's eyes. Evelyn eventually acquires agency, but the

FIGURE 4.2 *Fried Green Tomatoes* unpacks the struggle around female body images and the wrought relationship with eating and appetite as a tool that has often been used to limit women's agency.

scenes we just described help us to keep our distance from her. We are asked to view white, middle-class Evelyn with a mixture of pity and humor, perhaps glad that we are not in her shoes. The cinematography cautiously allows us to empathize with her without having to fear *becoming* her.[35]

In contrast, when Victor stuffs himself, we see him fighting tears and looking lost and alone. An eerie soundtrack makes us experience his pain. Rather than looking at him, we experience with him. *Heavy* ultimately places the blame for Victor's eating disorder on the oppressive, manipulative women in his life, in particular his mother. While Victor's figure offers a refreshing change from the status quo, the film undermines this by blaming his suffering on his mother and reiterating a very old, sexist trope that powerful women feminize and disempower men, especially their sons. The film explains Victor's obesity as a problem caused by his "henpecking" mother.

Unfortunately, this trope is not uncommon. *What's Eating Gilbert Grape* reverses the narrative so that the obese person is the mother of the lead character, Gilbert (Johnny Depp), while the son is "normal." The film tells the story of teenage Gilbert, whose mother, Bonnie (Darlene Cates), is so morbidly obese that she has not left her house in years.

Gilbert waits on his mother hand and foot and supports his impover-ished family. Throughout the course of the film he is finally able to sep-arate himself from her. Embedded in the small Iowa town of Endora, Gilbert watches life pass him by as he cares for his family and works in a small local grocery shop. When a new FoodLand supermarket moves in, symbolizing changes in the U.S. economy and culture, and Gilbert develops a crush on waif-like prepubescent-looking Becky (Juliette Lewis), Gilbert's world begins to change.

Throughout the film we see Gilbert cringe with embarrassment but also express fondness for his troubled family, which includes his developmen-tally disabled brother, Arnie (Leonardo DiCaprio). One evening, Gilbert neglects his brother while he and Becky are enjoying a private conver-sation. Arnie climbs to the top of a water tower and is arrested. Bonnie ventures out to help get her son Arnie released from the police, and she endures verbal and emotional abuse by onlookers who gawk at her and make fun of her. For the first time since her husband's death, Bonnie then climbs the stairs to her bedroom, where she dies. The children remove their belongings from and burn down the house with her corpse inside of it to spare her the humiliation of having to have her body removed by a crane. The mother becomes a symbol of a past that must be left behind for her children to move forward and lead better lives.

With the death of the mother, Gilbert can escape from his family's embarrassing low-income status and destructive eating habits. At the film's end he and Arnie wait by the roadside for Becky and her hip, mid-dle-class grandmother to pass through Endora in their Airstream trailer, a symbol of liberation and the broader world outside this claustrophobic town. Even though the film treats Bonnie kindly in its depiction of her, it is Gilbert with whom we are asked to identify. Gilbert is frustrated that his life has been cut off because he must feed and support his essentially disabled mother. Like Victor, Gilbert's life is limited because of his mother. In these films women are either victims of other women or dominators who try to control men and keep them from attaining power over their own lives. Betty Carver (Mary Steenburgen), a middle-aged woman who is having an affair with Gilbert, tries to control him through her sexuality much like Delores seeks to control Victor. Middle-aged women in these films have few options for self-realization and victimize young men, who must break free from their controlling grips. In both films the mothers limit sons through food (Victor's mother by keeping him heavy, Gilbert's mother by becoming so obese). In each case a thin, young woman offers reprieve from a downward spiraling life. The films offer the male protagonists refuge from their working-class worlds through alignment with the middle class, so that stories of gender, sexuality, and social class are woven together to create situations of entrapment and then release for men, who must move beyond their families' circumstances to experience individuation and productive, healthy adult sexuality.

At the same time, we note that both films take on mainstream food culture in ways that other food films do not. In *Heavy* Victor grapples with diet products that promise him salvation. The film dispels the myth that consuming more (light, low-fat products) represents the pathway to weighing less. *What's Eating Gilbert Grape* attacks corporatized eating culture as well in its representation of the contemporary supermarket. Considering our claim that food films engage in debates about citizenship through the lens of culture, this move is particularly interesting. Food studies scholar Sidney Mintz connects the formation of identity with the consumption of food goods. In both *Heavy* and *What's Eating Gilbert Grape* the critique of the dominant food system is a way of talking back to the idea that the "act of choosing to consume apparently can provide a temporary, even if most spurious, sense of choice, of self, and thereby of freedom."[36]

This pseudo-freedom that manifests itself in claims like the McDonald's "You deserve a break today" slogan is highly spurious and, as Susan Bordo points out, intricately woven into contemporary constructs of selfhood that link directly to economic structures: "An unstable, agonistic construction of personality is produced by the contradictory structure of economic life. On the one hand, as producers of goods and services we must sublimate, delay, repress desires for immediate gratification; we must cultivate the work ethic. On the other hand, as consumers we must display a boundless capacity to capitulate to desire and indulge in impulse; we must hunger for constant and immediate satisfaction. The regulation of desire thus becomes an ongoing problem, as we find ourselves continually besieged by temptation, while socially condemned for overindulgence."[37] While both films issue a critique of this "regulation of desire," they both succumb to traditional gender narratives that hold women responsible for men's suffering. Mothers and middle-aged, sexually deprived women serve as sources of suffering, while younger women provide salvation, a confusing configuration of femininity that offers few points of productive identification for women.

DRINK UP!

We cannot discuss shifting perceptions of masculinity and their relationship with food (in this case, wine) without considering *Sideways*. Unlike the other films we have discussed in this chapter, which ultimately hold women responsible for the ills that men face, *Sideways* points to men and their inability to manage relationships as a core part of the problem and offers honest, productive connections among people as a pathway for addressing loneliness and depression and for exploring life's riches. Food and wine consumption can either lead to more intense and direct emotional connections or to increased isolation. While the focus on wine appreciation points to an upper-middle-class and prevalently white environment, the male characters' vulnerability does suggest a shift in the perception of what mainstream masculinities may look like. Miles (Paul Giamatti) is an oenophile bachelor who is experiencing a significant life crisis after being left by his wife, Victoria, whom, we learn, he had cheated on because he felt threatened by her power. Something of a talentless and boorish person, Miles cannot seem to excel at anything other than his knowledge of wine: no one wants to publish a novel he is writing; he appears alienated from his role as high school English teacher; he consumes at least two medications to manage his anxiety and depression; and he drinks way too much wine (fig. 4.3). Despite his failures, Miles is marked by his white, middle-class privilege, which manifests itself in various degrees of self-absorption and the opportunities he has to taste great wines, regardless of his temporary financial woes. A road movie, *Sideways* depicts a weeklong trip that Miles and college buddy, wannabe-actor Jack (Thomas Haden Church), take to drink wine along California's central coast as a way of celebrating the final days before Jack's wedding. In a style bordering at times on slapstick, the

FIGURE 4.3 Wine connoisseurship, which is considered both legitimate work and a hobby for men, is explored in *Sideways* as a site of contested masculinity, at a time when women are making headway in wine-related professions.

two men, whose personalities are diametrically opposed, pursue their fulfillment respectively in wine (Miles) and women (Jack).

Often shot in tight frames with shallow focus, we see Miles as he struggles to come to grips with his life. Throughout the film he unravels to the point that he grabs and attempts to drink, in a state of anxiety and rage, the spit bucket at a lower-end winery. Unlike the other films we examine in this chapter, women are never blamed for Miles's feelings. Instead relationships with women make him question his own fragility, which he articulates through a description of his favorite grape, pinot noir, to Maya (Virginia Madsen), with whom he has fallen in love during the trip:

> Um, it's a hard grape to grow, as you know. Right? It's, uh, it's thin-skinned, temperamental, ripens early. It's, you know, it's not a survivor like Cabernet, which can just grow anywhere and, uh, thrive even when it's neglected. No, Pinot needs constant care and attention. You know? And in fact it can only grow in these really specific, little, tucked-away corners

of the world. And, and only the most patient and nurturing of growers can do it, really. Only somebody who really takes the time to understand Pinot's potential can then coax it into its fullest expression. Then, I mean, oh its flavors, they're just the most haunting and brilliant and thrilling and subtle and . . . ancient on the planet.

Maya, who delivers the film's most beautiful, poignant lines, describes wine as "a living thing." Wine, like people, changes, peaks, and eventually declines:

> I like to think about what was going on the year the grapes were growing; how the sun was shining; if it rained. I like to think about all the people who tended and picked the grapes. And if it's an old wine, how many of them must be dead by now. I like how wine continues to evolve, like if I opened a bottle of wine today it would taste different than if I'd opened it on any other day, because a bottle of wine is actually alive. And it's constantly evolving and gaining complexity. That is, until it peaks, like your '61. And then it begins its steady, inevitable decline.

Instead of reiterating men's disempowerment because of women, the film points to men themselves as holding responsibility for their feelings and behavior.

A scene on the golf course, where Miles and Jack attack fellow players in warrior-like fashion, seems to make fun of the notion of men as fighters. The men look ridiculous as they badger other men with a golf cart and clubs. Masculinity, and the socially defined gender-norming straitjacket it produces, becomes the actual object of criticism rather than men, and the film suggests that the gender norms we perform also entrap us in behavior patterns that limit our ability to live. Life peaks and then declines, just like Miles's prized possession of an extraordinary 1961 Château Cheval Blanc, which he drinks pitifully by himself, in a fast-food restaurant out of a Styrofoam cup, after ruining yet another relationship with a woman.

Wine offers an apt focus for these reflections on masculinity and gender relations. Wine connoisseurship has, until lately, been considered a masculine endeavor. Expertise and determination in exploring a patently complicated field can turn into a respectable men's occupation. It is not surprising that Miles attributes so much emotional weight to wine and, above all, to his capacity to be a discerning expert in the field. But his single-mindedness and obsessive focus on the object of his interest jeopardize his ability to express himself and create meaningful relationships. Like chefs that use their profession and their expertise to assert themselves as men—and as alpha men at that—Miles tries to increase his self-worth through connoisseurship. *Sideways*, released in 2004, complicates any received assumptions about mainstream masculinity, reflecting slow but undeniable changes in U.S. culture and social dynamics.

GENTLEMEN, YOU CAN HAVE YOUR STEAK AND EAT IT TOO!

The films we have examined in this chapter use food and eating to explore alternative models of masculinity and fluid gender relationships in the United States. Embracing a more critical approach to U.S. society, it is surprising that they also ask us to reflect on identity by raising questions about consumption. While carefully—and discreetly—reasserting white male privilege, the films point to a shift in men's experiences that is intricately linked to social changes that coalesce in the 1990s, when these films (other than *Spanglish* and *Sideways*) were released. Robert Connell argues that along with tremendous growth of men's material power comes "an intensification of crisis tendencies in the gender order."[38] According to Connell, this perceived crisis in masculinity, in particular in white masculinity, "damaged patriarchy's legitimacy and has left men to manage this loss in a range of ways."[39] That the media should become one of the sites where this looming crisis is negotiated and played out was inevitable. Collectively, however, these food films fail to recognize the social, political, and economic structures that govern gender, power, and citizenship.

The characters in these films point to dysfunctions in the contemporary gender order. The desire to reawaken the "fire in the belly"—to quote Sam Keen's book about reconquering manhood—appears in the knives on Chu's wall and in Victor's violent outbreak in the diner.[40] These characters combine "warrior and nurturer, provider and playful child."[41] In doing so, they ask us to identify with men's suffering and blame needy, voracious, and all-consuming women that scholars like Susan Bordo have identified in the discourse about anorexia nervosa and the way Western society has come to think of femininity.[42] With the exception of *Sideways*, which places responsibility fully on men's side, the controlling female figures in these food films keep the sensitive male from reaching his full potential. Although these films criticize hierarchies that exist *among* men, they fail to express a criticism of the overall gender order or even to represent masculinity within a larger social, cultural, or economic framework, taking into full account issues of class, race, and ethnicity. We believe these films offer insight into how dominant U.S. culture views—or is willing to view—men in relationship to food. They also provide some insights into the ways that ideas change. Men who cook—at least in these films—can take on softer, more feminine roles, without risking the loss of their masculinity. At face value this trend seems to challenge traditional notions of Western masculinity. Yet, as we have illustrated, the films strategically reinforce white masculinity as the dominant source of power, often vilifying women and holding them—especially mothers—responsible for men's suffering. In these stories men are allowed to be soft and hard, vulnerable and powerful without losing their power. The implications for what it means to participate as a full-fledged citizen in U.S. culture are tremendous, viewed from this vantage point. While many of the films we have explored thus far in this book make an effort to break with tradition, they tend to revert to dominant, traditional gender structures that suggest women should and do hold less power than men.

In many ways these films are in dialogue with the food films focused on women that we explored in the previous two chapters, as well as with those focused on restaurant life, which we discussed in chapter 1, and seem to point to diverse forms of "successful" masculinities, which are nevertheless inflected by class, race, ethnicity, and age dynamics. The tug-of-war around domesticity and the public sphere virtually mirrors itself, with women moving back into the home and men escaping the domestic hold to reassert themselves in the public sphere and realize their full masculinity. It appears that to assert their place in the world, men need to trust themselves, use their unique talents, and stick to their projects even when the world around them seems to think otherwise. As we will see in the next chapter, a new crop of feature-length animated movies embraces food as an arena for men to develop these life projects.

5

WHEN WEIRDOS STIR THE POT

Cooking Identity in Animated Movies

In the summer of 2007 an unusual new character joined the selected elite of celebrity chefs. Remy, the rodent protagonist of the smash hit *Ratatouille* (Bird and Pinkava, 2007), appeared on the silver screen, providing new fodder for the imagination of worldwide audiences increasingly passionate about food and cooking (fig. 5.1).

Filmgoers of all ages and backgrounds seemed to appreciate the culinary adventures of the little rodent and of his human coprotagonists. The thought of a rat meddling with pots and pans and a whole colony of pests invading a restaurant to cook gourmet meals came across as fun, not scary or disgusting. This is quite an accomplishment, considering that the animals were represented very realistically, although hands, eyes, and mouths were drawn to make them appear more human and less threatening. The movie's spotlight on the drive and commitment necessary to make it in the world of fine dining highlighted self-actualization, as well as the ever-present contrast between innate capacities and acquired skills. Attention to food preparation and consumption also allowed the story to deal with friendship, love, and community—always powerful and widely beloved topics—and to hint at less heartwarming issues, such as social status, cultural capital, gender, and ethnicity. Within a three-year period four more feature-length animated films placed food at the core of their narratives, setting them apart from other successful animated movies released in the same period: *Bee Movie* (Hickner and Smith, 2007), *Kung Fu Panda*

FIGURE 5.1 Remy the rat, the protagonist of *Ratatouille*, who quickly became a symbol of all things culinary around the world, aims to boost children's confidence by declaring that "everybody can cook."

(Osborne and Stevenson, 2008), *The Tale of Despereaux* (Fell and Stevenhagen, 2008), and *Cloudy with a Chance of Meatballs* (Lord and Miller, 2009). These films deserve special attention, especially considering that they have been watched and enjoyed by children all over the world, regardless of their cultural background and social context. Unlike the material we have discussed in previous chapters, these films specifically address young audiences as their main marketing target. Gadgets and video games built around the films' heroes illustrate the movie industry's high level of awareness of the business potential of these productions, using cross-marketing like figurines in fast-food meals, packaging, and all kinds of advertising and commercials.[1]

Another shared trait is that they all feature young male protagonists who, despite their oddities and struggles to find their place in the world, achieve success in the end. The plots glorify masculine traits, including determination, courage, and professionalism. Once again, food turns into an arena that determines what behaviors and identities are acceptable in terms of U.S. cultural citizenship, a move that becomes blatant when the films introduce "ethnic" characters. Although these cartoons deliberately present themselves as apolitical, they offer narratives about food and models of masculinity that can potentially influence the way children are socialized and, eventually, what kind of adults they will grow up to be. In the highly globalized distribution of U.S. animated features, it would be interesting to assess the impact of the ideas, behaviors, and norms illustrated in food-related narratives on children growing up in cultures where issues of age, social status, and gender are dealt with in very different ways.

What makes the recent animated films we examine in this chapter different from previous ones? Food has always been featured in cartoons to generate amusing situations and unadulterated physical comedy. The familiarity with food and related practices arguably facilitates the viewers' identification with characters and events, making the movie experience more engaging. Children, in particular, can immediately relate to food out of personal experience, even when other topics might go over their heads. In the five movies we discuss in this chapter, food is far more than just a narrative tool or a gimmick to draw viewers in with easy references and funny shenanigans. Instead, it functions as a protagonist, one that is as important as the main characters themselves. For this reason the way food appears onscreen has changed. Using sophisticated graphic technology, these five movies have introduced a visually arresting approach to food in cartoons. Ingredients and dishes, represented with precision and attention to detail, have turned into very realistic elements in the films' fictional worlds. For example, in the whimsical *Bee Movie*, although cooking plays a less crucial role, the glistening and transparent honey drips, flows, and whirls in ways that accurately mimic the real substance.

To a certain extent these cartoons embrace many aspects of food porn's aesthetic approach, providing fetishistic extreme close-ups, amplified sounds, and attention to gleaming and textured ingredients.[2] *Ratatouille* even experiments with the graphic representation of the internal sensory experience of Remy and his brother Emile while they taste and attempt to pair various ingredients. In this case the movie shifts from realistic representations toward more abstract, but still very accessible, reflections about personal perceptions of flavors and aromas. Accuracy in the visual description of edible matter obviously signals its relevance in the plot and in the protagonists' individual stories and elevates the importance of food in ways that correspond to mainstream representations, while at the same time downplaying the cultural politics of food and consumption in the United States. We argue that these films train young audiences to adopt viewing strategies that prepare them to become future consumers of food and food media, with the values and norms that come with them. The cartoons simultaneously target adults through tongue-in-cheek jokes that children do not usually get, thus creating a large audience segment that will consume both the messages in the film and the marketing tie-ins. This strategy capitalizes on the notion that themes that work for younger viewers will also resonate, at least in part, with the adults who ultimately are the ones who take them to the movies, purchase the DVDs and Blu-rays, or buy streaming access to the cartoons so that children can watch them over and over again at home.

In the past few years adult audiences worldwide have shown a growing interest in animation as a visual medium, as demonstrated by the growing popularity on anime and the establishment of the Academy Award for Best Animated Feature since 2001. Successful animated series such as *South Park*, *Family Guy*, and the shows featured on Cartoon Network's Adult Swim network, which shares channel space with the Cartoon Network but targets older audiences, contribute to the success of the medium. In many ways this constitutes a return to the past rather than a new development. In fact, cartoons were originally produced as adult entertainment and shown before feature films. Only after the success of Walt Disney's *Snow White and the Seven Dwarfs* in 1937 did feature-length and short animated movies come to consider children as their main intended audience.[3] Nevertheless, at times cartoons still appeared hesitant to focus exclusively on younger viewers, often including elements geared toward an older crowd. The *Looney Tunes* and *Merrie Melodies* stories, for instance, showcased highly exaggerated slapstick comedy that maintained elements of the original adult vaudeville spirit and could simultaneously entertain children.

The animated movies we discuss in this chapter maintain this ambivalence between the elements targeting children and grown-ups, while building the relevance of food and ingestion into the genre. In these films, eating offers viewers untapped opportunities to reflect on what constitutes acceptable models of behavior, especially focusing on the development of masculine identities in the context of social status, prestige, and success.

While it is important to understand what these male food protagonists enjoy and ingest, far more significant in the context of cultural citizenship is teasing out how these ideas and practices around eating might contribute to the formation of gender, ethnic, and class identity.

Using food provisioning, production, cooking, and eating as seemingly innocent and entertaining topics, the issue of who fits and who does not in the protagonists' communities—in other words, who can claim power and full cultural citizenship—dominates the narratives. More specifically, the plots in all five movies develop around themes of masculinity, coming of age, tensions between parents and children, and food as a tool of self-expression and personal fulfillment. The events unfurl against backgrounds and dynamics that often hint at issues of social status and ethnicity that play a crucial role in the determination of U.S. cultural citizenship. The previous chapter examined how food movies appear to propose alternative models of manhood, while in reality they end up reinforcing mainstream stereotypes. The pervasiveness of these cultural elements is amplified by the success of these movies in theaters, on DVD, and in other digital media. Of particular concern here is that the films discussed in this chapter primarily target children, engaging consistently in subtle political debates surrounding gender, ethnicity, class, and power.

This chapter aims to unpack how food in animated movies engages children about what it means to become an adult, more specifically, a man. Our analysis attempts to lay bare the personal and collective negotiations around food, identity, and community rather than assuming that the prevalent approaches are given or, worse, natural occurrences.[4] What norms and practices are marked as acceptable when the cartoon characters define their identity around food? How do these films participate in a process of inculcation and cultural reproduction that defines what it means to be a successful citizen of the United States?

THERE'S A RAT IN THE KITCHEN!

We start our exploration with *Ratatouille*. Released by Pixar Animation Studios for Walt Disney, it became an immediate global hit, banking more than $47 million in its opening weekend in July 2007. Produced with an estimated budget of $150 million, it grossed a total of almost $616 million at box offices worldwide.[5] The story's uniqueness lies in its ability to combine two elements that would appear otherwise mutually exclusive: rats and haute cuisine. And maybe that's the reason for the movie's wild popularity. Besides generating innumerable reviews in newspapers, magazines, and websites, *Ratatouille* has been analyzed as reflecting the relevance of cooking in the civilizing process,[6] as an instance of the complex relationship between haute cuisines in France and America,[7] as an introduction to the historical dimension of French culinary culture,[8] and even as an example of how movies have been dealing with business failure around the global financial crisis of 2008.[9] In the context of our analysis of the use of food in the negotiation around cultural citizenship, we focus instead on issues of gender, particularly masculinity. After all, only one main character is female, while many of the emotional and dramatic elements of the narrative hinge on father-son and male mentor-mentee relationships.[10] We also explore the movie's negotiation of cultural norms and class, particularly in relation to gender, to assess what model of acceptable masculinities it offers to its viewers, many of which—despite the enormous success among adults—are children on their journey toward adulthood.

Country rat Remy is gifted with innate culinary good taste and uncanny cooking skills that put him at odds with the rest of his community, especially his father, who prefers to steal and feed on garbage. Although he cannot speak, Remy can understand humans and is literate. He is attracted to the humans' ability to approach food in creative ways, independently from simple appetites and instincts. He is especially fascinated by the motto "everybody can cook," from the late celebrity chef Gusteau, whose books and TV shows ignited Remy's love for food. When his colony has to abandon its lair because of his culinary mishaps, Remy gets lost in the sewers and ends up in Gusteau's restaurant in Paris. Here he befriends the hapless Alfred Linguini, a young man devoid of culinary flair who is happy to be working as a garbage boy. Remy learns how to control Linguini's movements by hiding under his toque and yanking his unruly red hair. The young man can finally cook, although vicariously, and his (actually Remy's) culinary creations manage to muster attention from both patrons and critics.

The restaurant's current owner, chef Skinner, who is only interested in banking on Gusteau's name to launch ethnic frozen products, discovers that Linguini is actually Gusteau's son, a fact that not even the youngster knows. Despite Skinner's attempts to hide this fact, the truth comes to light and Linguini becomes a media star with help from Remy and the tough-but-honest Colette, the only female chef at Gusteau's. Unnerved by the challenging attitude of food critic Anton Ego, Linguini quarrels with Remy and is forced to reveal the existence of a secret animal helper to all the cooks in the restaurant. Everybody abandons him but Colette, while Remy tries to get back at him by allowing the rats from this colony into the restaurant pantry. Eventually, with the collaboration of his fellow rats, Remy saves Linguini's dinner service and prepares a ratatouille for Ego. The simple, but perfectly executed country dish reminds the food critic of his childhood, when his mother used to make it to comfort him. Despite Ego's glowing review, the health department shuts down Gusteau's restaurant owing to the presence of rodents. In the end the critic finances Colette and Linguini's new hip bistro, where Remy can finally express his talent and the rats can enjoy their own space, dining on good food rather than stolen garbage.

With its pervasiveness and visual impact, food plays a central role in this film. To ensure detailed representations of dishes and restaurant work, the producers made sure that all talent involved got hands-on experience in restaurant and food preparation. As the *San Francisco Chronicle* reported, "For six years, members of Pixar Animation Studios took classes at Bay Area cooking schools and channeled the artistry of Thomas Keller, the chef-owner of Napa Valley's critically acclaimed French Laundry restaurant."[11] Keller also created the film's modern version of the traditional ratatouille. Subsurface light scattering, a technique that had been used in previous Pixar films like *The Incredibles*, makes the ingredients appear translucent, and new CG techniques render the food appetizing and realistic.[12] According to a promotional podcast, graphic simulations were conducted on pictures of actual dishes prepared in the studio so that artists could make food relax and drape on itself, while great attention was paid to the textural and optical qualities of steam, heat waves, and bubbling sauces.[13] Highlighting the physical attributes of food introduces children to the aesthetics of food in kid-friendly ways that prepare them for the hypersexualized, glorified images they will experience as adults when they become consumers of food television, movies, magazines, and websites. At the same time, the imagery appeals to adult food enthusiasts, widening the audience base for the film.

The movie's worldwide success was based in part on its reception by captive audiences who are fully attuned to the urban foodie culture thriving on media hype, the vast popularity of star chefs, and issues such as local sourcing, sustainability, and health. Critic Ego's explanation of the movie's motto "everybody can cook" confirms this connection, which also reveals the dreams of many food lovers to become famous professionals: "Not everyone can become a great artist, but a great artist can come from anywhere." Remy fully embodies this democratic approach, represented in real life by many contemporary star chefs who were not classically trained but use their creativity to assert themselves.[14] The possibility of making it into the big time resonates with those who, feeding on the media frenzy and TV shows like *MasterChef*, fancy themselves advanced domestic cooks or want to turn their passion for food into a career.[15]

Banking on the widespread interest in kitchen cultures, the film documents the functioning of a classic French restaurant, the structure of the kitchen brigade, and the role of each member with great detail. It pays attention to the intricacies of ingredients and preparation, both from visual and technical points of view. Audiences have become familiar with these elements thanks to the success of reality shows like *Top Chef* and *Hell's Kitchen*, books, and websites focusing on what happens inside professional kitchens where patrons are not usually allowed, seemingly eroding the front- and backstage nature of the restaurant business.[16]

Ratatouille managed to open this world to younger viewers as well. In an explicit move to interest children in food, prepping them to become more engaged future consumers, Mattel marketed a *Kitchen Chaos* playset, which included culinary instruments and accessories and a less gastronomic *Sewer Splashdown* playset, inspired by Remy's adventures in the underbelly of Paris. LeapFrog Leapster released a *Ratatouille*-themed game that can help children learn to recognize and classify foods, while helping Linguini with recipes. THQ issued the video games *Ratatouille:*

Food Frenzy for Nintendo DS and *Ratatouille* for other console systems, to mediocre reviews. Like the action figures that now accompany big-budget animated movies, *Ratatouille*'s toys represent a move to build cultural capital around children's curiosity in the kinds of food and cooking that are presented as particularly significant and prestigious in the rat's story.

The film embraces French culinary traditions, both *haute cuisine* and *cuisine de pays*, as the epitome of good taste and refinement. Despite being a rat, Remy embodies these superior qualities. For example, he is clean and refuses to walk on all fours to avoid soiling food with dirty front paws, differentiating him from the rest of his rat colony, stuck in a lower social status. Besides being apparently all male, the other rats live in close quarters, near humans but hidden in abject places (under roofs, in the sewers), and proliferate in huge numbers, literally dwelling on top of each other. They are dirty and uncouth, as they feed on garbage, leftovers, and stolen food. They need to be steamed clean and purified before they are allowed to help Remy prepare food in the restaurant. They, too, understand humans but are not able to speak to them. This silent and efficient—although unskilled—labor force can be taught repetitive and mindless tasks whose precise completion allows the civilized, creative chef to take on the role of guide and leader. Without making too large of a stretch, we might see in the rat workers a reflection of the quiet and omnipresent immigrant workers who allow the U.S. restaurant industry to thrive but are often treated as foreign and inscrutable.

When meeting after a long period of separation, Remy's father teases him, pointing out that he has lost weight, either out of lack of food or excess of snobbery—the older rat attributes this change to his proximity to humans. In his mind they are not only physically different, but they belong to a superior and resented social group. Eventually, Remy's openness carries the day. The whole rat tribe stops stealing food and accepts that they need to be steamed clean, undergoing a symbolic process of purification that allows them to follow the proper and hygienic way to relate to food. From starving proletarians feeding off the scraps of the better-off, they become participants in the bourgeois project of French cuisine. Their scruffy, undisciplined, and underworld manhood—remember, we are not introduced to any female rats—morphs into more urban, sophisticated manners. In the final scene we see them sitting around proper tables eating proper food that has been properly prepared. This embedded message clearly points to taste and food behaviors as markers of class distinction, presented as an upward-bound ladder to social success.

Tensions in social structures also play a crucial role in *The Tale of Despereaux*, produced by Universal Pictures and Relativity Media and based on the children's book by Kate DiCamillo. The movie, which also bets on rodents as protagonists, grossed only around $50 million during its theatrical release in the United States, claiming a meager $10 million during its opening weekend in December 2008. Viewers are introduced to the parallel stories of Roscuro the rat and Despereaux, the little mouse. Roscuro is a sailor, brought by his curiosity to Dor, a kingdom where once a year a new soup is created for the king and his family, for the joy of the whole population. When Roscuro manages to enter the royal dining hall, attracted by the aroma, he ends up falling into the queen's dish right when she is about to taste the new soup. The queen is so terrified that she dies with her face in the dish, throwing the king into a state of desperation so profound that he outlaws "the making of soup, the selling of soup, or the eating of soup" and declares rats "unlawful creatures." Roscuro finds refuge in the sewers, where he joins a community of rats that live in hiding and feed on garbage, but he cannot fit in.

Meanwhile, another outsider is becoming a teenager in the back of the royal kitchen: the mouse Despereaux, who, unlike the other members of his community, does not know fear, does not cower at the sight of danger, and is curious about his surroundings. Just like Remy, he learns how to read books, identifying with human models—in his case not a celebrity chef but knights and heroes. The mouse eventually meets the princess, who asks him to keep on reading and reporting on the stories he reads. Despereaux's lack of fear and bravery are not acceptable to his community, which interprets them as recklessness and stupidity. He is exiled to the sewers, where he befriends Roscuro. Still feeling guilty about the soup incident, Roscuro decides to talk to the princess, just as Despereaux did. But when he tries, the princess gets scared and has him chased by her guards. The embittered Roscuro decides to take his revenge, allowing the evil rats to take her prisoner into their underworld. In the end Despereaux saves her, a narrative turn that allows Roscuro to realize his error and initiates a series of events that push the royal chef to cook again. The scent of the new soup creation wakes the king from his stupor, and the kingdom comes back to life.

Like *Ratatouille*, *The Tale of Despereaux* focuses on the interaction between humans and animals, the latter of which are graphically enhanced and detailed to a degree that verges on realism, even though these rodents wear clothes and speak and act like humans. The artwork is less original than that of *Ratatouille*, and the story follows lines that feel already familiar because of their fairy-tale themes. Although the protagonists do not cook, they express their identities and personalities through food and eating. Social distinctions are clear, as not everybody has access to the same fare, and characters display different degrees of refinement. The fictional kingdom of Dor is organized along class lines, with the soup-loving humans on top. The king showcases his royalty through the annual soup ceremony, in which the products of his land are brought to the capital to be transformed and cooked for his pleasure and his family's enjoyment. Without even participating in the manual work of the kitchen, the king and his family set the tone of what is considered tasty and refined in his kingdom.

The French chef, Andre, commands precisely what is needed for the soup and, in organizing its production, reflects current perceptions about celebrity chefs as detail-driven, creative, and domineering professionals who lead their kitchen thanks to healthy doses of alpha-male testosterone. Reminiscent of *Ratatouille*, Andre reinforces the dying stereotype of the supremacy of French cuisine, which appears to go unquestioned by moviegoers and is used by filmmakers to frame characters, backgrounds, and stories. Andre's expertise is only a facade, however; he actually uses a magic book that conjures a character made of vegetables that is inspired by Arcimboldo's visual creations and that speaks with an Italian accent, always adding garlic to food. Rustic traditions and humble ingredients emerge as the foundational strength of Andre's culinary style, complicating the apparently high-class nature of his creations.

Mice live in an intermediate environment—close to humans yet hidden from them. They have access to kitchen pantries and consume the same kind of food as humans, although in smaller quantities. Their manners are polite and refined; they consume their meals sitting around the table, chewing on small morsels, and using silverware. As they mimic the canons of urbanity of the more respectable classes and are content with their position, humans do not seem too scared or even disgusted by them. At the other end of the social ladder the rats are represented as sneaky, cruel, dangerous, and ready to consume garbage without any composure or social refinement. All the rats except Roscuro display an excess of uncouthness, refusing all bourgeois appearances. In the movie they actually represent the underbelly of all societies, a reality that is often far from view but nevertheless present and menacing.

THE DISCREET CHARM OF THE BOURGEOISIE

Social status, particularly middle-class respectability, is also a central theme in DreamWorks' *Bee Movie*, revealing how important status and class are in the construction of masculine identities that are acceptable in terms of cultural citizenship. What does it take to become a respected and successful male? Are there models to avoid that deserve to become the target of comedy? The film asserts the theme of Fordist production as potentially emasculating but necessary to the smooth functioning of society. Like in *Ratatouille*, to appeal to younger viewers, these adult topics are embedded in a narrative built around food—a sweet substance, honey—and a familiar animal, a nonthreatening bee. Produced with an estimated budget of $150 million, the film grossed around $38 million during its opening week in the States in early November 2007, with a total national gross of about $126 million during its theatrical release. Though the movie's action figures were sold with McDonald's Happy Meals at the end of 2007 and Activision released a video game geared toward young children, the characters did not enjoy the same popularity as *Ratatouille*'s Remy.

In *Bee Movie* a beehive becomes a symbol for consumerist society, where workers toil in mindless jobs in order to acquire the goods that are supposed to mark their success but in reality anchor them to their immutable status. The first time viewers see the protagonist, Barry the bee, he is graduating after "three days of grade school, three days of high school, and three days of college," an element that highlights the insect's limited life span while revealing middle-class obsession with education as a gateway to social success. Barry needs to choose what his job will be for the rest of his life. All bees enjoy long-term employment, another middle-class pillar that is nevertheless increasingly threatened by the transformation of the production system. Barry refuses to adapt to a secure but boring future before experiencing the world outside the hive, so he decides to accept the challenge ironically thrown at him by the pollen jocks, the hypermasculine, aviator-like bees who scout the meadows to gather precious pollen. Following them in an expedition into New York City, Barry ends up in a human apartment. He befriends a young woman, Vanessa, who dreams of being a florist, although her parents want her to be a doctor or a lawyer. Vanessa and Barry are experiencing the same conundrum: they both want to be useful to their community but not in the way the community expects them to be.

Going with Vanessa to a grocery store, Barry is shocked to see bottled, branded, and even discounted honey. Surprised that humans consume it (since they have so much available food), Barry is also dismayed to know that they take it from bees without any form of compensation. Bees are the exploited labor, while a more powerful group takes advantage of the fruit of their work. Barry decides to sting human honey bottlers where it really matters, successfully suing them for profiting off the bees' work. As a consequence of the court's decision, bee farms are shut down, and the bees in the artificial hives are freed. All of the honey is restituted to the bees, and this sudden abundance forces them to shut down production for the first time in their history. The bees also stop pollinating plants, nearly causing an environmental catastrophe. Vanessa and Barry gather all the remaining pollen in a plane that they manage to land with the help of the pollen jocks, who literally lift the plane and fly it in an insect-like pattern, thanks to their community instincts. Eventually, Barry convinces the bees to participate in the pollination, and nature is saved. In the last scene, we see Barry in his new law office in the back of Vanessa's florist shop, while he talks to a cow complaining that she does not get a nickel off all the products made with cow milk. In the final scene of the movie Barry is called into action, and he flies away with the pollen jocks, enjoying his double life as a lawyer and as a flying marvel. Exploitation is still an issue, but now downtrodden workers know they have a defender in Barry, whose success transcends his humble origins.

In *Bee Movie* the protagonist asserts himself by refusing the trappings of bourgeois life. The first time we see Barry, he flies down to the family room without using the stairs for which, as his mother points out, "his father has paid good money." The staircase, in its utter uselessness for flying bees, is presented as a symbol of middle-class aspirations to a better lifestyle that is nonetheless costly, and at the same time as a mark of the effectiveness of Barry's father as provider. In the *Bee Movie* hive, lifelong white- and blue-collar jobs, uniformity in clothing, housing, and locomotion vehicles, and even the home design style, hairdos, and eyeglasses reminiscent of the 1950s ironically point to a society where there is not much room for difference or individual initiative. The hive provides the perfect background for Barry to express his weird individuality and his difference from the stolid masses. He rejects the working ethos of his father, who is happy with the status quo. Raving about his job stirring honey day-in and day-out, Barry's father buys into the respectability and comfort of suburban life, as well as into the satisfaction that comes with his position within the family. His house has a TV set and a swimming pool, symbols of affordable luxury. For him and his wife, it is unthinkable that their son might not be interested in working in honey, produced in a very streamlined system with machinery, pipes, vats, and chemist-looking individuals working with vials. This textbook example of Fordist organization presents honey as mass production for the masses by the masses. The filmmakers assume that viewers can enjoy this kind of irony, sharing an outlook where consumption, consumer choices, and distinct lifestyles define individual identities, while mindless factory work becomes the object of ridicule.[17]

The contrast between social expectations and individual aspirations that we have identified in Remy's and Barry's involvement with food and food production emerges as a pivotal theme for yet another animal character: Po, the protagonist of *Kung Fu Panda*. With a lower production budget than *Ratatouille* ($130 million), the martial arts–themed cartoon boasted better results in the United States during its release week in June 2008, grossing around $60 million and reaching $633 million at box offices worldwide during the entire duration of its theatrical release. The film was followed by two shorts (a 2009 video about the secrets of the Furious Five, the movie's kung fu champions, and an NBC Holiday special in 2010); a sequel (*Kung Fu Panda 2* [Yuh 2011]); and a TV series (*Kung Fu Panda: Legends of Awesomeness*, started in 2011).

The box-office success of *Kung Fu Panda* was sustained by significant marketing initiatives, including the action figures that feature prominently in the movie itself. In fact, at the beginning we see that Po the panda imagines his adventures while engaging with action figures of his martial arts heroes, the Furious Five. In an intriguing turn, the marketing of the movie has somehow doubled as product placement. In 2008 Po ended up on the boxes of the Kellogg's Crunchers Cereal and in 2012 on General Mills' product packaging, which contained spin fighter toys featuring *Kung Fu Panda* characters. Small action figures also were included in McDonald's Happy Meals in 2011, when the sequel was released. In 2008 DreamWorks also developed a video game for various platforms, maximizing the marketing campaign. The film's promotion through a variety of products, but most specifically with industrial breakfast cereal, connects its message about the importance of personal initiative and originality with their accomplishment through mass consumption. Individuals carry out "choices" that are limited to the ongoing flow of commercial products drummed up by food television and other media. These dynamics parallel the TV marketing strategies of the Food Network, which delivers a steady blur of mixed messages about food and lifestyle.[18] The film also presents an interesting case of cultural appropriation, abundantly featuring Chinese martial arts, graphic motifs, mythology, architecture, and, of course, culinary culture. The film elicited mixed reactions in China, from amusement to annoyance at the use of the Chinese theme, especially since the Chinese animation industry at the time did not have the means to generate such an expensive product.[19] Earning more than $12 million in its first two weeks of distribution, the film became a huge hit, despite calls from critics and artists to boycott it.[20]

The story and personality of Po, a lovable panda, are endearing and entertaining for audiences of all ages (fig. 5.2). As is often the case in animated movies, however, the fun factor ends up working as a screen for subtle messages about the impact of body image, gender, and class—let alone ethnicity—on a person's social relevance. Po works in his father's

FIGURE 5.2 Po's unbridled appetite for food turns from a liability to an asset in *Kung Fu Panda*, showing children (and especially boys) that a full-figured body is acceptable and lovable.

(a goose) noodle restaurant, while dreaming of becoming a kung fu legend. The contrast between his fantasies and the bleak reality of his job as kitchen help comes to an end when, through a series of fortuitous accidents, the supreme kung fu master Oogwey (a turtle) chooses him as the Dragon Warrior, much to the dismay of the famous champions known as the Furious Five (a tigress, a monkey, a female snake, a mantis, and a crane) and their trainer, master Shifu (a little red panda). When the evil Tai Lung, a rogue snow leopard that Shifu had trained, escapes from prison, Po finds himself in the situation of facing an actual danger. At first despised by the Furious Five and master Shifu, when the evil Tai Lung defeats the kung fu champions, Shifu decides to train Po, cunningly using the panda's bottomless hunger to bring the warrior out of him. The master teases him with cookies and dumplings, thus forcing him to explore his physical potential and his determination. Eventually Po defeats Tai Lung using his rotund body and his capacity to take beatings. As it turns out, the very qualities that first made him an outcast turn him into the Dragon Warrior.

The panda's overweight body, unstoppable appetite, and total lack of athleticism are not the only roots of the initial tension between the protagonist and the kung fu master. Master Shifu and his acolytes enjoy a higher social status than Po—they live in a serene and beautiful temple at the top of a mountain, physically separated from the hustle and bustle of the village. Commoners are rarely admitted, except on extraordinary occasions like the choice of the new Dragon Warrior. An impossible long and steep flight of stairs leads from the village to the temple, underlining distance both in terms of location and prestige. It remains unclear how the masters survive or who provides them with food. Their world is removed from the daily preoccupations that the panda's father, Mr. Ping, has in his struggle to understand his son's aspirations.

FOOD ADVENTURES: FROM MISFITS TO HEROES

All the movies we discuss use food, from production to preparation to consumption, to emphasize the idea that growing individuals with a special talent must be ready to go through all kinds of trials and tribulations to achieve their potential and make their uniqueness shine. It does not matter if it makes them different from everybody else or if pursuing and expressing it means going against the advice of their elders: that's what becoming an adult means, at least in the fictional reality of cartoons. Each individual is presented as the only true judge of his own uniqueness, with self-actualization as its core. This value seems deeply embedded in U.S. culture, to the point of being recently critiqued in a much-discussed article in the *New York Times Magazine*, which described this attitude as the result of "our fetish for the authentically homespun and the American affliction of ignoring volumes of evidence in favor of the flashes that meet the eye, the hunches that seize the gut."[21]

This overarching theme is exemplified by the first sentences we hear from Flint, the protagonist of Sony Pictures' *Cloudy with a Chance of Meatballs*, as a disembodied narrator: "Have you ever felt that you were a little bit different? That you had something unique to offer the world? Then you know exactly how it felt to be me." As we hear these words, the frame zooms in from an aerial view to a close-up of the wide-eyed child, the protagonist in the past. Flint is giving a presentation of a scientific invention to his classmates: spray-on shoes that, unfortunately, cannot be taken off. Of course, the other children make fun of him. We can almost feel his humiliation when he runs home in the rain, trying to find consolation in his role models, the great scientists of the past whose posters decorate his room. "The world needs your originality, Flint," his mom consoles him. "You only need to grow into it."

The movie, based on the book by Judi Barrett, grossed a respectable $30 million in the States during its opening week in September 2009 and a total of $126 million during its theatrical release. Flint is a nerdy genius who, since childhood, has lacked interpersonal skills and is confined to his own world. He is unable to communicate with his widowed father and keeps a monkey as his lab assistant while he works on his mad-scientist projects. Flint lives on the tiny island of Swallow Falls, which, in the past, had built its fortune on fishing and canning sardines until the world realized that "sardines are super gross." As a consequence of this recent global realization, the island dwellers have lost their source of livelihood and are forced to consume the sardines that nobody else wants. Flint's father, tired of his mishaps, tries to get the young man to work at the family bait-and-tackle shop. Eventually, Flint manages to launch a machine that turns the atmosphere into food, giving Sam, a young female meteorologist to whom he is attracted, the opportunity to become a TV anchor.

Flint's exploit strokes the interest of the island's mayor, whose hunger for success and money is rivaled only by his gluttonous capacity to ingest portentous amounts of food. Leveraging Flint's desire for recognition and attention, the mayor convinces him to keep making it rain food three times a day to turn the island into a tourist attraction. The whole city goes into a gorging frenzy, excited at the idea of eating food other than sardines. Leftovers are not a problem at first because Flint invents an "out-of-sighter," a machine that sweeps foods from the streets and catapults it outside the town limits. Soon a spaghetti twister hits Swallow Falls, the first of a series of giant foods—including pancakes, watermelons, and donuts—that pile up to form a mountain that in the end crumbles, threatening to destroy everything in sight (fig. 5.3). While everybody abandons the island on makeshift sliced bread rafts, Flint flies in a rocket inside the food formation in the sky, eventually stopping the machine and saving the day.

FIGURE 5.3 Nerds can be heroes too. In *Cloudy with a Chance of Meatballs*, Flint turns children's favorite foods into edible landscapes that, unfortunately, become nightmares, reminding viewers that junk food is ultimately not good for you.

The opening of *Cloudy with a Chance of Meatballs* provides us with a key to interpret the movies we have discussed in this chapter. Viewers, including the younger ones, can easily identify with the trials and tribulations of their heroes, who feel different, misunderstood, and eager to show to everybody that they deserve admiration. Negotiating one's identity between one's self-perception and the world's expectations and judgments is an important part of personal development. At the same time, adults are reminded of their own potential and what they have achieved in their lives. Plus, they can be satisfied with providing their children with entertainment that also promotes a positive message. Apparently innocuous cartoons can become uncomfortable expressions of the continuous social pressure to perform and excel at one's best.

In each of the five movies discussed in this chapter, the narrative arc that allows the protagonists, all of whom are male, to find their true selves develops around food. One way or another, food becomes the instrument of the protagonists' redemption, even when it is seemingly the origin of their weirdness and a cause for social isolation. Female characters are absent or in the background. When they are featured in more visible supporting roles, they often chafe at the traditional gender roles that allow the male protagonists to shine. In *Ratatouille* food is used to express one's uniqueness or embraced as the path to the easy life. We never see Remy gorging himself. As a matter of fact, eating for him seems mostly connected to tasting rather than to actual consumption; he is not moved by the need for fuel or by hunger but by the desire to develop his creativity for creativity's sake. Unlike the other rats, clearly marked as uncouth and lower class, Remy is not controlled by food. He controls it for a higher end, so girth is not an issue. In a way he is the fantasy embodiment of the perfect consumer, who can ingest without suffering any undesirable consequences.

Kung Fu Panda's Po has a more ambivalent relationship with food. He loves eating, but his roundness creates problems in his training. He openly admits that his desire to eat increases when he is under stress, a trait that, as we discussed in the previous chapter, contemporary popular culture often attributes to women. But food ultimately becomes the instrument of Po's redemption. In fact, the first signs of Po's acceptance by the other kung fu warriors happen around the table. After training, the panda prepares soup for them, and the warriors express their enjoyment, praising Po, who charms them with his modest self-deprecation and his sense of humor. Thanks to his master's intuition, Po's desire for food is turned to his advantage as a powerful source of motivation. Using a bowl of dumplings as bait and enticement, Master Shifu pushes the panda to his limits in terms of strength, agility, perseverance, reflexes, and speed. A final battle fought with bowl and chopsticks to get to the last dumpling proves that Po has completed his training, and although he is now able to conquer the food, he voluntarily gives it up, declaring he is not hungry. Po has finally tamed his body, which is not just weight that pulls him down—it can be finally used as a weapon. In the narrative's resolution it is actually Po's heaviness that allows him to resist the attacks of Tai Lung and to eventually defeat him.

GROWING INTO MEN

As we have emphasized, the protagonists in the five animated films explored in this chapter are all male. The theme of gender and its relationship to food deserves particular attention, as it is featured front and center in these narratives. Nevertheless, as we have already pointed out, even when we focus on this specific identity trait, we can never discount other dynamics connected to age, social status, and ethnicity, which all contribute to define specific experiences of masculinity. Food contributes to the growth and success of male characters despite the fact that it is still often represented in popular culture as an element of the domestic, feminine sphere. This shift is possible because there is nothing domestic or ordinary about food in these movies. Even common dishes like noodles, meatballs, and soup allow the protagonists to assert themselves as extraordinary—either as chefs or scientists—in a very public and professional, and, as such, inherently masculine, way. Their success is made even more visible by contrast with secondary male characters that by class, ethnicity, or just intellectual or emotional endowment cannot compare with them, despite the embodiment of more mainstream models of masculinity. The main characters' conquest of masculinity as legitimate and socially acceptable, even when it pushes the envelope of conventional norms and behaviors, is also vetted by the presence of their father figures, whose symbolic resistance to change is eventually replaced with the young males' acceptance into the community. Po's masculinity is not only questioned by his body type but also by his relationship with other paternal figures. Unlike the other villagers in the Valley of Peace whose progeny openly belong to the same species, the panda is supposed to be a goose's son. This oddity underlines the essential difference between Po and his father, who embodies matter-of-factness, hard work, lack of imagination, and compliance with tradition. The goose's nurturing traits appear as acceptable because they align with his ethnic otherness, underlined by his foreign-sounding accent. Similar to many immigrants to the United States, Mr. Ping does not measure with the mainstream standards of successful masculinity. He is no chef. He lacks creativity and does not strive to distinguish himself or assert himself professionally. He is content with satisfying his clients and making a living. "We are noodle folks. Broth runs through our veins," he says. This representation of Mr. Ping employs Eurocentric strategies that scholars Ella Shohat and Robert Stam observe in mainstream U.S. media.[22] When it comes to masculinity, models from other cultures can be measured against dominant standards established in

U.S. culture and marked as weaker or less prestigious.[23] The treatment of Ping as a less-than-standard male through his depiction as an Asian naturalizes a set of recognizable, exotic, but ultimately debasing traits that are often not a reflection of actual elements from the other culture but rather a projection of the fantasies and biases through which a dominant culture reinforces its position of superiority.[24] His father expects Po to take on his profession and his role in society, but eventually it is he who helps his son to understand that there is no secret ingredient for his transformation to a kung fu hero and that he just needs to believe he is special.

Despereaux's father, in contrast, is not able to build a real dialogue with his son, and when the little mouse is banned, he responds to the pressure from his community by not intervening to defend him. Despereaux, however, does not seem very affected. He has developed coping mechanisms that allow him to thrive within his imagination, where the boisterous and valiant knights with whom he identifies eat together, consuming huge chunks of meat. At dinner, when the other family members eat dainty morsels of cheese with a fork, Despereaux spears a big piece of cheese with a loud "Whoopee!" The little mouse embodies the qualities that male children are supposed to develop as they grow: inquisitiveness and courage, like a knight who can fight and take care of damsels in distress. The story makes these positive traits more appealing to viewers by presenting them as Despereaux's acts of insubordination, which certainly intrigues children more than the fulfillment of adults' expectations. Even the mouse's desire to read is presented as somewhat reckless.

Flint's father, in *Cloudy with a Chance of Meatballs*, is not big on communication either. His son tries to build a machine to produce food out of water only to enjoy everybody's admiration. There is no sense of nurturing in his effort, and as a consequence the dishes he programs in his computers are all children's favorites that do not take health and nutrition into consideration but also indicate a relationship to food that is all about mindless consumption and fun. Flint's father is not big on nurturing either. Since the death of his wife, he has not been able to really communicate with his son, but he has a strong sense of responsibility that he expresses in his attachment to his bait-and-tackle shop, a symbol of the blue-collar economy that does not exist any longer on the island. "Technofood is too complicated for an old fisherman," he mutters sadly. Earl, however, the local policeman and only man of color in the movie, despite his attempts at mimicking the cops we can assume he admires on TV, has a clear understanding of food as expression of affection. When he asks for a special treat to celebrate his beloved son's birthday, Flint covers the whole town in ice cream, a vision reminiscent of Willy Wonka's imaginary factory.

In *Bee Movie* Barry's father is not the only male figure providing standards against which Barry tries to build his identity. The young bee is fascinated by the pollen jocks, who are bred differently and have a distinctive look: tall, brawny, and dressed like World War II aviators. They are covered in pollen, which attracts female bees. Their days are never the same, as they get to leave the hive and explore, even if some of them never come back. Risking their lives to get pollen for the hive, their palpable maleness derives from the fact that they are providers and are not involved in food transformation and preparation, processes marked as less masculine since they take place indoors, in the less dangerous and more domestic environment of the hive. Incidentally, the masculine bees are also in charge of pollinating flowers, thus enabling reproduction and the survival of nature.

In *Ratatouille* Remy's contrast with his father, articulated around the fearless pursuit of creativity as opposed to the stubborn attachment to mundane but stable behaviors, is also built around food. Remy's father is happy with garbage and stolen food, content with creating a colony in hidden places, and clearly at ease with dirt. Conversely, Remy wants to eat food in human kitchens, a practice his father perceives as dangerous. The difference between the two is not only a question of adherence to tradition but one of class tension, with the young rat bent on achieving his lofty goals and the older one, seemingly unrefined and ignorant, disinterested in improvement and change. Ultimately, Remy's father realizes the potential and value of his son's gift, and the presence of the whole rat community in the new bistro symbolizes complete acceptance and respect for Remy, the rat chef. From this point of view Remy, and the model of masculinity he embodies, manages to become socially acceptable through paternal approval.

Rather than modeling himself on his father, Remy is inspired by the chef Gusteau, whom the viewers only see in a TV show and as a figment of Remy's imagination in many internal conversations. He reminds Remy of the chops it takes to become a successful chef: "Great cooking is not for the faint of heart. You must be imaginative, strong hearted. You must try things that might not work, and you must not let anybody define your limits because of where you come from. Your only limit is your soul. What I say is true; anyone can cook, but only the fearless can be great." Serious cooking requires fearlessness, and Remy's relationship to food affirms the alignment of courage with masculinity in that his involvement with food does not move him closer to a position of disempowerment. After all, he expresses himself in the restaurant, a male-dominated and professional field. The soft and ample Gusteau is still a real man, who, besides having an illegitimate child, was also a businessman running a successful restaurant, publishing popular cookbooks, and who expanded the aura of his celebrity through the media.

At the opposite end of the spectrum, the skeleton-like and clearly anorexic food critic Anton Ego has a much more complicated relationship with ingestion (fig. 5.4). He angrily barks, "I don't like food. I love it. If I don't love it, I don't swallow." Food for him is about intellectual

FIGURE 5.4 The gaunt and irascible food critic Anton Ego in *Ratatouille* embodies a model of masculinity that reveals how complicated men's relationships with food can be.

analysis until he experiences Remy's ratatouille, which breaks down all his defenses and turns him into a happier man who can finally enjoy eating. Ego's gender development seems suspended between his sad childhood, where his mother loomed large, and his powerful, albeit even sadder, adulthood. While his professional authority would safely place his masculinity within the mainstream, his excessive control over food and ingestion evokes the eating disorders whose incidence is increasingly acknowledged among men.[25] Eventually he sheds this troubled element of his personality to embrace the more acceptable model of the successful entrepreneur who finances Linguini's restaurant and who can enjoy the food prepared for him in his establishment.

The theme of masculinity, although not immediately apparent, is woven into the whole narrative of *Ratatouille*, sending not-so-subliminal messages to the viewers. The action does not take place in a domestic kitchen. Gusteau's restaurant is not a nurturing place but a well-oiled machine that produces high-quality food for discerning clients. Remy and the other cooks, who all seem to hide mysterious past lives, do not express any supposedly feminine traits as they do not use food to nourish others. They embody professional cooking as the exclusive domain of trained professionals, which was the basis of the expansion and success of French cuisine both nationally and abroad. For many years the presence of a chef from France ensured the authenticity of French cuisine and secured the successful employment of those who went through traditional culinary French training.[26] As the only female chef at Gusteau's, Colette angrily acknowledges, "Haute cuisine is an antiquated hierarchy built upon rules written by stupid old men, rules designed to make it impossible for women to enter this world." Colette has been forced to adapt to these rules and negotiate them, as many female chefs experience daily in their attempt to achieve success in a male-dominated environment.[27] For example, Colette's vehicle of choice is a motorbike. She wears a black helmet and sleek leather gear when she rides, masculine attire that reflects her toughness and differentiates her professional work from women who feed families in domestic environments.[28] When she is given the apparently nurturing task to train Linguini, Colette is very resentful, as she had fought hard for her position in the kitchen. Being the only woman in the kitchen, she cannot commit errors or lose her focus by wasting time with the young man.

The gender politics of the kitchen, as represented in *Ratatouille*, privilege an unforgiving approach to food that is based on prestige and professionalism connected to a successful career. As alpha males asserting their authority over weaker males, celebrity chefs establish their dominance over lesser cooks and armies of busboys and dishwashers, whose social status, ethnic origin, and lack of education and cultural capital put them at a disadvantage. The chef's initiative and creativity acquire visibility when contrasted with the repetitive tasks of kitchen staff. This allows for a seemingly domestic and manual occupation to achieve higher status and social respectability, two traits that popular culture often indicates as fundamental for successful and well-adjusted adult manhood.

HUNGRY BOYS DON'T CRY

The tensions lingering in the movies we have examined in this chapter reflect larger issues surrounding cultural citizenship and the acculturation processes of children through media in the United States. In all of them the male characters' identities are defined in their relationships with food production and consumption. Manhood can be conquered, and many movies do embrace the narrative of the young man trying to succeed in his goal while proving his worth as a real man. When we scratch the surface, it becomes immediately clear that masculinity is far from solid and unchanging. Rather, it is socially and culturally negotiated around practices and behaviors linked to food preparation, food provisioning, eating, and even the fear of being eaten.[29] In the animated movies we have explored, the comedic approach allows for a more relaxed evaluation of masculinity, which is called into question under amusing circumstances. Nevertheless, our analysis has pointed out how the apparent oddness of the cartoon characters eventually gets normalized into social acceptance, a move that reinforces mainstream practices and values about manhood. In all five films this crucial shift takes place around food, a narrative choice that is meant to assuage anxieties around such a relevant issue.

These cartoons appear to function not only as a commentary on food as an important element around which gender identity is constructed and negotiated but also as a reflection on how those dynamics often play out within the family, in particular in the complex relationships between fathers and sons. The fathers embody the status quo, tradition, accepted norms, and acceptable behaviors, while the sons strive to modify the system, create new alternatives, and develop their own unique individuality beyond the accepted limits. In none of the movies does this contrast usher a definitive rupture but rather creates a soft transformation that demonstrates society's ability to accept change and thrive thanks to its supposed openness to diversity. The father figure is necessary for the main characters to achieve manhood, often through contrasts that develop around food issues.

In fact, the reflection about what can be considered normal, and to what point society can deal with transformation and unique individuals, constitutes the core of these movies. Food assumes important metaphorical values, allowing "weird" characters to express themselves while participating in the bettering of their communities. By dealing with an aspect of life often perceived as simply innate and motivated by biological needs, movies can reinforce values, behaviors, and practices that are far from neutral. Cultural biases, social dynamics, and power hierarchies can appear natural states, while the negotiations and the tensions that underpin them are erased. This is particularly relevant given that an important segment of the audience consists of children who might absorb and mimic some of the behaviors performed by their beloved characters. Cultural critic Henri Giroux reminds us that films and other forms of electronic communication function as a "powerful pedagogical force, veritable teaching machines in shaping the social imaginary."[30] We cannot forget that young children ask to watch their favorite movies over and over again, often to their parents' dismay. Viewing and reviewing teaches children—and adults alike—how to participate in society.

These films teach children, especially boys, how to empower themselves to belong, despite the fact that they may not all come to the table with the right ingredients from the outset. Food emerges as a legitimate arena for the construction and the negotiation of adulthood, social status, and success, which can be interpreted as a result of the increased visibility and prestige of cooking at the beginning of the twenty-first century.[31] Certainly, these films also teach lessons about femininity, but the focus is clearly on male characters and food. Although including aspects of material life usually attributed uniquely to women may soften and widen the rigid limits of acceptable models of maleness, the films separate the domestic, nurturing, daily aspects of cooking from the professional, self-asserting, moneymaking ones. The characters in these cartoons, as unusual as they are, become respected warriors, artists, lawyers, and scientists, falling again into the normalized expectations of what young boys should become. They also take full advantage of their privileged positions in terms of class and, at times metaphorically, ethnicity.

Far from being framed as elements of the domestic and feminine sphere, in these films eating and cooking are not domestic activities and do not appear related to care work. The ethnic connotations of dishes and cooks—although quite visible—remain mostly in the background, obliquely pointing to relevance of ethnicity and race—in their complex interplay with gender, class, and age—in the negotiations surrounding cultural citizenship. In the next chapter we will see how some food films embrace these components but neutralize their subversive potential by framing them in forms of culinary tourism that allow mainstream viewers to quench their curiosity without questioning their privilege. This approach becomes particularly sensitive as food films widely circulate globally among moviegoers and in particular among the new cosmopolitan and international communities of "foodies."

6

CONSUMING THE OTHER

Food Films as Culinary Tourism

Ethnic foods have historically played a crucial role in shaping U.S. food culture, which developed out of a range of different food traditions. At any given time and place the definition of what was considered "American" and "foreign" or "ethnic" depended less on material elements than on ideological contexts. Food culture in eighteenth-century South Carolina, for example, openly embraced what we would now refer to as multiethnic, global fusion cuisine. A hundred years later, southern European immigrants to East Coast cities were instructed by settlement house workers to abandon their highly flavored foods in favor of bland, boiled "American" dishes. Today, many formerly rejected cuisines have found their way into mainstream American diets. The elevated status of Italian food in the United States serves as but one example of how much a moving target the concept of "ethnic" food is. Food scholar Donna Gabaccia points to debates that erupted between the late nineteenth and early twentieth century about food, culture, and belonging: "nativism and xenophobia—both prominent features of U.S. politics in the early twentieth century—had expressed themselves in opinions about the foods Americans should consume. Between 1880 and 1940, a veritable 'food fight' erupted over what it meant not only to be, but to eat, American. Here again, however, the preference for variety and novelty would win over those intellectuals and home economists who would define patriotic eating by the regional eating habits of the New England past."[1]

What comes to be defined as ethnic, foreign, or full-fledged American (consider, for a moment the role of pizza, hot dogs, and salsa in the contemporary United States) has deep links not only to who can claim membership to the States but also to what assertions America has allowed itself to make on foods that, historically, might have been defined as foreign. Following the moving target of what is perceived as ethnic food can help us tease out the power and privilege that are assigned to or taken away from the respective groups whose food falls into this category at any given time. Historically, issues of ethnicity have interacted with other markers of identity, from sexuality to gender, to social class, to religion, complicating the concept of what it means for someone or something to be "ethnic." In the late nineteenth century, being an Italian ice cream vendor in the streets of New York's Lower East Side was perceived very differently than was an Italian maître d' at the prestigious Del Monico restaurant. Nowadays, a female tamale vendor selling handmade products out of a shopping cart does not enjoy the same social status as a female Mexican chef and restaurant owner, who is likely to encounter larger problems in running a business than her male counterparts in Mexican communities, independent of the obstacles they may face when compared to white chefs who are entrepreneurs.[2]

Consistent with its "melting pot" history, the United States has recently developed an intense appetite for foreign and ethnic foods. Scholars often point to February 11, 1963, when Julia Child's cooking show, *The French Chef*, first aired on television as a point of major shift in American food history.[3] The show's relevance is reflected also in its visibility in the box-office hit *Julie & Julia*, starring Meryl Streep, discussed in chapter 2 (fig. 6.1). Child, however, worked within the realm of a cuisine that had all the prestige of a European tradition perceived as refined and upper class, which helped to mute its "ethnic" character. Thanks to Julia Child and others who followed her, few would think of French food as ethnic, although it is clearly a culinary tradition from another country. This example makes clear that cultural norms and values define what is "national" and what is "alien." With Child's show and the many other cooking shows that followed, the United States increasingly developed a greater appetite for international foods. From the popularity of Mexican food to the rise of sushi to the

FIGURE 6.1 Meryl Streep plays Julia Child in *Julie & Julia*, solidifying Child's position in the pantheon of the great innovators of U.S. cuisine and food media.

proliferation of fusion cuisine, ethnic food has an important place at the American table. In concert with our understanding of food culture as part of broader U.S. culture, it comes as no surprise that consumer and media culture are saturated with images of ethnic cuisine, from television to food magazines to tourism's public relationships strategies. Among "foodies," connoisseurship of ethnic culinary traditions is now often considered a mark of cultural capital and refinement: the more obscure the foreign cuisine is, the more impressive. Yet who decides what is ethnic? And why do some foreign foods, like French, Italian, and more recently Japanese, enjoy higher status than others? How have these ongoing shifts in prestige taken place, and what role do media play in helping transform foods from exotic to everyday?

Inevitably, the popularity of ethnic food leads us to ask deeper questions about food, power, and culture. Elspeth Probyn has argued that the United States possesses a "hearty enthusiasm for 'foreign food' that is supposed to hide the taste of racism."[4] This appetite is fueled, in part, by the wide availability of ethnic food, reflected through omnipresent representations across different forms of U.S. media. Food films, in particular, are replete with images of ethnic food. Whether they present African American,

Latino, Asian American, or Jewish characters, food films parade a series of assimilated people whose culinary traditions appear readily palatable for mainstream audiences. Food films like *The Joy Luck Club* (Wang, 1993), *Tortilla Soup* (Ripoll, 2001), *Soul Food* (Tillman, 1997), and *What's Cooking?* (Chadha, 2000) invite us to sit at the dinner tables of different American ethnic families as guests. In doing so, these films allow us to become tourists. More specifically, we turn into culinary tourists. As such, we can visit without any requirement to stay or even to actually engage with the place we choose to explore. The food habits, the flavors, and the imagined aromas of their dishes become a marketable commodity that is there just for our enjoyment.

In this chapter we focus on films that feature ethnic food in the United States, exploring them as part of the broader cultural landscape of the U.S. culinary identity. We do so in such a way that investigates the relationship of race and ethnicity to other markers of identity, especially gender and sexuality. Nonetheless, our primary focus is on ethnicity because these films position themselves as films about ethnic families and were marketed as such. Certainly, issues related to race and ethnicity emerge in all the food films we have examined so far, as in the case of the ethnic chefs in chapter 1 or the magic women in chapter 3. But those ethnic characters were examined primarily in their role of professionals or providers in the public sphere, even when their private and family lives were shown to provide background and emotional content to their stories. Not surprisingly, the seminal *Eat Drink Man Woman* stands as an exception, as its main audience was supposed to be Chinese, just like the characters. As we will see, its U.S. remake, *Tortilla Soup*, presents a different approach in its focus on a family of Mexican descent who live in a white environment, for the delight of both Latino and white viewers.

The particular body of films we explore in this chapter allows viewers unfettered access to the characters' intimate life and their family dynamics. The films have been designed to appeal to both ethnic and mainstream white audiences. *Soul Food*, for example, was heavily marketed to African Americans but also to white audiences. Looking at these films through the lens of cultural citizenship, we recognize a strategy that enables white spectators to safely visit the world of ethnic others and consume images of food and family in a comforting, inviting environment. This move seems to invite and favor cross-cultural learning. Yet the films maintain a careful distance, ensuring that the tourist experience doesn't bring viewers too close to experiences of difference that might otherwise be perceived as threatening. We can experience diversity via the images on the screen, gazing at difference from a distance that might feel safer than direct interaction.[5]

Scholarship on food films that depict ethnic groups often ignores the films' tensions among stereotypes, idealized or utopian representations, and the material circumstances of the respective ethnic groups represented. Food studies scholars have also focused on *Tortilla Soup*'s dazzling food, eschewing any discussions of race, ethnicity, class, and gender. Jim Stark applauds Martín's cooking as "the glue that holds together both the family and the film."[6] He calls *Tortilla Soup* a "culinary delight," stating, "[the] meticulous care with which the food is made, the vibrant colors of the Mexican sauces, the ache when Martín cannot even taste the wonder of what he has created—all of this makes for a film not only about the enduring love of family, but also about the timeless love of food." Like Stark, Robin Balthrope takes *Tortilla Soup* and *Soul Food*'s representations of food, ethnicity, race, and U.S. culture for granted in emphasizing how audiences are "fed as well with food for the soul that lingers on long after these cinematic feasts have concluded."[7] We question this celebratory approach to these films and dig deeper to ask how they help to (re)shape cultural politics in ways that reinforce the marginalization and disenfranchisement of some groups over others.

We argue that these films, which simultaneously pull us in and distance us from their characters, share some common elements. Their plots push eating and culinary traditions—as unfamiliar as they may appear—to the forefront, allowing viewers to peek at intimate aspects of the characters' material and emotional existence. This culinary tourism experience is reinforced by the frequency and intensity of food shots and sequences that embrace the "food porn" aesthetics we discussed earlier in this book. This kind of food film, already a mainstay in the States, has started appearing in other countries that have become more multiethnic in the past decades and started experiencing new ethnic and racial tensions. We mention, for instance, *The Secret of the Grain* (*La graine et le mulet* [Kechiche, 2007]), which explores the attempts of a Moroccan family to start a couscous restaurant on a boat in the port of Marseille, in southern France. *Soul Kitchen* (Akin, 2009), which examines the vicissitudes of a restaurant in multiethnic Hamburg, is also worth noting. But these European films present more nuanced perspectives on ethnic food, with a critical eye on how foreign culinary traditions are understood, practiced, hybridized, and commodified.[8] We stress that not all U.S. films that look at the food traditions of ethnic or racial minorities adopt the culinary tourism approach. A great example, *Daughters of the Dust* (Dash, 1991), although not a food film per se, explores the culinary traditions of the Gullah communities in the Sea Islands off the U.S. coast of Georgia and South Carolina.

By positioning us as tourists, the films we examine in this chapter present themselves as educational tools, implying that the information we gather from stories, characters, and images can improve our knowledge and understanding of other cultures. This attitude of benign curiosity and cultural engagement is a slippery slope. It can reassure us of our goodwill, liberal open-minded approach, and distance from bigotry and racism. At the same time, these movies carefully navigate our expectations as audience members, sometimes aligning characters with racial and ethnic stereotypes that underline their unique traits, sometimes positioning them as fully assimilated. The films reaffirm a dominant pattern in the United States that aggregates certain ethnic groups into one large homogenized whole, reiterating dominant beliefs and attitudes about ethnicity. This pattern frequently emerges, for instance, in the usage of the term *Latinos*, underpinning the false assumption of race-based similarities between Mexican Americans and Cuban Americans. In doing so, they grant whiteness a special privilege to observe and monitor unfamiliar nonwhite neighbors. Ultimately, this matters very much in the way we think about cultural citizenship in the States, as these patterns contribute to a discreet but effective form of control and containment of ethnic distinctiveness. As political debates about immigration escalate in the United States, it is clear that the country is deeply divided about who gets a full seat at the citizenship table and who does not. In this context the use of food is especially insidious; oftentimes the foodways of certain groups become Americanized, while the people who developed these foods are marginalized. Consider, for example, the prevalence of tacos and salsa in the United States and the ongoing disempowerment of people of Mexican descent.

Food films serve as a platform for experiencing nonmainstream populations and cultures. In the words of bell hooks, such "encounters with Otherness are clearly marked as more exciting, more intense, and more threatening."[9] In inviting tourists to the virtual table, food films show how easy it is to turn ethnic differences into commodities at the same time that ethnic groups are so often positioned within U.S. visions of multiculturalism in ways that increase their marginalization and disempowerment. This move is linked, in part, to what some refer to as postethnicity—the idea that ethnicity and race are voluntary.[10] From this vantage point ethnicity and race appear as something that people can choose to be or practice rather than something that society ascribes and that impacts individuals and groups on a daily basis. Ethnicity and race appear together in this configuration as inclinations, relegated to issues of style and choice that ultimately privilege whiteness.

Indeed, the films reflect this tendency in that they often focus on those minority groups who can assimilate with greater ease than others as a way of suggesting a cultural openness to difference. This move tends to hide the very real social and economic ethnic inequality that persists in the United States.[11] Food media maintain these differences, encouraging the consumption of otherness without promoting a deep understanding of how ethnicity and race operate in the States and how they interact with other elements of identity formation such as gender, sex, age, or social status. The films offer safe, commodifiable experiences that do not require viewers to reflect on their own positions and attitudes. Beautified ethnic food creates a sense of safety and acceptability that leaves whiteness and the privileges that accompany it intact. Our intention is to question these images and to understand how they converge with broader societal questions of power and belonging. In other words we intend to shed light on the role these films play in the politics of cultural citizenship.

We engage these questions by looking across a number of food films to understand how this experience of culinary tourism is constructed. We identify three central strategies these films collectively adopt to engage viewers as visitors. First, we provide examples of films that utilize a "tour guide" to introduce their characters. The guide is, on the one hand, an insider, allowing viewers to enjoy the illusion of special access; on the other hand, she or he serves as cultural mediator, explaining all that could come across as obscurities to outsiders. Second, we highlight how these films privilege assimilation, reinforcing the homogenization of different ethnic groups into conglomerated categories based on the idea of fundamental racial difference. Third, we explore how the films turn ethnic and racial identities into commodities, both figuratively and literally. Delving into these strategies can help us to understand how storytelling can advance relationships of power that are deeply embedded in U.S. history and social structures, operating as a key force in shaping norms and practices of cultural citizenship. Before we explore these three strategies across a number of food films, we turn our attention to the concept of culinary tourism and its relationship to media.

VIRTUAL CULINARY TOURISM: GETTING CLOSE TO DIFFERENCE

According to folklore scholar Lucy Long, culinary tourism is an intentional mode of experiencing the food and foodways of other cultures that represents a well-established paradigm in Western culture.[12] Culinary tourism can range from consuming meals to learning about food cultures different from one's own, without necessarily leaving one's environment. Tourism experiences are increasingly linked with culinary experiences. When they travel, growing numbers of tourists are interested in tasting local specialties, especially those that enjoy fame and are often considered representative of a place. In the States, when we visit New Orleans, we may want to savor beignets and pralines. While making our way through Tennessee, the itinerary is likely to include a stop at a BBQ pit. As a matter of fact we may not even need to leave our hometowns, where we can find creole or BBQ restaurants that offer surrogate but acceptable experiences. And, if we do not feel like going out, we can buy dehydrated creole rice in a box that only requires a little water. The same approach works for foreign countries, especially those whose culinary traditions enjoy worldwide popularity. One of the clearest embodiments of this link between food and tourism is the World Food Travel Association, which centers on "preserving and promoting the world's food and drink cultures through travel."[13] We also see this phenomenon across a wide range of travel magazines like *Condé Nast* and *Travel and Leisure*, as well as in food magazines, like *Saveur* and *Bon Appétit*, that routinely include special features about travel destinations and food. Food magazines regularly include promotion for new food films; for example, advertisements for both *What's Cooking?* and *Tortilla Soup* were present in the now defunct *Gourmet* magazine on full-page spreads. While films that highlight food and eating from other cultures and groups do not provide viewers with literal opportunities for consumption, they offer a form of indirect, vicarious participation.

Culinary tourism is linked more generally to how dominant U.S. culture tends to think about ethnic food. Food culture frequently commercializes ethnicity and race, positioning ethnic identity as an object of consumption.[14] Supermarkets sell ethnic and foreign foods, while advertising employs the words *authentic* and *real* to market mass-produced food products that have little or no relationship to the ethnic traditions on which they are supposedly based. While consuming ethnic food can indeed facilitate learning,[15] we have to consider food consumption in the broader context of how power and hierarchies operate along the lines of ethnicity, race, gender, sexuality, and national identity within the United States.[16]

Culinary tourism is embedded in a larger media and cultural framework that commercializes the desire for authenticity. A visible component of the experience economy we discussed in chapter 1, tourism often functions as a kind of ritual designed to facilitate experiences thought to be more "authentic" than everyday occurrences, although definitions of what counts as authentic are subjective and therefore open to debate. A key element in these experiences is the excitement generated by the exposure to supposed "primitive" elements. According to this line of thinking, too much civilization distances us from "authentic" reality, so visiting the "primitive" environments and communities in all safety can provide some approximation of this feeling of returns to the origins and to truer selves.[17]

This mode of viewing ethnic families and their food is ambivalent and deeply connected to Western colonialism because it reiterates hierarchies that grant whiteness privilege above groups of color. A more direct access to nature, enjoyment, and sensuality, attributed to supposedly less advanced people, is longed for with nostalgia, as something that we have lost as the necessary prices to achieve higher levels of civilization. At the same time, privileged groups are reassured about their cultural and material superiority, even if their access to them comes at a price. For this reason culinary tourism can demonstrate both respect and denigration toward groups perceived as different.[18] Dominant hierarchies can easily disguise themselves as expressions of everyday ingestion, masking the politics of food and emphasizing instead its ordinary nature as devoid of broader political consequences.[19] Culinary tourism represents a deeply complicated means of learning about foodways and cultural values. Celebratory images of ethnic food traditions tend to promote an agenda that ignores issues of power, advancing the idea that assimilation and appropriation are the proper strategy for living together in the United States. The key message communicated is that it is acceptable to be different but only to a minor degree that does not fundamentally disrupt the status quo. The pervasiveness and almost invisibility of this message underlines the importance of analyzing food films as a way of becoming more aware of how we experience other cultures through food and how this experience may reiterate the legacy of colonialism. The lure of ethnic others as exotic or different often justifies the appropriation and commodification of communities outside the mainstream, and culinary tourism frequently reiterates this perspective.

THE TOURIST GUIDE

As much as culinary tourism places film viewers in a position of power, they still need an invitation to dine at foreign tables, as well as the presence of somebody who presides over the necessary introductions. From this point of view food films embrace a narrative strategy that is far from original. From Virgil in Dante's *Divine Comedy* to Nick Carraway in Fitzgerald's

The Great Gatsby, Western literature and culture is full of guides who accompany readers as narratives unfold. In food films these guides take on a special function: they shepherd viewers into new, unfamiliar contexts to ensure a safe visit and a safe return. We offer two examples of this phenomenon, one from *The Joy Luck Club*, a film that focuses on the experience of Chinese mothers and their Chinese American daughters, and the other from *Soul Food*, a film that tells the story of a Chicago-based African American family.

A key scene in *The Joy Luck Club* illustrates how a character in a food film serves as a cultural bridge between an ethnic family and a supposedly non-Chinese spectator. Based on Amy Tan's 1989 novel of the same name, the film tells the poignant story of the relationships between four middle-class, educated Chinese American women and their Chinese mothers. Throughout the course of the film the background stories of the four mothers unravel, while we watch their daughters try and fail to maintain distance, hoping to distance their experience from that of their unassimilated mothers. In one particular scene one of the Chinese American daughters, Waverly (Tamlyn Tomita), brings her white fiancé, Rich (Christopher Rich), home to meet her family for the first time. Rich's presence is clearly a threat to her mother, Lindo (Tsai Chin), who envisions Waverly marrying a Chinese man and adhering to Chinese cultural traditions. The camera cuts back and forth between Rich, a first-time dinner guest in a Chinese American home, Waverly, and Lindo, who has already expressed her distaste for this interethnic relationship in a previous scene. Seated at the family table, we see Rich raising his wine glass for a toast, pouring more wine, serving himself a large portion of shrimp, fumbling with his chopsticks until one of the shrimps lands on his tie, and then pouring soy sauce over a fish dish that Lindo proclaims to be "not salty enough, no flavor. It's too bad to eat" (fig. 6.2).

The camera cuts from medium close-ups of Rich to Waverly and Linda, both of whom observe Rich, unaware that his behavior is being scrutinized, with critical disdain as he fumbles his way through the meal. The viewer watches Rich from Waverly and Linda's perspectives. Throughout we hear Waverly in a voice-over, explaining the nature of Rich's faux pas:

FIGURE 6.2 In *The Joy Luck Club* the comical representation of a white man's inability to behave properly during a formal meal in a Chinese household is meant to ease non-Chinese viewers' anxieties about their lack of culinary knowledge and cosmopolitanism.

Of course the night was still young. Thank God I had already prepped him on the Emily Post of Chinese manners. Actually, there were a few things I forgot to mention. He shouldn't have had that second glass when everyone else had had just a half inch . . . for taste. He should have taken only a small taste of the best dish until everyone had had a helping. He shouldn't have bragged he was a fast learner. But the worst was when Rich criticized my mother's cooking, and he didn't even know what he had done. As is the Chinese cook's custom, my mother always insults her own cooking, but only with the dishes she serves for special occasions. That was our cue to eat some and proclaim it the best she'd ever made.

The scene anticipates a spectator who is not versed in Chinese culinary culture and requires explicit narration of events to understand the cultural norms that Rich's behavior transgresses. Without Waverly's role as storyteller, the rules that Rich breaks are only visible to those with deeper cultural insight into Chinese food culture. In this film about two generations of women—Chinese mothers and Chinese American daughters—and the conflicts and heartaches that they face in navigating life in the States, the film functions as a teacher who instructs us in proper behavior. "Foodie" viewers are invited to distance themselves from the inept Rich and his lack of connoisseurship of foreign cuisines and table manners, while acquiring useful knowledge that can increase cultural capital in their real-life interactions. Experiencing the scene from Waverly's perspective, we are able to get the joke. As cultural mediator, Waverly guarantees the authenticity and insights that the film allows audiences to enjoy. Certainly, director Wayne Wang, who comes from the position of Chinese cultural insider, can make jabs at Chinese culture that are acceptable, yet this context is lost on most non-Chinese viewers.

Similar to *The Joy Luck Club*, George Tillman's 1997 hit film *Soul Food* makes use of a narrator who serves as a tourist guide for viewers. Focused on an African American family in Chicago, the story is told through the eyes of a prepubescent character, Ahmad, who introduces us to the relationships among three generations of the Joseph family. We hear Ahmad's voice, gentle, small, and sweet, as he introduces us to his kin, "My grandma always said—family pulling together in times of need makes you strong. This is a story about my family, about our family—about the things that pulled us together and the things that tried to pull us apart. Les' see—where should I begin?" As he speaks, we see the happy family dancing and cut to shots of food on large metal trays: collard greens, potatoes, ham.

The film follows these relationships focusing on the ritualistic Sunday soul food dinner at Mama Joe's (otherwise known as Big Mama) (fig. 6.3). Ahmad (Brandon Hammond) is Big Mama's grandson, and through him, we meet Big Mama, her brother, and her three daughters, along with their husbands and children. Throughout the course of the film we experience the many trials and tribulations of the Joseph family. Mama Joe suffers from diabetes and is forced to have her leg amputated. After lying in a coma for some time, she dies. With the onset of her hospital stay and then her death, the family begins to disintegrate. The family dinner ritual falls apart as family members drift further away from each other. Young Ahmad takes it on himself to pull the family back together, and through a series of manipulations he manages to reunite the family for a Sunday dinner. In the

FIGURE 6.3 Food films such as *Soul Food* provide U.S. viewers with cultural mediators who help them get acquainted with the food customs of ethnic and racial minorities, without abandoning the safety of the privileged position of external observers.

end the family has managed to reconstitute itself, with daughter Maxine assuming her mother's role of heading up the Sunday meal preparation.

Soul Food provided many African American viewers with a story line and the types of characters they felt were lacking in mainstream U.S. cinema. Through the representation of a Chicago family that meets weekly over Sunday dinner at their mother/grandmother's house, Tillman's treatment of the family members appears in some regard as a deviation from the generic Hollywood depiction of African Americans as gangsters, criminals, welfare mothers, and hypersexualized animalistic objects of desire. From its beginning the film carefully weaves us into the nostalgic, comforting, and relatable world of the Joseph family, and Ahmad assures a safe connection between the viewer and the film's world. But the depiction of the African American foodways is much more geared toward outsiders, and meant to appear appealing and reassuring, than food representations in films such as *Daughters of the Dust* and *Once upon a Time . . . When We Were Colored* (Reid, 1996).

Soul Food produces an intimate, personal relationship through the nonthreatening, young narrator. As the main storyteller, Ahmad helps to situate viewers in the world of a middle-class African American family and avert any fear of identifying too closely with a racialized other.[20] Putting us in comfortable, danger-free proximity to the family, the film follows the pattern of many television shows from the 1980s and 1990s that were set in the domestic realm.[21] The foods that we see in the film are familiar. For example, we hear about chitterlings—or chitlins, the stewed smaller intestine of a pig—but never actually see them.

At the same time, though, the narrative structure enables the film to reinforce destructive stereotypes about blackness. African American characters, in particular, are caught between mainstream tensions that emphasize their supposed racialized difference, while turning them into commodified spectacles. Greg Tate writes, "In a world where we're seen as both the most loathed and the most alluring of creatures, we remain the most co-optable and erasable of cultures too."[22] In its opening sequence the film highlights a number of racial stereotypes, all witnessed through the eyes of Ahmad, who introduces us to various family members as the camera moves across the dance floor at the wedding of one of Big Mama's daughters, Bird (Nia Long). As we progress across the dance floor, we see the groom, Lem (Mekhi Phifer), dancing with an inappropriately attired woman who gyrates her hips and humps him. The hem of her dress reaching barely below her underwear, the woman lifts the corner of her skin-tight dress, presses her backside against Lem's groin, and jiggles her body so that her breasts and rear-end shake. "Who is that hoochie-coochie mama with her big butt all over my husband out there on the dance floor?" we hear Bird say, the camera capturing her and her sisters in the bathroom as they try to calm her down. Bird's sister Maxine (Vivica Fox) comforts her, saying, "Everybody's happy, but we'd be more happy if we'd go out there and beat that ho down!" These derogatory terms specifically play not only on the characters' gender and race but also on their perceived social status, a source of tension in the family. One of the sisters, Teri (Vanessa Williams), who has a successful career as a lawyer and has moved toward an upper-middle-class lifestyle, avoids vulgarity in her language and in her food, displaying preference for light salads over the hearty soul food fare of the Sunday meals. Ahmad's narration holds us at a safe distance from which to observe (and pass judgment on) the family's behavior.

Visiting this African American family through the eyes of a child enables viewers to perceive themselves as "experiencing" the family, while also distancing themselves from the African American experience.

The film makes a similar move with regard to its treatment of soul food. As food studies scholar Psyche Williams-Forson emphasizes, "On some levels, *Soul Food* really ended up being more about what American culture (and many blacks) thinks about African American food consumption as opposed to the reality of our consumption."[23] Rather than providing a more nuanced, historically, and sociologically specific, detailed account of the relationship between a black family and its foodways, the film appeals to the stereotypical ways in which many U.S. consumers are accustomed to experiencing and consuming African American eating culture and black bodies. The term *soul food* for many nonblack Americans conjures up stereotypical images of fried chicken, collard greens, chitterlings, and sweet potato pie. Among food studies scholars, however, the term is contested. Doris Witt contrasts the term to Black Power movements during the civil rights era, while Psyche Williams-Forson emphasizes the relationship that most cookbooks make between soul food and its culinary origins during the slavery period.[24] Williams-Forson emphasizes that most people who characterize their own foodways as linked to the term *soul food* rarely link their foodways to the 1960s "soul" movement.[25] The history of soul food is itself very complex, and southern black cooking has often been usurped by the term *southern* cooking, coding the culinary history as white and denying the tradition of recipes and cooking that was handed down by black women.[26] It encompasses a broad range of foods from different geographical locations and historical periods, its variety accentuated by social and political dynamics. Yet mainstream white American culture, in particular media culture, reduces soul food to a narrow range of food practices, equating any black American cooking with this term.[27]

What Greg Tate writes on the appropriation of black culture holds true within culinary history as well: "the Black body, and subsequently Black culture, has become a hungered-after taboo item and a nightmarish bugbear in the badlands of the American racial imagination. . . . Paul Whiteman, Elvis Presley, the Rolling Stones, Sting, Britney Spears, 'N Sync, Pink, Eminem—all of those contrived and promoted to do away with bodily reminders of the Black origins of American pop pleasure."[28] Furthermore, the assumption that all African Americans cook and eat this narrow diet of "soul food" positions the soul food tradition as well as other cuisines of African American traditions and African American chefs as inferior to other ethnic cuisines. In mainstream media the "alimentary signs of blackness" are generally limited to southern foods, and *Soul Food* provides no exception to this tendency.[29]

Attempting to strike an across-the-board appeal, the film *Soul Food* reiterates this pattern by dehistoricizing soul food, unilaterally relegating it to the stereotypical domain of "finger-licking" home cooking. The film's treatment of soul food as—in Mama Joe's words—"cooking from the heart" obscures the history of diaspora and slavery that lies behind the history of soul food. Only one vague comment provides any link between the term *soul food* and African American history. Young Ahmad describes Sunday dinners as a "tradition started down in Mississippi when the ol' folks got together to talk smack and chow down on some good ol' soul food." No further references to the history of soul food are mentioned, and this statement simply helps to reaffirm that soul food is "southern" cooking.

In both *The Joy Luck Club* and *Soul Food* a nonthreatening character assumes the role of shepherding mainstream viewers into an experience of otherness that carefully avoids direct and upfront confrontations about race and ethnicity. In other food films that focus on communities deemed ethnic by mainstream audiences, the narrative strategy may employ both insiders and outsiders, usually a white character who functions as a stand-in for the viewer's curiosity, confusion, and lack of comfort. Through the plot's positive resolution and the outsider's integration in the unfamiliar communities, audiences can enjoy the actualization of a postethnic harmony fantasy.

In *My Big Fat Greek Wedding* (Zwick, 2002) a Greek woman experiences the tension between her immigrant family, which adheres to its tradition despite making its living through an American-style diner, and the outside world. Her voice and her insider position allow viewers to familiarize themselves with Greek customs, while maintaining an ironic gaze on exotic and sometimes comical customs and ideas without running the risk of being accused of cultural insensitivity. Eventually, she finds herself mediating between her vegetarian Anglo boyfriend and her overbearing family. His attempts at embracing the culture of his bride-to-be and his parents' puzzlement at the physicality and unbridled rambunctiousness of their son's future in-laws, played out around food and celebrations, allows viewers a vicarious but safe experience of what being integrated in a different ethnic community would feel like. We observe a similar dynamic in Ang Lee's *The Wedding Banquet* (1993), which we discussed previously. Here, the estrangement of the white newcomer is increased by the fact of his being in a same-sex relationship with a Chinese immigrant in the United States who marries a Chinese woman to hide his sexual orientation. The traditions of the Chinese nuptials provide a colorful and entertaining background for the development of greater understanding across ethnic boundaries, while allowing non-Chinese viewers to have access to dishes and customs that otherwise would remain unknown.

PRIVILEGING ASSIMILATION: WORLD BEAT MULTICULTURALISM MEETS FUSION CUISINE

Across the body of food films we discuss in this book, the ones that represent ethnic communities and individuals—actually, the majority of the films—dance along the delicate lines of making ethnicity something novel and exciting, while also ensuring it is safe, beautiful, and clean. The films often draw on the concept of authenticity to affirm that their representations reflect reality, when indeed these images are deeply ideologically constructed. Here, we illustrate this trend with examples that show the range of ways in which the films present food and identity as *authentic*, while also promoting assimilation—blending into the white mainstream—as the preferred strategy for addressing multiculturalism. Furthermore, as we have already noticed in *Soul Food*, the films tend to homogenize and thus obscure the distinctive histories and experiences of ethnic groups in the States. We argue that this cleansed version of storytelling ensures that the tourist's visit reaffirms dominant narratives about whiteness and ethnic otherness. Focusing specifically on how the films both aim to assimilate and homogenize diverse communities while at the same time glorifying their authenticity, we explore two films: *Tortilla Soup* and *What's Cooking?*

That *Tortilla Soup*, along with films such as *Woman on Top* (discussed in chapter 3), *Tortilla Heaven* (Dumontet, 2007), and *Nothing like the Holidays* (De Villa, 2008), focuses on Latinos, America's "fastest growing minority," is significant; that a number of food films represent Mexican American families specifically leads us to consider how cinema engages in a charged debate about Mexican American identity, food, and belonging. Released in 2001, *Tortilla Soup* emerged amid turbulent decades of ongoing anti-immigrant legislation and activism, especially against Mexican Americans in California. The concept of illegality positions Mexican Americans as permanent outsiders who are not entitled to any form of citizenship, be it political, economic, or cultural.[30] During the 1990s Mexicans were frequently perceived as creating the most problems out of any recent immigrant groups.[31] *Tortilla Soup*'s representation of Mexican Americans as middle-class, educated, English-speaking, and "legal" challenges Hollywood's stereotypes and counters negative metaphors of Mexicans as animals, weeds, diseases, parasites, and invaders, simultaneously assuaging white middle-class anxieties.[32] Representing the Mexican American family as light-but-exotic entertainment advances a version of multiculturalism that addresses fears of a burgeoning Latino population and an increasing, racialized economic gap that privileges whiteness.[33]

Firmly anchored in the secure world of the middle class, *Tortilla Soup*'s representation of Mexican American identity as both assimilated and unfamiliar lends voice and power to the film's characters, while simultaneously undermining this authority. The film specifies the characters as Mexican or Mexican American, only to then flatten and subsume this specificity into a pan-ethnic, generic Latin construction. Based on Ang Lee's 1994 Taiwanese/American film *Eat Drink Man Woman* (discussed in chapter 4), *Tortilla Soup* revolves around the domestic life of a former professional chef. When the Samuel Goldwyn Company acquired the rights to distribute *Eat Drink Man Woman*, it simultaneously purchased the rights to rework the story in an American context. Seven years later, *Tortilla Soup* opened in U.S. theaters. Director Maria Ripoll and a team of writers reworked the tale of a Taiwanese star chef into the story of a Mexican-born widower living in Southern California.

The former owner of a successful upscale L.A. Mexican restaurant, Martín Naranjo (Hector Elizondo) has raised his three now adult daughters on his own, after the death of his wife fifteen years ago (fig. 6.4). The eldest, Leticia, is an uptight, born-again Christian schoolteacher who eventually falls in love with easygoing Orlando, the school's baseball coach. Middle sister Carmen, a successful yuppie business executive, spends her free time sleeping with her ex-boyfriend and dreaming of a career as a professional fusion chef. Youngest daughter Maribel feels that no one in the family listens to her. Throughout the course of this contemporary "Fiddler on the Roof" tale, each daughter rebels against her father's wishes by proclaiming, "I have an announcement," at the Sunday dinner table. Each time, the meal and the father's sense of cultural continuity are disrupted. Leticia announces that she has eloped with Orlando; Carmen buys a condominium in L.A. but then decides to take a job in Barcelona; and Maribel postpones going to college and moves in with her Brazilian boyfriend.

FIGURE 6.4 A male Mexican chef struggles to define his relationship with U.S. culture and his Americanized daughters in *Tortilla Soup*, in which Mexican food is represented as exotic and appealing in ways that non-Mexican viewers can relate to.

Martín eventually adjusts to the changing dynamics of his family and steps forward at the film's end with his own announcement: he intends to marry Leticia's friend Yolanda, whose intrusive mother, Hortensia, has been making passes at him. In a happy-end sequence we see the reconstructed family, including now pregnant Yolanda, seated at a table in Carmen's Latin fusion restaurant. Martín, who had lost his ability to taste and smell, regains both senses at the end of the film.

The food in *Tortilla Soup*, as in so many food films, is dazzling and erotic, definitely more so than its precursor *Eat Drink Man Woman*. Fetishistic images of food invite us to engage in a supposedly value-free consumption and enjoyment of these images. The opening sequence focuses on the preparation of the Sunday meal, its ingredients, its dishes, and the awesome set of skills necessary to prepare it. We see chef Martín rubbing water on a banana leaf in close-up, the bright green glistening with beads of water. Water reflects on the highly lit food, making the dishes appear sensuous, luscious, and desirable. The images are coded as Mexican in their sensuality and exoticism. We see traditional Mexican cooking utensils alongside Mexican cooking ingredients (banana leaves, zucchini flowers, jalapenos, huge exotic squash, nopales). Scrumptious plates of salad appear next to grilled bass with a ground-red-pepper sauce on a table decorated with banana leaves, candles, more platters of beautiful food and handsome place settings. While highlighting the refinement and complexity of Mexican culinary traditions, the film also blurs Mexican identity with other Latino identities. The soundtrack, for example, combines Brazilian, Venezuelan, Latin-French fusion, Cuban, Jamaican, Mexican American, and Caribbean music. In the same vein the food, touted by so many reviewers and the film itself as authentic, was actually designed by Milliken and Feniger, neither of whom claims Mexican descent. The choice to focus the film's website on Milliken and Feniger's expertise reflects tropes that stage authenticity for a white gaze. Certainly there are numerous Mexican chefs raised in the culture of Mexican and Mexican American foodways who could have served as consultants for this project.

While the actual dishes that Martín cooks have traditional roots, the film represents only certain types of Mexican dishes, namely the kinds of Mexican food that mainstream Americans are willing to consume. Just as traditional dishes such as barbecued beef head (*barbacoa de cabeza*) and ones made with entrails of goat do not find their way into mainstream U.S. Mexican restaurants, the food in this film appears an assimilated version of traditional Mexican cuisine that tends to be overtly romanticized and beautified, especially when transformed into southwestern U.S. cuisine.[34] At the same time, the food also differentiates itself from the pervasive presence of Tex-Mex cuisine and fast food that most Americans assume to be "real" Mexican food. The film continually emphasizes the authenticity of Martín's cooking and contrasts it to his daughter Carmen's Latin fusion cuisine, in reality both safely situated in middle-class social and economic security, quite distant from the living situations of many Mexican Americans. This move ultimately reinforces assimilation over cultural pluralism. Martín represents the traditional Mexican chef, a "cultural purist," as the daughters call him, who disdains the mixing of ingredients as much as the fusing of languages. Latin fusion specialist Carmen creates dishes such as "tamarind glazed lamb on cumin cabbage with a tangerine salsa." "The lamb is French-South American," she explains; "the cabbage is pure Mexican, and the salsa is Caribbean." Although Martín refers to her dishes as "mutts," it is Carmen's "Nuevo Latino" cuisine (along with his entry back into the heterosexist mainstream with his new, young wife) that helps him regain his taste buds. This neatly packages assimilated Mexican American identity when it closes with the family in Carmen's restaurant, a symbolic gesture that favors hybrid, postethnic identity and the alignment of Latin fusion cuisine (and identity) with middle-class values and white mainstream culture.[35]

Positioning fusion over traditional cuisine suggests that Mexican Americans, like Asian Americans, can become "model minorities" if they blend their identities with white U.S. value systems. The popularity of chefs like Ming Tsai and Padma Lakshmi, both of whom appear on television's Food Network, lies in their ability to appear simultaneously exotic and assimilated.[36] *Tortilla Soup* mirrors this duality. Indeed, one of the most popular celebrity chefs in the United States associated with Mexican cuisine is Rick Bayless, who has published multiple cookbooks on Mexican food and owns a number of renowned restaurants, all of which are based on extensive research and experience in Mexico.

Reviews of *Tortilla Soup* emphasized the food's beauty and allure, aligning the film with other food films while avoiding discussion of the representation of Mexican American identity. Stephen Hunter, from the *Washington Post*, states, "The food is the star."[37] Virtually all reviewers note the film's reworking of *Eat Drink Man Woman*, while ignoring that the earlier film's family is adapting to changing times within its own country, whereas the characters in *Tortilla Soup* struggle with issues of assimilation and cultural preservation in a new country. Several reviewers comment on the "authenticity" of the Mexican cuisine, pointing out how the film avoids reducing Mexican food to tacos and burritos. Given the social, political, and economic positioning of Mexican Americans and other Latinos in the United States, it is troubling to divorce *Tortilla Soup* from the history of representations of Latinos and from political legislation such as California's Proposition 187, which denied public social services, publicly funded health care, and public education to people suspected of being illegal immigrants, who, in California, come predominantly from Mexico.[38] Unequal access to social services, education, and other resources based on ethnicity impacts Latinos on a daily basis and has helped to fuel recent discussions in the United States on immigration. At the same time, U.S. film and marketing tend to package sanitized images of Latino identity and culture for mainstream audiences.

At the root of this fusion move is the idea that we can "all just get along." Gurinder Chadha's *What's Cooking?* reinforces this concept through the idea that things will be fine if we can just eat together. *What's Cooking?* is an ensemble film that depicts four ethnic families living in L.A.'s Fairfax neighborhood as they prepare for and celebrate Thanksgiving. A Latino family (the Avilas), a newly immigrated Vietnamese family (the Nguyens), an African American family (the Williamses), and a Jewish family (the Seeligs) all experience conflicts between traditional and newer, more liberal, value systems. Crosscutting among the four families, the film depicts their respective Thanksgiving experiences and the tensions that arise on this quintessentially American day.

From the outset *What's Cooking?* presents Los Angeles (and by extension the United States) as a hybrid culture. The film opens to a shot of a white family surrounding a glistening Thanksgiving turkey to the tune of the Star Spangled Banner. As the camera pulls away, we see that the image is an advertisement on an L.A. Metro bus that proceeds to drive through the city. As the bus travels through various ethnic neighborhoods, the soundtrack morphs from a traditional version of the Star Spangled Banner into Latino, African American, Vietnamese, and Klezmer tunes ("Hava Nagila"), paralleling the diverse families we are about to meet. Filled with people from diverse ethnic communities, the bus itself signifies the notion of a white, mainstream U.S. society as an image of the past, appropriated and sanitized by marketing. L.A. appears as fundamentally ethnically diverse. We see the city through the bus window. Its walls depict paintings of multicultural families, while camera shots of Canter's Deli and Little Tokyo present the cityscape as fundamentally diverse. The notion of the all-American family as a white family emerges as a myth as the final shot of the opening credits lands on a park bench with the words *Feliz Día de Gracias* and an image of a happy Latino family on it. The soundtrack transitions back to the Star Spangled Banner to confirm the film's adherence to a liberal, multicultural interpretation of American citizenship. The film seems to suggest that all of these differences are important parts of U.S. culture and that it is precisely this blending of difference that we should celebrate.

We follow the families as they prepare ethnically influenced variations of the Thanksgiving turkey and all its trimmings. Simultaneously, we learn about the families' struggles as the film devolves into sitcom-like stereotypes. The Vietnamese family faces the threat of the son having a gun and being part of a gang. The African American family faces tension between the father's adherence to white, upper-middle-class social values and the son's desire to connect with his African American heritage. The Latino family must deal with a group of patriarchal males who are angry with their mother for starting a new relationship after a divorce. The Jewish family struggles with the fact that their daughter is a lesbian who is expecting her first child with her partner. Rather than challenging the complex ways that race and ethnicity function in mainstream U.S. society, *What's Cooking?* uses food as a metaphor to bridge the four families who, as we learn at the end of the film, live across from each other. This depiction of the neighborhood represents a microcosm of Los Angeles, which in turn represents a microcosm of the United States. In this sense *What's Cooking?* (and numerous other food films) deploys food as a means of celebrating difference. Yet this celebration hovers at a superficial level that fails to interrogate how race and ethnicity actually impact people's lived experiences. As such, these films tend to participate in discourses that sometimes treat ethnic differences as racial stereotypes, sometimes as postethnic and assimilated.

ETHNICITY FOR SALE

Walking through any American supermarket, shoppers can find aisles of ethnic and foreign foods. Advertising successfully promotes these products that have little or no relationship to the ethnic traditions on which they are supposedly based as "authentic" and "real." As such, food culture in the States mirrors broader patterns that turn ethnicity and race into objects of consumption, and food films contribute to a media landscape that commercializes otherness in ways that strike appeal across a broad range of audiences. Films like *Tortilla Soup, Soul Food,* and many others use food to make ethnicity and otherness accessible to mainstream consumers on their terms, without any need to negotiate what is made available or how. This move is troubling because it reaffirms a relationship that posits ethnicity as an object of desire and commodification for the mainstream. As bell hooks writes, "Within current debates about race and difference, mass culture is the contemporary location that both publicly declares and perpetuates the idea that there is pleasure to be found in the acknowledgement and enjoyment of racial difference. The commodification of Otherness has been so successful because it is offered as a new delight, more intense, more satisfying than normal ways of doing and feeling."[39] Food functions within consumer culture as an arena where people can "experience" differences in ways that mark it as "more exciting, more intense, and more threatening."[40] This reinforces contradictory ideas about ethnicity. On the one hand, it implies that purchasing goods can bring consumers closer to unfamiliar ethnic groups, even enabling them to try on difference for size, a move that reinforces the tenets of postethnicity we discussed at the beginning of this chapter. This mode supports the notion that people can "shop" for ethnicity without inheriting the burden of racial discrimination.[41] On the other hand, this supports essentialist, biological notions that refuse to consider race and ethnicity as social and cultural construction, which are heavily influenced by class, gender, and location. By doing so, these ideas associate stereotypes with specific people and bodies without considering the role of the many privileges of whiteness in establishing ethnicity and race as crucial categories in all sorts of social interactions.

Food films, although they may not directly market food, play a role in turning ethnic identities into commodities. As we saw in chapter 1, films like *Big Night* promote consumption, even while appearing to critique habits of consumption. In doing so, the films also affirm and reinforce certain social norms through an appeal to middle-class beliefs of what constitutes style and good taste. When food films represent Latino and African American characters, their promotion of consumption takes on a different flavor altogether. While *Big Night*—both through the film itself and the products that accompanied the film—sells a specific Americanized version of Italian culture, it reaffirms Italian identity as part of white, middle-class values and norms. Films that focus on communities of color tend to do so with deeper contradictions. They exploit ethnicity as different and exciting, while glossing over cultural differences and ensuring that consuming otherness is safe. In these films the narratives tend to privilege individual characters that can assimilate with greater ease than others as a way of suggesting a cultural openness to difference. In this final section we turn to some examples that illustrate how food films turn ethnicity and race into commodities.

Soul Food, considered broadly a "black" film because it was produced, written, and directed by African Americans, describes African American characters and their foodways in ways that reinforce blackness as an object of consumption. *Soul Food* jockeyed around attracting the lucrative market sectors both of black moviegoers and white mainstream audiences. With food as its focus the film draws heavily on strategies employed by the food advertising industry and food television. Analyzing these strategies helps us understand how the film positions blackness as an object of consumption.

Big Mama, one of the film's key characters, illustrates this tendency. While Big Mama exudes warmth, strength, and kindness, the physical image of her standing in her kitchen preparing food for the family with a scarf around her head unmistakably calls up nostalgic images of Aunt Jemima on the syrup bottle, an icon stereotypical of black women that has continually been contested in the United States given its ties to the history of slavery. This image has become "too well inscribed on the collective American unconscious" to be coincidental.[42] The association of Big Mama with Aunt Jemima taps into a long-standing racialized tradition in the States of reducing black women to caretakers.[43] The Aunt Jemima figure was specifically designed to appeal to white consumers, although over the years her appearance has been altered to conform to "politically correct" imagery as a means of appeasing African Americans.[44] Combining Big Mama with this historically burdened image reinforces her position as caretaker and brings the film into line with dominant commercial culture (fig. 6.5).

The choice to cast Vanessa Williams as the professional, upper-middle-class daughter, Terri, represents another way in which the film links blackness to dominant commercial culture. *Soul Food* marketed Williams in an attempt to use her crossover appeal to generate interest across diverse audiences. Williams, the first African American woman to be crowned

FIGURE 6.5 *Soul Food*'s Big Mama reflects many stereotypes about African American women and their cooking abilities; at the same time, though, the film shows her in loving interactions with her own family and community.

Miss America, was already well established with black and white audiences by the time *Soul Food* was released. The film's poster strategically features a large image of Williams's face in the center with smaller images of all the other characters around her, even though Terri is not one of the film's most central characters. In fact, if anyone's face should be front and center, it should be young Ahmad's, who serves as the narrator and is involved in most scenes in the film. Within the film Terri is positioned as a white-washed foil to her otherwise black family. She is the only daughter who speaks "white" English, and her social-class affiliation, fair complexion, and green eyes distinguish her from her sisters. Terri cannot cook because her parents apparently forced her out of the kitchen and into her studies, a point that the film emphasizes. Terri's lack of interest in cooking and markers of class and ethnicity differentiate her from her family, and using her image to market the film reinforces the film's commercialization of blackness. Similarly, the film's trailer highlights an otherwise minor scene in the film that features hypersexualized stereotypes of black women and perpetuates an association of black female sexual wantonness with animal-istic tendencies. This type of marketing enabled the film to target white audiences in ways that emphasize stereotypes but also make the visit to this African American family seem safe, inviting, and enticing.

After the release of the film, *Soul Food* developed into a spin-off television series on Showtime cable network and ran from 2000 to 2004. The show featured a black cast, and it eventually led to a book series authored by Leslie E. Banks. Clearly, the need for mass media that represent black families on film and television helped drive the popularity of the film. The film's commercialization of blackness also advanced its broad audience popularity.

Even though some food films, *Big Night* in particular, appear to critique consumption, they ultimately promote it. We see evidence of this in the numerous marketing tie-ins associated with them, including novelizations, movie soundtracks, DVDs with extra features, and cookbooks. The way food films commercialize ethnic identity in the context of food deserves special attention because it helps us understand the kinds of power and access to which underrepresented minorities have access and where their power is limited. *Tortilla Soup*'s marketing follows other food films in that it commercializes "Mexicanness" while affirming white middle-class values.

The "*Tortilla Soup* Store" on surlatable.com marketed items associated with the film, including the *Mesa Mexicana* cookbook, the film's soundtrack, the traditional lava mortar (molcajete) and tortilla presses, and the "Too Hot Tamales Peppermills," named after the team of chefs, Mary Sue Milliken and Susan Feniger, who, as we have noted, created the food for the film. Milliken and Feniger, who are also known as the "Border Girls," own the L.A.-based restaurants Border Grill and Ciudad and are former hosts of the Food Network's cooking show *Too Hot Tamales*. The website provided links to recipes for dishes from the film such as "Porcupine Cookies," "Quinoa Fritters with Romesco Sauce," and, of course, "Tortilla Soup," presenting Mexican dishes as fashionable Americanized commodities packaged for a white, middle-class audience.

Tortilla Soup made its appearance at a time when Hollywood was making significant efforts to attract Latino audiences.[45] In addition to the popularity of some films that address Latino issues and characters, stars like Jennifer Lopez and Ricky Martin now enjoy crossover fandom.[46] At the same time, Hispanic advertising increasingly tends to favor white-looking actors and actresses over more "ethnic" types.[47] That these characters often appear as assimilated and postethnic would resonate with some Latino viewers, even if these stories tend to rewrite history and certain cultural specificities. Pressures to assimilate to mainstream culture are tremendous, and the film purports to demonstrate how those who have been marginalized can become part of the American dream.

Latino groups, in particular, have been vulnerable to contemporary marketing strategies that encourage corporate clients to view them as authentic and marketable yet simultaneously as an exotic other.[48] As debates about U.S. citizenship, anti-immigration, and antibilingual legislation mount, "hunger pangs for Latino talent" have grown in the entertainment industry.[49] *Tortilla Soup* emerged amid this complicated "love affair" with Latinidad, presenting it as a kind of "world beat multiculturalism" that flattens differences among Latino groups.[50] Given the enormous popularity and marketability of Mexican foods in the United States (salsa, for example, outsells ketchup on the condiment market),[51] films that attempt to represent Mexicanness require further scrutiny, particularly when this representation focuses on the highly marketable commodity of Mexican food.

A SOBERING DIGESTIF

How we represent different groups of people has significant bearing on what kind of power these groups are able to hold. The everyday nature of food, as we have illustrated throughout this book, invites us to forget how politically charged food actually is. Films representing food and eating offer a perception of involvement with unfamiliar food cultures that links to the broader culture of tourism in the United States. This linkage encourages us to think about certain foods and practices as "authentic," even when they may deviate significantly from how communities engage with and through food.[52] Food films help to create the illusion that we are experiencing ethnicity in its most genuine form and, at the same time, help us maintain enough distance to feel protected and safe. Any complexities connected with class, gender, age, geographical location, and other factors that could generate political or economic reflections are often overlooked or ignored. In doing so, these films help to draw lines between who does and does not belong to mainstream society, ultimately the key question surrounding issues of citizenship.

The chapters of this book have explored a variety of ways in which narrative food films engage us as viewers and consumers. But food does not only appear in fictional stories. In our conclusion we turn our attention to a growing body of documentary food films focusing on different aspects of food systems, from production to consumption, and presenting approaches that vary from the political critique to the glorification of culinary excellence. Viewers are still consumers, but this time the films' goal is actually to have them change their behaviors in real life, make political choices, or change their consumption patterns. Although documentary films are far from being a neutral reflection of reality given that filmmakers intervene at all levels—from narrative structure to editing and even shot choices—they require a different engagement from audiences. In our conclusion we explore this genre and reflect on how some of its approaches could help bring new life and energy to fictional food films and drive different conversations about food and cultural citizenship.

CONCLUSION

When we feast our eyes on food films, we do so in deeply complicated and layered ways that engage us simultaneously as citizens and consumers. Food films offer the opportunity to examine how we participate—both consciously and unconsciously, willingly and unwillingly—in diverse discourses, practices, and structures that determine our role and position in the communities in which we operate. The success of the food-film genre reminds us that we cannot so easily separate our behaviors as consumers—purchasing meals at Olive Garden and jars of chutney at Trader Joe's—from our participation in culture and from our decision-making processes as political citizens. Economic, political, and cultural citizenships matter collectively to how we live our lives. Studying food films and other forms of food media pushes us to move beyond documenting what appears as simple reflections of the reality surrounding us to ask how these representations matter in our daily lives and in the choices we make.

Food asks us to think on multiple levels simultaneously. It challenges us to move outside of our comfort zones. We can never simply take a meal at face value; rather, we must continually unravel food's grammar and meanings. Food—prepared, cooked, and consumed every day—runs the risk of appearing ordinary and uncomplicated, an inevitable part of human life. Yet it is precisely this seeming normalcy that provides us with an important push to unpack the socioeconomic, political, and cultural complexities of lived experience and the ramifications of our everyday choices as citizens.

Food-themed fiction films, in their apparent lightness, constitute a unique entryway into questions of cultural citizenship. Restaurants, kitchens, and dining rooms become the background for intriguing dynamics among characters, objects, and environments to unfold, indicating how much food is entangled with who we are, who we think we are, and who we like others to think we are. In the films we have explored in this book, gender, sexuality, race, ethnicity, age, and class all emerge as relevant components of contemporary identities, both shaping the way we relate to food and being shaped by it. Producing, cooking, and eating are far from being simple expressions of biological needs but rather reflect crucial cultural, social, and political issues. The films we have discussed, all products of the U.S. media industry, tend to treat these delicate topics only tangentially, almost as an involuntary by-product, while focusing on food as an experience of great aesthetic and sensorial value. Although films such as *Heavy* and *Waitress* complicate this outlook, the positive appreciation for food as an expression of love, community, and tradition remains prevalent, even when characters go through difficult events to achieve a final positive resolution.

What these fictional food films say about food and identity is as significant as what they fail to represent: the environmental impact of the food system, its political implications, and its power over individuals and communities not only in the United States but also all over the world, as flows of goods, people, ideas, information, and money become increasingly globalized. Largely, the films we examined in this book neither engage with food policy, nor do they address the labor issues that underlie the production of industrialized food. Instead, with few exceptions they tend to treat food as sublime and enjoyable, erasing the traces of reproduction that underlie our dominant food system and ignoring the emergence of alternative networks and practices. In short, food films produced within the mainstream U.S. system largely support the commodification and fetishization of food.

Although inevitably touching on issues ranging from gender to race and class, and often apparently embracing progressive positions that seem to question mainstream social arrangements and cultural approaches, mainstream food films reinforce many of the dynamics that, at first blush, they seem to want to critique. Food-themed films are not, however, inevitably doomed to become cogs in the propaganda wheel for the contemporary alimentary complex. Some films have tried to take a different approach to food, which produces an interesting counterpoint to the utopian perspective. These films deserve some attention as we conclude this book.

DOCUMENTARY FOOD FILMS: A PALATABLE ALTERNATIVE?

As of this writing few fictional films have focused on the structural issues of the food system. Although food becomes increasingly relevant as a topic in cultural and social debates in the United States, and as an important component in identity formation at the individual and communal level, filmmakers in the mainstream industry have avoided the less pleasurable aspects of food production, distribution, and consumption. As fictional food films have developed into a recognizable genre, conquering growing audiences and reflecting the media frenzy for all things cuisine, the past two decades have also witnessed the emergence and growth of a body of documentary films that collectively addresses a variety of topics that are often invisible in their fictional counterparts. *The Future of Food* (Koons, 2004), *Super Size Me* (Spurlock, 2004), and *How to Cook Your Life* (Dörrie, 2007) focus on food, health, and identity, pointing out the impact of systemic issues and corporate power on personal choices and well-being. Some of the films deal with the production and consumption of specific commodities, such as *Black Gold* (Francis and Francis, 2006), about coffee, and *King Corn* (Woolf, 2007), about corn. Others, such as *The Real Dirt on Farmer John* (Siegel, 2005), *Fight* (Taylore, 2008), *Food, Inc.* (Kenner, 2009), and *Fresh* (Joanes, 2009), critique the broader food industry and food system and offer solutions for alternative foodways. One film, *Big River* (Ellis, 2010), frames its discussion of the food system around the environmental impact of the corn industry. Other films, such as *Food Stamped* (Potash and Potash, 2010) and *The Garden* (Kennedy, 2008), deal with issues of equity, power, and food.

Although this list is not exhaustive, it provides an overview of the range of films that have been circulating in the United States while fictional food films captured the imagination of audiences already attuned to fascination with cooking and eating and their aesthetic appreciation. These documentary films focus specifically on problems with the U.S. food system. They all share a concerted effort to engage people as active citizens and political agents of change. Form, style, and content are also important indicators of a film's ability to challenge the status quo. Ultimately, the films' ability to effect change rests on their ability to move people to action. Many of the films' websites, designed to keep viewers informed of changes and concerns, have calls for action and enable people to sign up for listservs that keep them apprised of (and hopefully involved in) food-related issues. For instance, the film *Fresh* touted its website as "a gateway to action. Our aim is to help grow FRESH food, ideas, and become active participants in an exciting, vibrant, and fast-growing movement."[1] The websites of *Food, Inc.*, *Food Fight, King Corn*, and others included similar descriptions and links to become more engaged in food activism.

Fast Food Nation (Linklater, 2006), loosely inspired by Eric Schlosser's 2001 best seller of the same title, looks at the production of fast-food hamburgers through the eyes of a company executive, a young student working part-time in a store, and Mexican undocumented workers being exploited in the meat plant (fig. 7.1). The issue of the presence of manure in the burgers becomes the entry point to examine the horrors of the whole industry from structural and social points of view, while drawing audiences in through the individual journey of the various characters. The theme of food production provides the backdrop for the sport film *McFarland, USA* (Caro, 2015), which takes place in a California town where Mexican immigrants grow fruits and vegetables, struggling to make a better life for themselves but often isolated both culturally and socially from their Anglo neighbors. The story focuses on a white coach (Kevin Costner) who recognizes the skills and endurance of his young Mexican students who would run back and forth to the fields to work long hours before getting to school. The characters are obviously stereotyped, and the white protagonist takes on the role of savior. At the same time, the film depicts a difficult process of acculturation that includes

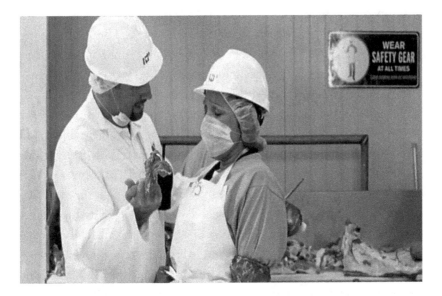

FIGURE 7.1 The docufiction *Fast Food Nation* forces viewers to face the hidden aspects of the U.S. food industry, including the exploitation of immigrant workers and the lack of attention to consumers' safety.

the coach letting his daughter date a Latino young man. The film never glosses over the hardships of rural work but rather highlights them to emphasize the athletes' achievements. The satiric comedy *Butter* (Smith, 2011) uses food, in particular the butter-sculpting competition at the Iowa State Fair, to poke fun at a small-town bourgeoisie, its pretenses, small-mindedness, and political aspirations. A thriller released in 2015, *Consumed*, by Daryl Wien, focuses on the controversies surrounding GMOs. The press kit provides information about the film's main topic and its political impact: "Emotionally gripping performances in combination with intriguing sociopolitical issues cast the landscape for a powerful original story that begs the audience to question what we as Americans are eating every day."[2]

Food, Inc. and the other documentary films in this group tend to privilege issues of people and future generations, framing them from the perspective of human concerns such as health and economic stability. Embracing an anthropocentric perspective is more likely to encourage behavior change. Appealing to what people care about can even serve as a bridge to getting them to care about other issues that are less at the forefront of their awareness and less apparently significant to their daily lives.

Articulating the context within which these films are consumed and understanding the various ways in which they move people to action, or fail to do so, requires analysis of people's behavior and their ability and desire to take action, as well as the limitations to creating change. This also requires consideration of the dominant messages that viewers receive about food in mainstream media and the degree to which they are persuasive and influence individual choices. Power and creativity themselves are always situated within the ideology of a given social and cultural context, and it is important to understand the broader culture in which these critical documentary films circulate, the roles that they have, and the opportunities for change that they offer, as well as the limitations placed on them. Documentary food films try to engage viewers by challenging dominant messages about the food industry that appear continually in advertising, television, and film, and this engagement seeks to motivate action. We must ask, however, if the context in which these films are consumed enables them to have such an impact and, if not, how we might alter that context.

Documentary films face significant challenges in reaching broad audiences through mainstream media channels. Since they express critical points of view about contemporary food systems, they are likely to suffer from limited distribution, and even considering their sales in terms of DVDs, pay-per-view, and streaming, their viewership is not as wide as that for fictional food films. As Cynthia Baron observes, the reasons for this phenomenon lie in "the film industry's deep-rooted policy to work with, rather than against, other industries," with the consequence that "the film-industry profit-focused distribution and exhibition practices ensure that even films with theatrical releases reach limited audiences."[3] Furthermore, Baron notes the limited box-office returns, compared to the necessary production and distribution expenses; the movie theaters' resistance to showing films with unrated status; and investors' and producers' fear of lawsuits and litigation from the food industry.

While conversations about food systems with regard to production, safety, health, equity, and even environmental impact increasingly become part of the dominant discourse, the circulation and consumption of these films appear tiny in comparison to the amount of time U.S. citizens spend watching The Food Network and mainstream food films and television. Documentary films typically struggle at the box office and face tremendous challenges in reaching their target audiences. Next to *Super Size Me*, with its box-office revenues of $11,529,368, *Food, Inc.* has had the widest circulation and received a great deal of attention in the United States with its relatively high box-office returns for a documentary film: $4,467,205.[4]

In the documentary sector "fewer than two dozen titles have ever topped $4 million" in the United States.[5] *Food, Inc.* (fig. 7.2) surprised the industry with its ability to break this barrier. Behind the film's success was a strong marketing campaign by its producer, Participant Films, which "did everything from promoting the film on Stonyfield yogurt lids to encouraging

FIGURE 7.2 Food documentaries such as *Food, Inc.* embrace an activist approach to stimulate viewers to participate directly in the attempts at changing the U.S. food system.

Mexican fast-food chain Chipotle to buy out screenings, targeting the foodie-activist audience."[6] *Food, Inc.* is an exceptional documentary film, and most of the other food films pale in comparison to the success that it has experienced. Increasingly, documentary films "have virtually disappeared from the big screen in all but a few major markets," as the market primarily supports narrative films produced by mainstream media outlets.[7] As filmmaker Steve James remarks, "Today there are so many more docs being made, and many of them are terrific, inventive films. There's this creative explosion going on, but it's nearly impossible for those filmmakers to make a living off their work."[8] Compared to the dominant film industry, very few viewers actually watch documentary food films, and this has the potential to undermine the broad-based radical impact that these films might have if larger audiences viewed them. Producing and disseminating documentary food films remains a challenge that must be taken into consideration when thinking about how much impact these films can have.

At the same time, organizing and activating communities around food documentaries at the local level can provide remarkable opportunities for change. Film screenings and festivals that feature documentary food films often fill auditoriums and enable people with similar values to launch collaborative efforts geared toward positive change. More research would help to determine the role that films play in encouraging participation in urban farming, community-supported agriculture, and other local efforts to support sustainable foodways.

Furthermore, it is important to consider the role that the Internet can play as an alternative venue for circulating messages that do not travel through mainstream media channels. Web venues such as YouTube and Vimeo enable individuals to have access to audiences they may not otherwise be able to reach, and social networking sites provide opportunities for discussion and collective action. Roger Doiron, founder of Kitchen Gardeners International, had enormous success with a video campaign entitled "This Lawn Is Your Lawn."[9] The short video features Doiron digging up his front lawn in front of his white house and transforming it into a vegetable garden. The film's message, "Eat the View," was designed to persuade the Obamas to plant an organic garden on the front of the White House lawn. Although the Obamas never directly referenced Doiron's campaign, many believe that this viral video campaign played a decisive role in encouraging the Obamas to create a White House lawn garden.

These works embrace a participatory ethos that often includes calls to action based on the principle that individual choices in terms of consumption can influence macroeconomic dynamics. Personal desires to maintain one's health by eating nutritious food are reinforced by dedication to consumption of local, organic, and possibly artisanal foods. Dehumanized commercial relationships are expected to acquire new life through direct connections with producers. The invitation to "vote with one's dollar" allows viewers to participate in the public sphere without engaging in traditional politics, while unintentionally reflecting neoliberal principles that consider markets the most efficient instrument to bring innovation and usher efficiency into contemporary societies.

Documentary filmmakers aim to engage audiences not to provide entertainment but to prompt reflection and stimulate action. These films remind us of two things. First, reflections about ethnicity, race, gender, and sexuality (similar to those we have explored in previous chapters) emerge more visibly and intentionally in noncommercial films that aspire to counter many of the problematic tendencies in fictional food films. Second, documentary films offer opportunities for hope because they are trying to think outside the box and to reconsider how media can communicate about food, identity, and power. In other words they have the potential to become effective tools in discussions about cultural citizenship. Many focus on how we can actually change the way that we consume to create more sustainable futures for ourselves and the planet and to achieve a stronger sense of social justice among diverse groups of people with competing interests.

Activism, however, is not the only theme dominating nonfiction feature-length films on food. The potential for social change and innovation that the documentaries may engender is not a direct consequence of the genre per se in terms of narrative form, visual material, and editing. While many documentaries use these communication strategies to draw attention to the structural issues plaguing contemporary food systems, others employ the same approach to reinforce audiences' fascination with the pleasurable and aesthetic aspects of the food world, and in particular fine dining.

Several documentaries focused on celebrity chefs—*Three Stars* (Drei Sterne—*Die Köche und die Sterne* [Hachmeister, 2010]), *A Matter of Taste: Serving Up Paul Liebrandt* (Rowe, 2011), *El Bulli: Cooking in Progress* (Wetzel, 2011), *Jiro Dreams of Sushi* (Gelb, 2011), and *Step Up to the Plate* (Entre les Bras [Lacoste, 2012])—were released between 2010 and 2012. Although not U.S. productions, they enjoyed some success among American "foodie" audiences and showed the potential of the genre. Since 2012, the U.S. Public Broadcasting System (PBS) has broadcast four seasons of short documentaries, *The Mind of the Chef*, and in 2015 Netflix released its own streaming series, *Chef's Table*. In these works countless shots document the preparation of food and the supple movements that assemble it almost magically. The chefs' hands exude a hypnotic quality, drawing viewers into an emotional and material reality that is understandable yet foreign enough to remain fascinating. Besides the usual documentary techniques, filmmakers employ many of the trappings of the popular visual style we have referred to as "food porn." Audiences for this kind of documentary, who we can safely assume are interested in food and culture, cannot but appreciate the exceptionality of the artisans' skills, honed by decades of absolute dedication, creativity, and professionalism.

As with any media representations, these documentaries actually participate in the construction of the very social field—in this case, fine dining—in which they find themselves operating. By so doing, they also have an impact on practices, power dynamics, social relationships, economic interests, and cultural debates in which the filmmakers are stakeholders as invested as restaurateurs, critics, food producers, and patrons. The more or less contrasting or aligning interests of all these actors, who are vying to assert their specific points of view as dominant, are shaping the ever-changing discursive field of fine dining. What emerges is a set of underlying tensions around the shift from the classical French conception of culinary excellence to a more culturally diverse and chef-centric approach to gastronomy, strongly influenced by media trends, financial pressures, and global dynamics, as well as by the relevance that food has acquired as an arena for social and political change. The analysis of these documentaries suggests that they do not merely reflect but actually contribute to the formation of a cosmopolitan canon of practices, norms, and values that naturalize the concept of the knowledgeable chef trained in a prestigious culinary tradition as the professional ideal.

Documentaries participate in the often-unspoken negotiations about cultural citizenship. They provide audiences with a repository of images, ideas, and values that are perceived as based on reality rather than fiction and, as such, are likely to interact with their worldview and their practices. Although more ideologically intentional in their choices of characters, stories, and images than mainstream fictional food films, they reach fewer viewers and primarily those who are already sensitive to and well-informed about the themes they address. To date, very few mainstream films—*Fast Food Nation* is an example—have embraced sensitive or controversial topics about the food system as their narrative focus. The fear of being perceived as preachy, boring, or at worst politically unacceptable has dissuaded most filmmakers from delving into uncomfortable plots and topics. Nevertheless, the success of food films builds on the effort to remain entertaining while apparently adopting a liberal or progressive position on important issues. In reality, as we have attempted to demonstrate, these films end up reinforcing traditional or conservative values and ideas.

FOOD FOR THOUGHT, THOUGHTFUL ACTION

At a powerful turning point in the film *Big Night*, Pascal, the ruthless and shrewd businessman, articulates his theory of how to influence people. Commenting on the highly Americanized spaghetti and meatballs that he pawns off as "authentic" Italian food and reaffirming his love of the high-quality cuisine prepared by Primo and Secondo, he states, "Give people what they want; then later you can give them what you want." Pascal's line troubles and yet entices us. It implies that taste can and should be influenced as a means of economic and social gain. It also implies that people's tastes can and do change and that engagement with new ideas and experiences can influence this taste.

Food is clearly an important site for studying the contestation of who belongs to a community—defined at various scales—and who doesn't.

The cultural aspect of citizenship, albeit a crucial one, often slips under the surface of what we define to be normal, when indeed it is deeply influenced by a variety of factors, including media. Gender and cultural studies scholar Elspeth Probyn asks compelling questions about the nature of food in its relationship to our identities and ultimately to the power that we can enact on the world: "Do we eat what we are, or are we what we eat? Do we eat or are we eaten? In less cryptic terms, in eating, do we confirm our identities, or are our identities reforged, and refracted by what and how we eat?"[10] It is our hope that this book can enable us to think through the complex relationships among identity, citizenship, and food media. This project grew out of a desire to learn more about food and film. As fans and consumers of food films, we felt compelled to understand more thoroughly the pleasure we encounter when we consume these films, a pleasure we clearly share with many other people. We wanted to deepen our understanding of the stakes inherent in this pleasure and to think through how easy it is to consume these food films in a casual manner.

We have drawn on different bodies of knowledge to inquire into food films, food culture, and cultural citizenship. Narrowing this focus to the study of U.S. food from the 1990s to the early twenty-first century has enabled us to identify links between these films and social anxiety about food, eating, bodies, and sexuality. Scholars such as Richard Klein and Elspeth Probyn have argued that the AIDS epidemic has impacted the relationship among food, bodies, and sexuality. The growth of "food porn" certainly represents a shift in how we visualize food and sexuality. The way we prepare, consume, and relate to food has also shifted dramatically over the past fifty years, and the decade of the 1980s, as historian Harvey Levenstein writes, ushered in a host of new paradoxes that live on in dominant culture today.[11] The culture of eating has shifted so that many of us consume more meals outside of the home than within it. A change in the type of media that U.S. viewers consume is inevitable as part of a process of grappling with these changes. As we have demonstrated throughout this book, there are stakes to this pleasure: the consumption of food films is vested with political, social, and economic implications. Although the emergent body of documentary films seeks to encourage citizens to act as political agents through cultural engagement, the majority of food films limits itself to reflect a utopian and ludic approach to eating and cooking. Luscious images of ingredients and dishes, joyful scenes around the table, and the excitement of the restaurant kitchen are pervasive, stimulating the imagination of viewers all over the world. Consuming film, in this case, does not provide much basis for engaging individuals as political, economic, and cultural citizens, even when important themes emerge in the narrative. While some documentary films refuse to divorce different types of citizenship from each other, the fictional ones tend to cater to the desires and fantasies of the viewers as consumers only. In doing so, they ignore—or at best sideline—citizens' political power beyond their participation in culinary practices and rituals.

What change might we hope to foster? What food for thought, and what thought for change might we hope to inspire? There are clearly powerful interests at play in media and food industries, over which we as individuals may not have much direct control. We chose to frame this book through the lens of citizenship for a reason: the concept of citizenship implies that individuals can participate, contribute, and make a difference. As this book draws to a close, we ask you to think about what role you might play in fostering productive, equitable change.

As a consumer, you can communicate with others to bring attention to the way that food media gloss over issues of power and make us feel safely distant from the troubling parts of food production and consumption. You can talk with your friends, colleagues, and families; write blogs; participate in conversations on social media; and find other venues for promoting a more nuanced conversation about how we feast our eyes. You can make deliberate choices about what you do and do not wish to consume, in terms of food and media. If you are an educator or a scholar, you can write and teach about food to help others engage in critical conversations about what we eat, what we watch, and how these influence each other. So many people are already doing this, and we are personally heartened by the growth in food studies, which allows many young citizens to better understand food systems and the innovative role they can play in them. We hope to see more and for food and media to enter the conversation in more academic disciplines. For those in the field of media production, you can think through the implications of what you represent in your films, ads, television shows, websites, and magazines. We are heartened by the increase in new films that draw attention to the politics of food. We value entertainment and love—as much as many of you—to relish the pleasures of food and movies. Perhaps we can envision entertainment that reminds us that food—and media—interweave pleasure and politics in deeply complex ways. When we feast our eyes, we do indeed feast. Let us feast our eyes, bodies, and minds in wise, responsible ways that foster respect for each other and for our planet.

NOTES

INTRODUCTION

1. Steve Chagollan, "Eat Drink Make Movie: Hollywood's Next Course," *New York Times*, July 9, 2009.
2. Marion Nestle, *Food Politics: How the Food Industry Influences Nutrition and Health* (Berkeley: University of California Press, 2002); Michael Pollan, *In Defense of Food: An Eater's Manifesto* (New York: Penguin, 2008); Eric Schlosser, *Fast Food Nation: The Dark Side of the All-American Meal* (Boston: Houghton Mifflin, 2001).
3. Food Festival Amsterdam, 2015, http://foodfestivalamsterdam.nl/; Lee Seung-ah, "Take a Culinary Trip at the Seoul Food Film Festival," Korea.net, July 9, 2015, www.korea.net/NewsFocus/Culture/view?articleId=128631; Associazione Montagna Italia, Food Film Fest, 2015, www.montagnaitalia.com/foodfilmfest2015.html.
4. See, e.g., David Theo Goldberg, *Multiculturalism: A Critical Reader* (Cambridge, MA: Blackwell, 1994); and Avery Gordon and Christopher Newfield, *Mapping Multiculturalism* (Minneapolis: University of Minnesota Press, 1996).
5. David R. Roediger, *The Wages of Whiteness: Race and the Making of the American Working Class*, rev. ed. (London: Verso, 2007).
6. Steve Zimmerman and Ken Weiss, *Food in the Movies* (Jefferson, NC: McFarland, 2005).
7. Ibid., 1–2.
8. Anya Hoffman, "Chef," in *Lights! Camera! Taste! Spotlight on Food & Film*, ed. James Beard Foundation (New York: James Beard Foundation, 2013).
9. Kathleen Collins, *Watching What We Eat: The Evolution of Television Cooking Shows* (New York: Continuum, 2009); Allen Salkin, *From Scratch: The Uncensored History of the Food Network* (New York: Putnam, 2013).
10. Alexander Cockburn, "Gastro-Porn," *New York Review of Books* 24, no. 20 (1977): 18.
11. Molly O'Neill, "Food Porn," *Columbia Journalism Review* 42, no. 3 (2003): 39.

12. Andrew Chan, "*La grande bouffe*: Cooking Shows as Pornography," *Gastronomica* 3, no. 4 (2003): 47–53.

13. Pauline Adema, "Vicarious Consumption: Food, Television and the Ambiguity of Modernity," *Journal of American & Comparative Cultures* 23, no. 3 (2000): 118.

14. Richard Klein, *Eat Fat* (New York: Pantheon, 1996); Peter N. Stearns, *Fat History: Bodies and Beauty in the Modern West* (New York: New York University Press, 1997).

15. Signe Rousseau, *Food Media: Celebrity Chefs and the Politics of Everyday Interference* (London: Berg, 2012).

16. Susan Jeffords, *Hard Bodies: Hollywood Masculinity in the Reagan Era* (New Brunswick, NJ: Rutgers University Press, 1994).

17. Dennis Bingham, *Acting Male: Masculinities in the Films of James Stewart, Jack Nicholson, and Clint Eastwood* (New Brunswick, NJ: Rutgers University Press, 1994); Steven Cohan and Ina Rae Hark, *Screening the Male: Exploring Masculinities in Hollywood Cinema* (London: Routledge, 1993); Fred Pfeil, *White Guys: Studies in Postmodern Domination and Difference* (London: Verso, 1995).

18. Gerald Auten, Geoffrey Gee, and Nicholas Turner, "Income Inequality, Mobility, and Turnover at the Top in the US, 1987–2010," *American Economic Review* 103, no. 3 (2013): 168–172; Nathan J. Kelly, *The Politics of Income Inequality in the United States* (New York: Cambridge University Press, 2011).

19. James Chapman, *Cinemas of the World* (London: Reaktion, 2003); Bill Nichols, *Movies and Methods: An Anthology*, 2 vols. (Berkeley: University of California Press, 1976, 1985).

20. Nick Browne, *Refiguring American Film Genres: History and Theory* (Berkeley: University of California Press, 1998); Stephen Neale, *Genre and Hollywood* (London: Routledge, 2000).

21. Rick Altman, *Film/Genre* (London: BFI, 1999).

22. Günther Beckstein, "An Approach to the Guiding Culture," in *Germany in Transit: Nation and Migration, 1955–2005*, ed. Deniz Göktürk, David Gramling, and Anton Kaes (Berkeley: University of California Press, 2007).

23. Robert Stam and Louise Spence, "Colonialism, Racism and Representation," *Screen* 24, no. 2 (1983): 2–20.

24. Barry Langford, *Film Genre: Hollywood and Beyond* (Edinburgh: Edinburgh University Press, 2005).

25. Mervyn Nicholson, "My Dinner with Stanley: Kubrick, Food, and the Logic of Images," *Literature Film Quarterly* 29, no. 4 (2001): 279–289.

26. Robin Balthrope, "Food as Representative of Ethnicity and Culture in George Tillman Jr.'s *Soul Food*, Maria Ripoll's *Tortilla Soup*, and Tim Reid's *Once upon a Time . . . When We Were Colored*," in *Reel Food: Essays on Food and Film*, ed. Anne Bower (New York: Routledge, 2004); Anne Bower, "Watching Food," in *Reel Food: Essays on Food and Film*, ed. Anne Bower (New York: Routledge, 2004); James R. Keller, *Food, Film and Culture: A Genre Study* (Jefferson, NC: McFarland, 2006); Gaye Poole, *Reel Meals, Set Meals: Food in Film and Theatre* (Sydney: Currency Press, 1999).

27. Bower, "Watching Food," 6.

28. Cynthia Baron, "Dinner and a Movie: Analyzing Food and Film," *Food, Culture and Society* 9, no. 1 (2006): 103.

29. Keller, *Food, Film and Culture*, 5.

30. Zimmerman and Weiss, *Food in the Movies*, 395.

31. Altman, *Film/Genre*; Neale, *Genre and Hollywood*.

32. Roger Ebert, review of *Big Night*, *Chicago Sun Times*, www.rogerebert.com /reviews/big-night-1996.

33. Kenneth Turan, "'Big Night': A Feast of Fine Character," *Los Angeles Times*, http://articles.latimes.com/1996-09-20/entertainment/ca-45581_1_big-night.

34. Peter Stack, "*Big Night*'s Winning Recipe: Tucci Whips up Delicious Food Film," *San Francisco Chronicle*, www.sfgate.com/movies/article/Big-Night-s-Winning -Recipe-Tucci-whips-up-2964971.php.

35. James Berardinelli, review of *Julie & Julia*, www.reelviews.net/reelviews/julie -julia; Roger Ebert, review of *Julie & Julia*, www.rogerebert.com/reviews/julie -and-julia-2009.

36. Anne E. McBride, "Food Porn," *Gastronomica* 10 (2003): 38–46; Elspeth Probyn, *Carnal Appetites: Foodsexidentities* (London: Routledge, 2000); Terrie L. Wilson, "Tasty Selections: An Evaluation of Gourmet Food Magazines," *Journal of Agricultural & Food Information* 5, no. 2 (2003): 49–66.

37. Frederick Kaufman, "Debbie Does Salad: The Food Network at the Frontiers of Pornography," *Harper's Magazine*, Oct. 2005, 55.

38. Arjun Appadurai, *Modernity at Large: Cultural Dimensions of Globalization* (Minneapolis: University of Minnesota Press, 1996); Warren James Belasco and Philip Scranton, *Food Nations: Selling Taste in Consumer Societies* (New York: Routledge, 2002); Sylvia Ferrero, "Comida sin par. Consumption of Mexican Food in Los Angeles: 'Foodscapes' in a Transnational Consumer Society," in *Food Nations: Selling Taste in Consumer Societies*, ed. Warren Belasco and Phillip Scranton (New York: Routledge, 2002).

39. Walter Benjamin, *Reflections: Essays, Aphorisms, Autobiographical Writings*, ed. Peter Demetz (New York: Harcourt Brace Jovanovich, 1978).

40. Linda Williams, "Film Bodies: Gender, Genre, and Excess," *Film Quarterly* 44, no. 4 (1991): 2; see also "World Food Travel," www.worldfoodtravel.org/.

41. See Adema, "Vicarious consumption"; Jonathan Crary, *Techniques of the Observer: On Vision and Modernity in the Nineteenth Century* (Cambridge, MA: MIT Press, 1990); Laura U. Marks, *The Skin of the Film: Intercultural Cinema, Embodiment, and the Senses* (Durham, NC: Duke University Press, 2000); Steven Shaviro, *The Cinematic Body* (Minneapolis: University of Minnesota Press, 1993); Vivian Sobchack, *The Address of the Eye: A Phenomenology of Film Experience* (Princeton, NJ: Princeton University Press, 1992); Linda Williams, *Hard Core: Power, Pleasure, and the "Frenzy of the Visible,"* exp. pbk. ed. (Berkeley: University of California Press, 1999).

42. Vivian Sobchack, *Carnal Thoughts: Embodiment and Moving Image Culture* (Berkeley: University of California Press, 2004), 60.

43. Keller, *Food, Film and Culture*, 1.

44. Martin W. Bauer, Nick Allum, and Steve Miller, "What Can We Learn from 25 Years of PUS Survey Research? Liberating and Expanding the Agenda," *Public Understanding of Science* 16, no. 1 (2007): 79–95.

45. Néstor García Canclini, *Consumers and Citizens: Globalization and Multicultural Conflicts* (Minneapolis: University of Minnesota Press, 2001).

46. Toby Miller, *Cultural Citizenship: Cosmopolitanism, Consumerism, and Television in a Neoliberal Age* (Philadelphia: Temple University Press, 2007).

47. Jean E. Burgess, Marcus Foth, and Helen G. Klaebe, "Everyday Creativity as Civic Engagement: A Cultural Citizenship View of New Media," in *Communications Policy & Research Forum* (Sydney, Australia: Network Insight Institute, 2006), 1.

48. Ibid., 2

49. Jim McGuigan, "The Cultural Public Sphere," *European Journal of Cultural Studies* 8, no. 4 (2005): 427–443.

50. Julie Guthman, *Weighing In: Obesity, Food Justice, and the Limits of Capitalism* (Berkeley: University of California Press, 2011).

51. Elspeth Probyn, "Choosing Choice: Images of Sexuality and 'Choiceoisie' in Popular Culture," in *Negotiating at the Margins: The Gendered Discourses of Power and Resistance*, ed. Sue Fisher and Kathy Davis (New Brunswick, NJ: Rutgers University Press, 1993), 278–294.

52. Raymond Williams, *Problems in Materialism and Culture: Selected Essays* (London: Verso, 1980), 41.

53. Ibid., 40.

54. John Fiske, *Television Culture* (London: Methuen, 1987), 15–16.

55. Deborah Root, *Cannibal Culture: Art, Appropriation, and the Commodification of Difference* (Boulder, CO: Westview Press, 1996).

56. Elizabeth Spelman, *Inessential Woman: Problems of Exclusion in Feminist Thought* (Boston: Beacon, 1988), 4.

57. Ibid., 115.

58. Gloria Anzaldúa, cited in Nikki Sullivan, *A Critical Introduction to Queer Theory* (New York: New York University Press, 2003), 71.

59. Patrick R. Grzanka, *Intersectionality: a Foundations and Frontiers Reader* (Boulder, CO: Westview Press, 2014), xv.

1. FOOD FILMS AND CONSUMPTION

1. George Ritzer, *The McDonaldization of Society: An Investigation into the Changing Character of Contemporary Social Life*, rev. ed. (Thousand Oaks, CA: Pine Forge Press, 1996), 1, xiii.

2. *Big Night*, Internet Movie Database, www.imdb.com.

3. Roger Ebert, review of *Big Night*, *Chicago Sun Times*, www.rogerebert.com /reviews/big-night-1996.

4. David Bell and Gill Valentine, *Consuming Geographies: We Are Where We Eat* (London: Routledge, 1997), 5.

5. Jon Lewis, *The New American Cinema* (Durham, NC: Duke University Press, 1998), 97. Lewis writes that this era is characterized by "increasing deregulation and a dramatic reinterpretation of antitrust guidelines, the introduction of junk-bond financing and its use in leveraged mergers and acquisitions, and the growing consolidation of assets and power by large corporations within the deeply incestuous and collusive industry subculture" (87).

6. David Ansen, "Way Beyond Spaghetti and Meatballs; Stanley Tucci's 'Big Night' Was Big at Sundance," *Newsweek*, Feb. 12, 1996, www.newsweek.com/way -beyond-spaghetti-and-meatballs-179802.

7. Judith Weinraub, "A 'Big Night' for Food Fans," *Washington Post*, Sept. 25, 1996, www.washingtonpost.com/wp-srv/style/longterm/review96/fbignight.htm.

8. Joan Tropiano Tucci, Gianni Scappin, and Mimi Taft, *Cucina & Famiglia: Two Italian Families Share Their Stories, Recipes, and Traditions* (New York: William Morrow, 1999), xi.

9. Ibid.

10. Ansen, "Way Beyond Spaghetti and Meatballs."

11. Weinraub, "Big Night."

12. Big Night, www.geocities.com/MotorCity/2380/cucina7.htm, Jan. 1996 (website no longer available).

13. Joanne Finkelstein, *Dining Out: A Sociology of Modern Manners* (New York: New York University Press, 1989), 2, 4.

14. B. Joseph Pine II and James H. Gilmore. "Welcome to the Experience Economy," *Harvard Business Review*, July-August 1998, 97–105; B. Joseph Pine II and James H. Gilmore, *The Experience Economy: Work Is Theater and Every Business a Stage* (Boston, MA: Harvard Business School Press, 1999).

15. Jens Christensen, *Global Experience Industries: The Business of the Experience Economy* (Aarhus: Aarhus University Press, 2009); Donna Quadri-Felitti and Ann Marie Fiore, "Experience Economy Constructs as a Framework for Understanding Wine Tourism," *Journal of Vacation Marketing* 18, no. 1 (2012): 3–15.

16. Anne-Mette Hjalager and Greg Richards, *Tourism and Gastronomy* (London: Routledge, 2003); Haemon Hoo, Anne Marie Fiore, and Miyoung Jeoung, "Measuring Experience Economy Concepts: Tourism Applications," *Journal of Travel Research* 46 (2007): 119–132; Lucy M. Long, *Culinary Tourism* (Lexington: University Press of Kentucky, 2004).

17. It is worth noting that Stanley Tucci committed himself to making *Big Night* in part out of the frustration he was experiencing with continually being typecast as a stereotypical Italian mafioso. Stanley Tucci, interview by Terri Gross, *Fresh Air*, NPR, Sept. 27, 1993.

18. See Laura Mulvey, "Visual Pleasure and Narrative Cinema," in *Issues in Feminist Film Criticism*, ed. Patricia Erens (Bloomington: Indiana University Press, 1990).

19. Katy McLaughlin, "Food Truck Nation," *Wall Street Journal*, June 5, 2009, www .wsj.com/articles/SB10001424052970204456604574201934018170554.

20. Sean Basinski, "Hot Dogs, Hipsters, and Xenophobia: Immigrant Street Food Vendors in New York," *Social Research* 81, no. 2 (2014): 397–408.

2. AUTONOMY IN THE KITCHEN?

1. Cynthia Baron, Diane Carson, and Mark Bernard, *Appetites and Anxieties: Food, Film, and the Politics of Representation* (Detroit: Wayne State University Press, 2014), 26–27.

2. Janice A. Radway, *Reading the Romance: Women, Patriarchy, and Popular Literature* (Chapel Hill: University of North Carolina Press, 1984); Mary Ann Doane, Patricia Mellencamp, and Linda Williams, *Re-vision: Essays in Feminist Film Criticism* (Frederick, MD: University Publications of America, 1984).

3. Susan Bordo, *Unbearable Weight: Feminism, Western Culture, and the Body*, 10th anniv. ed. (Berkeley: University of California Press, 2004); Catrina Brown and Karin Jasper, *Consuming Passions: Feminist Approaches to Weight Preoccupation and Eating Disorders* (Toronto: Second Story Press, 1993); Caroline Walker Bynum, *Holy Feast and Holy Fast: The Religious Significance of Food to Medieval Women* (Berkeley: University of California Press, 1987); Carole Counihan, *The Anthropology of Food and Body: Gender, Meaning, and Power* (New York: Routledge, 1999).

4. Marjorie L. DeVault, *Feeding the Family: The Social Organization of Caring as Gendered Work* (Chicago: University of Chicago Press, 1994), 118.

5. Bordo, *Unbearable Weight*, 110.

6. Shelley Bovey, *The Forbidden Body: Why Being Fat Is Not a Sin*, rev., updated, and exp. ed. (London: Pandora, 1994).

7. See Susan Faludi, *Backlash: The Undeclared War Against American Women* (New York: Crown, 1991).

8. Angela McRobbie, *The Aftermath of Feminism: Gender, Culture and Social Change* (Los Angeles: Sage, 2009).

9. Mark Palermo writes, "No motion picture subgenre has had so perplexing a success as the food movie. Generally defined as an arty romance centered around elegant cuisine, the food movie jumped to success with 1987's *Babette's Feast*, and kept its audience through such acclaimed sleepers as *Like Water for Chocolate* (the 1992 adaptation of Laura Esquivel's novel) and 1996's *Big Night* (a tale of two restaurant-owning Italians whose brotherhood is united through their culinary art)." Roger Ebert and Kenneth Turan both compare *Big Night* to *Babette's Feast* (see Ebert, review of *Big Night*; and Turan, "'Big Night'").

10. Rita Kempley, "Babette's Feast," *Washington Post*, April 8, 1988.

11. Counihan, *Anthropology of Food*, 73.

12. Elspeth Probyn, *Carnal Appetites: Foodsexidentities* (London: Routledge, 2000), 4.

13. Roger Ebert, review of *No Reservations*, www.rogerebert.com/reviews/no-reservations-2007.

14. Gisela Hoecherl-Alden and Laura Lindenfeld, "Thawing the North: *Mostly Martha* as a German-Italian Eatopia," *Journal of International and Intercultural Communication* 3, no. 2 (2010): 114–135.

15. See Edward W. Said, *Orientalism* (New York: Pantheon, 1978); and Ella Shohat and Robert Stam, *Unthinking Eurocentrism: Multiculturalism and the Media* (London: Routledge, 1994).

16. Ella Shohat and Robert Stam, "Contested Histories: Eurocentrism, Multiculturalism, and the Media," in *Multiculturalism: A Critical Reader*, ed. David Theo Goldberg (Cambridge, MA: Blackwell, 1994).

17. Barbara Welter, "The Cult of True Womanhood: 1820–1860," *American Quarterly* 18, no. 2 (1966): 151–174.

18. Nigella Lawson, www.nigella.com/books/view/how-to-be-a-domestic-goddess-12.

19. Lynn Andriani, "*Mastering the Art of French Cooking* Reaches Young Readers Again," *Publishers Weekly*, July 20, 2009, Internet Archive, http://web.archive.org/web/20091009162330/http://www.publishersweekly.com/article/CA6671678.html?nid=4599&source=link&rid=840626276.

20. Michael O'Sullivan, review of *It's Complicated*, *Washington Post*, Dec. 25, 2009, www.washingtonpost.com/gog/movies/its-complicated,1158864.html.

21. Ibid.

22. See Wendy Varney, "The Briar around the Strawberry Patch: Toys, Women, and Food," *Women's Studies International Forum* 19, no. 3 (1996): 267–272.

23. See, e.g., Nancy Fraser, *Justice Interruptus: Critical Reflections on the Postsocialist Condition* (New York: Routledge, 1997), esp. 73–74.

24. Seyla Benhabib, *The Claims of Culture: Equality and Diversity in the Global Era* (Princeton, NJ: Princeton University Press, 2002).

3. MAGICAL FOOD, LUSCIOUS BODIES

1. See, e.g., Julia Kristeva, *Desire in Language: A Semiotic Approach to Literature and Art* (New York: Columbia University Press, 1980).

2. Ibid., 22.

3. Stuart Hall, "Encoding/Decoding," in *Culture, Media, Language: Working Papers in Cultural Studies, 1972–79*, ed. Stuart Hall, Dorothy Hobson, Andrew Lowe, and Paul Willis (London: Hutchinson Centre for Contemporary Cultural Studies, University of Birmingham, 1980).

4. Laura Mulvey, "Visual Pleasure and Narrative Cinema," in *Issues in Feminist Film Criticism*, ed. Patricia Erens (Bloomington: Indiana University Press, 1990), 33.

5. See Janice A. Radway, *Reading the Romance: Women, Patriarchy, and Popular Literature* (Chapel Hill: University of North Carolina Press, 1984).

6. See Hall, "Encoding/Decoding."

7. James Berardinelli, *"Like Water for Chocolate*: A Movie Review by James Berardinelli," n.d., www.reelviews.net/reelviews/like-water-for-chocolate.

8. Chon A. Noriega and Steven Ricci, *The Mexican Cinema Project* (Los Angeles: UCLA Film and Television Archive, 1994).

9. Dianna C. Niebylski, "Heartburn, Humor, and Hyperbole in *Like Water for Chocolate*," in *Performing Gender and Comedy: Theories, Texts and Contexts*, ed. Shannon Hengen (Amsterdam, Netherlands: Gordon and Breach, 1998), 193.

10. Roger Ebert, review of *Simply Irresistible*, *Chicago Sun Times*, Feb. 5, 1999, www .rogerebert.com/reviews/simply-irresistible-1999.

11. Mick LaSalle, "Most of 'Simply's' Charms Are Easily Resistible but Gellar Shows She Can Play Grown-Up," *San Francisco Chronicle*, www.sfgate.com/cgi-bin /article.cgi?f=/c/a/1999/02/05/DD13974.DTL.

12. Emily Martin, "The Egg and the Sperm: How Science Has Constructed a Romance Based on Stereotypical Male-Female Roles," *Signs: Journal of Women in Culture and Society* 16, no. 3 (1991): 485–501.

13. Barbara Ehrenreich and Deirdre English, *For Her Own Good: 150 Years of the Experts' Advice to Women* (New York: Anchor, 1989).

14. Roger Ebert, review of *Woman on Top*, *Chicago Sun Times*, Sept. 22, 2000, http:// www.rogerebert.com/reviews/woman-on-top-2000.

15. Ella Shohat and Robert Stam, *Unthinking Eurocentrism: Multiculturalism and the Media* (London: Routledge, 1994), 138.

16. Angharad N. Valdivia, *A Latina in the Land of Hollywood and Other Essays on Media Culture* (Tucson: University of Arizona Press, 2000), 2.

17. Shari Roberts, "The Lady in the Tutti-Frutti Hat: Carmen Miranda, a Spectacle of Ethnicity," *Cinema Journal* 32, no. 3 (1993): 11.

18. David Theo Goldberg, *Multiculturalism: A Critical Reader* (Cambridge, MA: Blackwell, 1994); Arlene M. Dávila, *Latinos, Inc.: The Marketing and Making of a People* (Berkeley: University of California Press, 2001); Deborah Root, *Cannibal Culture: Art, Appropriation, and the Commodification of Difference* (Boulder, CO: Westview Press, 1996).

19. Jeffrey M. Anderson, "Hollow 'Chocolat,'" Combustible Celluloid, www .combustiblecelluloid.com/2001/chocolat.shtml.

20. Roger Ebert, review of *Chocolat*, *Chicago Sun Times*, Dec. 22, 2000, www .rogerebert.com/reviews/chocolat-2000.

21. Alexander Cockburn, "Gastro-Porn," *New York Review of Books* 24, no. 20 (1977): 128.

22. Jane Juffer, *At Home with Pornography: Women, Sex, and Everyday Life* (New York: New York University Press, 1998), 3.

23. Ibid.

24. Anh Hua, "Homing Desire, Cultural Citizenship, and Diasporic Imaginings," *Journal of International Women's Studies* 12, no. 4 (2011): 45.

25. Ibid., 52.

4. CULINARY COMFORT

1. Cahal Milmo, "The Curse of 'Man and Baby': Athena, and the Birth of a Legend," *Independent*, Jan. 16, 2007.

2. Esther Dermott, *Intimate Fatherhood: A Sociological Analysis* (New York: Routledge, 2008); Melissa A. Milkie and Kathleen E. Denny, "Changes in the Cultural Model of Father Involvement: Descriptions of Benefits to Fathers, Children and Mothers in *Parents' Magazine*, 1926–2006," *Journal of Family Issues* 35, no. 2 (2014): 223–253; Jenny Owen, Alan Metcalfe, Caroline Dryden, and Geraldine Shipton, "'If They Don't Eat It, It's Not a Proper Meal': Images of Risk and Choice in Fathers' Accounts of Family Food Practices," *Health, Risk and Society* 12, no. 4 (2010): 395–406.

3. Susan Jeffords, *Hard Bodies: Hollywood Masculinity in the Reagan Era* (New Brunswick, NJ: Rutgers University Press, 1994).

4. Fred Pfeil, *White Guys: Studies in Postmodern Domination and Difference* (London: Verso, 1995).

5. Fred Pfeil, "Getting up There with Tom: The Politics of American 'Nice,'" in *Masculinity Studies and Feminist Theory: New Directions*, ed. Judith K. Gardiner (New York: Columbia University Press, 2002), 121 (emphasis in original).

6. Marjorie L. DeVault, *Feeding the Family: The Social Organization of Caring as Gendered Work* (Chicago: University of Chicago Press, 1994), 95.

7. Kari Sellaeg and Gwen E. Chapman, "Masculinity and Food Ideals of Men Who Live Alone," *Appetite* 51, no. 1 (2008): 120–128; Michelle Szabo, "Foodwork or Foodplay? Men's Domestic Cooking, Privilege and Leisure," *Sociology* 47, no. 4 (2012): 623–638; Michelle Szabo, "'I'm a Real Catch': The Blurring of Alternative and Hegemonic Masculinities in Men's Talk About Home Cooking," *Women's Studies International Forum* 44 (May-June 2014): 228–235.

8. Michael S. Kimmel, *The Politics of Manhood: Profeminist Men Respond to the Mythopoetic Men's Movement (and the Mythopoetic Leaders Answer)* (Philadelphia: Temple University Press, 1995), 17.

9. Barbara Ehrenreich and Deirdre English, *For Her Own Good: 150 Years of the Experts' Advice to Women* (New York: Anchor, 1989), 12.

10. See Alberto Godenzi, "Style or Substance: Men's Response to Feminist Challenge," *Men and Masculinities* 1, no. 4 (1999): 385–392.

11. See Arthur Brittan, *Masculinity and Power* (Oxford: Basil Blackwell, 1989).

12. See, e.g., R. W. Connell, *The Men and the Boys* (Cambridge: Polity, 2000).

13. Antonio Gramsci, *The Gramsci Reader: Selected Writings, 1916–1935*, ed. David Forgacs (New York: New York University Press, 2000).

14. Michael Kimmel, *The Gender of Desire: Essays on Male Sexuality* (Albany: State University of New York Press, 2005), 30.

15. R. W. Connell, *Masculinities* (Cambridge: Polity, 2005), 76–81; see also Lynne Segal, *Slow Motion: Changing Masculinities, Changing Men* (New Brunswick, NJ: Rutgers University Press, 1990).

16. Chantal Mouffe, "Feminism, Citizenship and Radical Democratic Politics," in *Feminists Theorize the Political*, ed. Judith Butler and Joan Wallach Scott (New York: Routledge, 1992), 372; see also Judith Butler, *The Psychic Life of Power: Theories in Subjection* (Stanford, CA: Stanford University Press, 1997).

17. Steve Garlick, "What Is a Man? Heterosexuality and the Technology of Masculinity," *Men and Masculinities* 6, no. 2 (2003): 156–172; Francine Deutsch, "Undoing Gender," *Gender & Society* 21, no. 1 (2007): 106–127.

18. Bethan Benwell, "Ironic Discourse: Evasive Masculinity in Men's Lifestyle Magazines," *Men and Masculinities* 7, no. 1 (2004): 3–21; Jaqueline Kacen, "Girrrl Power and Boyyy Nature: The Past, Present, and Paradisal Future of Consumer Gender Identity," *Marketing Intelligence and Planning* 18, no. 6/7 (2000): 345–355.

19. Mark Simpson, "Meet the Metrosexual," *Salon*, July 22, 2002.

20. Connell, *Masculinities*, 81.

21. William S. Pollack, *Real Boys: Rescuing Our Sons from the Myths of Boyhood* (New York: Henry Holt, 1999), 25.

22. Adam S. Beissel, Michael Giardina, and Joshua I. Newman, "Men of Steel: Social Class, Masculinity, and Cultural Citizenship in Post-Industrial Pittsburgh," *Sport in Society* 17, no. 7 (2014): 955.

23. Susan Bordo, *The Male Body: A New Look at Men in Public and in Private* (New York: Farrar, Straus and Giroux, 1999), 18.

24. Richard Dyer, *White* (London: Routledge, 1997).

25. Jeffords, *Hard Bodies*, 13.

26. Pfeil, *White Guys*, 54.

27. Peter Lehman, *Running Scared: Masculinity and the Representation of the Male Body*, new ed. (Detroit: Wayne State University Press, 2007); Mark Moss, *The Media and the Models of Masculinity* (Plymouth, UK: Lexington Books, 2012).

28. Susan Bordo, *Unbearable Weight: Feminism, Western Culture, and the Body*, 10th anniv. ed. (Berkeley: University of California Press, 2004); Joan Jacobs Brumberg, *Fasting Girls: The History of Anorexia Nervosa* (New York: Vintage, 2000); Caroline Walker Bynum, *Holy Feast and Holy Fast: The Religious Significance of Food to Medieval Women* (Berkeley: University of California Press, 1987).

29. Patricia Thomson, review of *Heavy*, *Independent*, Jan./Feb., 1996, 31.

30. Shelley Bovey, *The Forbidden Body: Why Being Fat Is Not a Sin*, rev., updated, and exp. ed. (London: Pandora, 1994); Richard Klein, *Eat Fat* (New York: Pantheon, 1996).

31. See Bordo, *Unbearable Weight*.

32. Peter N. Stearns, *Fat History: Bodies and Beauty in the Modern West* (New York: New York University Press, 1997).

33. Fabio Parasecoli, *Bite Me! Food in Popular Culture* (Oxford: Berg, 2008).

34. See Ehrenreich and English, *For Her Own Good*.

35. A similar approach inspires Henri Jaglom's scripted film *Eating* (1990), which poses as a documentary. Its treatment of women and food reminds us of the character of Evelyn in *Fried Green Tomatoes*. The women "interviewed" throughout

the film are represented as being obsessed with food and feeling out of control in their relationships to eating.

36. Sidney Wilfred Mintz, *Tasting Food, Tasting Freedom: Excursions into Eating, Culture, and the Past* (Boston: Beacon, 1996), 13.

37. Bordo, *Unbearable Weight*, 199.

38. Connell, *Masculinities*, 201.

39. Ibid., 202.

40. See Sam Keen, *Fire in the Belly: On Being a Man* (New York: Bantam, 1991).

41. Pfeil, *White Guys*, 191.

42. Bordo, *Unbearable Weight*, 160.

5. WHEN WEIRDOS STIR THE POT

1. Jennifer L. Harris, Marlene B. Schwartz, and Kelly D. Brownell, "Marketing Foods to Children and Adolescents: Licensed Characters and Other Promotions on Packaged Foods in the Supermarket," *Public Health Nutrition* 13, no. 3 (2010): 409–417; Kathryn C. Montgomery and Jeff Chester, "Interactive Food and Beverage Marketing: Targeting Adolescents in the Digital Age," *Journal of Adolescent Health* 45, no. 3 (2009): S18–S29; Jennifer J. Otten et al., "Food Marketing to Children Through Toys: Response of Restaurants to the First U.S. Toy Ordinance," *American Journal of Preventive Medicine* 42, no. 1 (2012): 56–60.

2. Anne E. McBride, "Food Porn," *Gastronomica* 10, no. 1 (2010): 38–46.

3. J. Michael Barrier, *Hollywood Cartoons: American Animation in Its Golden Age* (New York: Oxford University Press, 2003); Giannalberto Bendazzi, *Cartoons: One Hundred Years of Cinema Animation* (Bloomington: Indiana University Press, 1994).

4. S. Dudink, A. Clark, and K. Hagemann, *Representing Masculinity: Male Citizenship in Modern Western Culture* (New York: Palgrave Macmillan, 2007).

5. *Ratatouille*, Internet Movie Database, www.imdb.com.

6. Benjamin Anastas, "The Foul Reign of Emerson's 'Self-Reliance,'" *New York Times Magazine*, Dec. 4, 2011, 58–59; Stanley Brandes and Thor Anderson, "*Ratatouille*: An Animated Account of Cooking, Taste, and Human Evolution," *Ethnos* 76, no. 3 (2011): 277–299.

7. "Box Office for Food Inc.," www.imdb.com/title/tt1286537/business; James B. Simpkins, "Two Rats in the Kitchen: *Ratatouille* and an American Culinary Dream," *Contemporary French & Francophone Studies* 14, no. 2 (2010): 205–211.

8. Ann Lair, "*Ratatouille*: An Historical Approach toward Gastronomy," in *Diverse by Design*, ed. C. Bloom and M. Gascoigne, (Richmond, VA: Central States Conference on the Teaching of Foreign Languages, 2009), 121–130.

9. Rosamaria Bitetti, "Economics of Failure in Movies After the Big Crisis," *Mises Seminar*, Istituto Bruno Leoni, Turin, Oct. 7, 2012, https://prezi.com/qkpub8wkhnup/economics-of-failure-in-movies-after-the-big-crisis/.

10. Anastas, "The Foul Reign"; Edwin Michael et al., "A Comparative Study of Gender Roles in Animated Films," *Global Journal of Human Social Science* 12, no. 5 (2012): 73–78.

11. Stacy Finz, "Bay Area Flavors Food Tale: For Its New Film 'Ratatouille,' Pixar Explored Our Obsession with Cuisine," *San Francisco Chronicle*, June 28, 2007, www.sfgate.com/bayarea/article/BAY-AREA-FLAVORS-FOOD-TALE-For -its-new-film-2583956.php.

12. Anne Neumann, "Ratatouille Edit Bay Visit!" *Comingsoon.net*, 2007, www .comingsoon.net/movies/features/19939-ratatouille-edit-bay-visit.

13. Pixar, "*Ratatouille* Podcast #7: Cooking up CG Food," 2007, www.youtube.com /watch?v=eu-7olnY6Xs.

14. Jose Johnston and Shyon Baumann, "Democracy versus Distinction: A Study of Omnivorousness in Gourmet Food Writing," *American Journal of Sociology* 113, no. 1 (2007): 165–204.

15. Cheri Ketchum, "The Essence of Cooking Shows: How the Food Network Constructs Consumer Fantasies," *Journal of Communication Inquiry* 29, no. 3 (2005): 217–234.

16. Gary Alan Fine, *Kitchens: The Culture of Restaurant Work* (Berkeley: University of California Press, 1996).

17. Elspeth Probyn, *Sexing the Self: Gendered Positions in Cultural Studies* (London: Routledge, 1993); Elspeth Probyn, "Choosing Choice: Images of Sexuality and 'Choiceoisie' in Popular Culture," in *Negotiating at the Margins: The Gendered Discourses of Power and Resistance*, ed. Sue Fisher and Kathy Davis (New Brunswick, NJ: Rutgers University Press, 1993), 278–294.

18. Laura Lindenfeld, "On the Ethics of Food Television: Does Rachael Ray Really Promote Healthy Eating?" in *Whose Weight Is It Anyway? Essays on Ethics and Eating*, ed. Sofie Vandamme, Suzanne van de Vathorst, and Inez de Beaufort (Brussels: Acco, 2010).

19. Maureen Fan. "*Kung Fu Panda* Hits a Sore Spot in China," *Washington Post*, July 12, 2008, www.washingtonpost.com/wp-dyn/content/article/2008/07/11 /AR2008071103281.html.

20. David Barboza, "In China, Jeers and Cheers for *Kung Fu Panda*," *New York Times*, June 30, 2008.

21. Anastas. "The Foul Reign."

22. Ella Shohat and Robert Stam, *Unthinking Eurocentrism: Multiculturalism and the Media* (London: Routledge, 1994).

23. Mai Ghoussoub and Emma Sinclair-Webb, *Imagined Masculinities: Male Identity and Culture in the Modern Middle East* (London: Saqi, 2000).

24. Edward W. Said, *Orientalism* (New York: Pantheon, 1978).

25. Susan Bordo, *The Male Body: A New Look at Men in Public and in Private* (New York: Farrar, Straus and Giroux, 1999); Murray J. N. Drummond, "Men, Body Image, and Eating Disorders," *International Journal of Men's Health* 1, no. 1 (2002): 79–93; David Gal and James Wilkie, "Real Men Don't Eat Quiche: Regulation of

Gender-Expressive Choices by Men," *Social Psychological and Personality Science* 1, no. 4 (2010): 291–301; Brendan Gough, "Real Men Don't Diet: An Analysis of Contemporary Newspaper Representations of Men, Food and Health," *Social Science & Medicine* 64, no. 2 (2007): 226–237; Harrison G. Pope, Katharine A. Phillips, and Roberto Olivardia, *The Adonis* (New York: Touchstone, 2000).

26. Priscilla Parkhurst Ferguson, *Accounting for Taste: The Triumph of French Cuisine* (Chicago: University of Chicago Press, 2004); Amy B. Trubek, *Haute Cuisine: How the French Invented the Culinary Profession* (Philadelphia: University of Pennsylvania Press, 2000).

27. Charlotte Druckman, *Skirt Steak: Women Chefs on Standing the Heat and Staying in the Kitchen* (San Francisco: Chronicle, 2012).

28. Marjorie L. DeVault, *Feeding the Family: The Social Organization of Caring as Gendered Work* (Chicago: University of Chicago Press, 1994).

29. Fabio Parasecoli, *Bite Me: Food in Popular Culture* (Oxford: Berg, 2008).

30. Henry Giroux, "Racial Politics and the Pedagogy of Whiteness," in *Whiteness: A Critical Reader*, ed. Mike Hill (New York: New York University Press, 1997), 295.

31. Douglas Brownlie and Paul Hewer, "Prime Beef Cuts: Culinary Images for Thinking 'Men,'" *Consumption, Markets and Culture* 10, no. 3 (2007): 229–250; Rebecca Swenson, "Domestic Divo? Televised Treatments of Masculinity, Femininity and Food," *Critical Studies in Media Communication* 26, no. 1 (2009): 36–53.

6. CONSUMING THE OTHER

1. Donna R. Gabaccia, *We Are What We Eat: Ethnic Food and the Making of Americans* (Cambridge, MA: Harvard University Press, 1998), 21.

2. See Jacques Gautier, Roberto Santibañez, Mariana Suarez, and Maximo Tejada, "From Ethnic to Mainstream: Latino Chefs Conquering NYC," conference panel, New School for Public Engagement, New York City, Nov. 7, 2011; and Heather Carlucci, Charlotte Druckman, Cheryl Smith, Mona Talbott, and Sue Torres, "Breaking the Mold: Women in Restaurant Kitchens," conference panel, New School for Public Engagement, New York City, June 6, 2012.

3. Krishnendu Ray, "Domesticating Cuisine: Food and Aesthetics on American Television," *Gastronomica* 7, no. 1 (2007): 50–63.

4. Elspeth Probyn, *Carnal Appetites: Foodsexidentities* (London: Routledge, 2000), 2.

5. Coco Fusco, *English Is Broken Here: Notes on Cultural Fusion in the Americas* (New York City: New Press, 1995), 50.

6. Jim Stark, "At the Movies: *Tortilla Soup*," *Gastronomica* 2, no. 1 (2002): 100–101.

7. Robin Balthrope, "Food as Representative of Ethnicity and Culture in George Tillman Jr.'s *Soul Food*, Maria Ripoll's *Tortilla Soup*, and Tim Reid's *Once upon a Time . . . When We Were Colored*," in *Reel Food: Essays on Food and Film*, ed. Anne Bower (New York: Routledge, 2004), 112.

8. Gisela Hoecherl-Alden and Laura Lindenfeld, "Thawing the North: *Mostly Martha* as a German-Italian Eatopia," *Journal of International and Intercultural Communication* 3, no. 2 (2010): 114–135.

9. bell hooks, "Eating the Other: Desire and Resistance," in *Eating Culture*, ed. Ron Scapp and Brian Seitz (Albany: State University of New York Press, 1998), 186.

10. David A. Hollinger, *Postethnic America: Beyond Multiculturalism* (New York: Basic Books, 1995).

11. Marilyn Halter, *Shopping for Identity: The Marketing of Ethnicity* (New York: Schocken, 2000), 183.

12. Lucy M. Long, *Culinary Tourism* (Lexington: University Press of Kentucky, 2004).

13. World Food Travel Association, www.worldfoodtravel.org/.

14. Greg Tate, *Everything but the Burden: What White People Are Taking from Black Culture* (New York: Broadway Books, 2003).

15. See Long, *Culinary Tourism*.

16. See, among others, Carole Counihan, ed., *Food in the USA: A Reader* (New York: Routledge, 2002); Carole Counihan and Penny Van Esterik, *Food and Culture: A Reader*, 2nd ed. (New York: Routledge, 2008); Hoecherl-Alden and Lindenfeld, "Thawing the North"; Ron Scapp and Brian Seitz, eds., *Eating Culture* (Albany: State University of New York Press, 1998); and James L. Watson and Melissa L. Caldwell, *The Cultural Politics of Food and Eating: A Reader* (Malden, MA: Blackwell, 2005).

17. Dean MacCannell, *The Tourist: A New Theory of the Leisure Class* (New York: Schocken, 1976); Chris Rojek and John Urry, *Touring Cultures: Transformations of Travel and Theory* (London: Routledge, 1997).

18. Lisa M. Heldke, *Exotic Appetites: Ruminations of a Food Adventurer* (New York: Routledge, 2003).

19. Ella Shohat and Robert Stam, *Unthinking Eurocentrism: Multiculturalism and the Media* (London: Routledge, 1994).

20. Ed Guerrero, *Framing Blackness: The African American Image in Film* (Philadelphia: Temple University Press, 1993), 163.

21. Herman Gray, *Watching Race: Television and the Struggle for "Blackness"* (Minneapolis: University of Minnesota Press, 1995).

22. Tate, *Everything but the Burden*, 14.

23. Psyche Williams-Forson, "Building Houses out of Chicken Legs: African American Women, Material Culture, and the Powers of Self-Definition" (PhD diss., University of Maryland, College Park, 2002), 403.

24. Doris Witt, *Black Hunger: Food and the Politics of U.S. Identity* (New York: Oxford University Press, 1999).

25. Williams-Forson, "Building Houses out of Chicken Legs," 402.

26. See Rafia Zafar, "The Signifying Dish: Autobiography and History in Two Black Women's Cookbooks," in *Food in the USA: A Reader*, ed. Carole Counihan (New York: Routledge, 2002), 249–262.

27. Williams-Forson, "Building Houses out of Chicken Legs."

28. Tate, *Everything but the Burden*, 4.

29. Williams-Forson, "Building Houses out of Chicken Legs," 390.

30. Nicholas De Genova and Ana Y. Ramos-Zayas, *Latino Crossings: Mexicans, Puerto Ricans, and the Politics of Race and Citizenship* (New York: Routledge, 2003), 6.

31. Marcelo M. Suárez-Orozco and Mariela M. Páez, eds., *Latinos: Remaking America* (Berkeley: University of California Press, 2002), 76.

32. Otto Santa Ana, *Brown Tide Rising: Metaphors of Latinos in Contemporary American Public Discourse* (Austin: University of Texas Press, 2002), xvii.

33. Fusco, *English Is Broken Here*, 24.

34. Amy Bentley, "From Culinary Other to Mainstream America: Meanings and Uses of Southwestern Cuisine," *Southern Folklore* 55, no. 3 (1998): 238–252.

35. Arlene M. Dávila, *Latinos, Inc.: The Marketing and Making of a People* (Berkeley: University of California Press, 2001), 172.

36. Anita Mannur, "Model Minorities Can Cook: Fusion Cuisine in Asian America," in *East Main Street: Asian American Popular Culture*, ed. Shilpa Davé, LeiLani Nishime, and Tasha G. Oren (New York: New York University Press, 2005), 16.

37. Stephen Hunter, "*Tortilla Soup*: A Combo Plate. In Remake of *Eat Drink Man Woman*, the Food Is the Star," *Washington Post*, Nov. 21, 2001, C12.

38. Kent A. Ono and John M. Sloop, *Shifting Borders: Rhetoric, Immigration, and California's Proposition 187* (Philadelphia: Temple University Press, 2002).

39. hooks, "Eating the Other," 181.

40. Ibid., 186.

41. Halter, *Shopping for Identity*; Tate, *Everything but the Burden*.

42. Zafar, "The Signifying Dish," 449.

43. See Doris Witt, "Soul Food: Where the Chitterling Hits the (Primal) Pan," in *Eating Culture*, ed. Ron Scapp and Brian Seitz (Albany: State University of New York Press, 1998), 258–287.

44. Maurice M. Manring, *Slave in a Box: The Strange Career of Aunt Jemima* (Charlottesville: University Press of Virginia, 1998).

45. Halter, *Shopping for Identity*.

46. Mary C. Beltrán, "The Hollywood Latina Body as Site of Social Struggle: Media Constructions of Stardom and Jennifer Lopez's 'Cross-Over Butt,'" *Quarterly Review of Film & Video* 19, no. 1 (2002): 71–85; Frances Negrón-Muntaner, *Boricua Pop: Puerto Ricans and the Latinization of American Culture* (New York: New York University Press, 2004).

47. Dávila, *Latinos, Inc.*, 111.

48. Ibid.; see also Arlene M. Dávila, *Latino Spin: Public Image and the Whitewashing of Race* (New York: New York University Press, 2008).

49. Negrón-Muntaner, *Boricua Pop*.

50. Mary C. Beltrán, "The New Hollywood Racelessness: Only the Fast, Furious (and Multiracial) Will Survive," *Cinema Journal* 44, no. 2 (2005): 50–67; Halter, *Shopping for Identity*.

51. Michael J. Weiss, "The Salsa Sectors," *Atlantic Monthly*, May 1997, www
.theatlantic.com/magazine/archive/1997/05/the-salsa-sectors/376871/.
52. Barbara Kirshenblatt-Gimblett, "The Ethnographic Burlesque," *Drama Review* 42,
no. 2 (1998): 175–180; Martin Mowforth and Ian Munt, *Tourism and Sustainability:
Development, Globalisation and New Tourism in the Third World*, 3rd ed. (London:
Routledge, 2009); John Urry, *The Tourist Gaze*, 2nd ed. (London: Sage, 2002).

CONCLUSION

1. *Fresh*, www.freshthemovie.com.
2. *Consumed*, www.consumedthemovie.com/#intro.
3. Cynthia Baron, Dian Carson, and Mark Bernard, *Appetites and Anxieties: Food,
Film, and the Politics of Representation* (Detroit: Wayne State University Press),
202.
4. "Box Office for *Food, Inc.*," http://pro.boxoffice.com/statistics/movies/food
-inc-2009.
5. Dave McNary, "Lionsgate Hopes to Ride Moore's Wave," *Variety*, Sept. 18, 2009,
www.variety.com/article/VR1118008860.html?categoryid=2526&.
6. Ibid.
7. Matthew Ross, "Docs Drive Innovative Deals," *Variety*, Sept. 9, 2009, www
.variety.com/article/VR1118008354.html?categoryid=3720&cs=1.
8. Ibid.
9. Roger Doiron, "This Lawn Is Your Lawn," YouTube, www.youtube.com
/watch?v=sOXtNdQxGw8#action=share dkMVTMoGszw.
10. Elspeth Probyn, *Carnal Appetites: FoodSexIdentities* (London: Routledge, 2000), 11.
11. Harvey Levenstein, *Paradox of Plenty: A Social History of Eating in Modern America*
(New York: Oxford University Press, 1993).

BIBLIOGRAPHY

Adema, Pauline. "Vicarious Consumption: Food, Television and the Ambiguity of Modernity." *Journal of American & Comparative Cultures* 23, no. 3 (2000): 113–123.

Altman, Rick. *Film/Genre*. London: BFI, 1999.

Anastas, Benjamin. "The Foul Reign of Emerson's 'Self-Reliance.'" *New York Times Magazine*, Dec. 4, 2011. www.nytimes.com/2011/12/04/magazine/riff-ralph-waldo-emerson.html?_r=0.

Anderson, Jeffrey M. "Hollow 'Chocolat,'" Combustible Celluloid. www.combustiblecelluloid.com/2001/chocolat.shtml.

Andriani, Lynn. "*Mastering the Art of French Cooking* Reaches Young Readers Again." *Publishers Weekly*, July 20, 2009.

Ansen, David. "Way Beyond Spaghetti and Meatballs; Stanley Tucci's 'Big Night' Was Big at Sundance." *Newsweek*, Feb. 12, 1996.

Appadurai, Arjun. *Modernity at Large: Cultural Dimensions of Globalization*. Minneapolis: University of Minnesota Press, 1996.

Associazione Montagna Italia, Food Film Fest, 2015. www.montagnaitalia.com/foodfilmfest2015.html.

Auten, Gerald, Geoffrey Gee, and Nicholas Turner. "Income Inequality, Mobility, and Turnover at the Top in the US, 1987–2010." *American Economic Review* 103, no. 3 (2013): 168–172.

Balthrope, Robin. "Food as Representative of Ethnicity and Culture in George Tillman Jr.'s *Soul Food*, Maria Ripoll's *Tortilla Soup*, and Tim Reid's *Once upon a Time . . . When We Were Colored*." In *Reel Food: Essays on Food and Film*, edited by Anne Bower, 101–116. New York: Routledge, 2004.

Barboza, David. "In China, Jeers and Cheers for *Kung Fu Panda*." *New York Times*, June 30, 2008. www.nytimes.com/2008/06/30/business/media/30panda.html?pagewanted=all&_r=0.

Baron, Cynthia. "Dinner and a Movie: Analyzing Food and Film." *Food, Culture and Society: An International Journal of Multidisciplinary Research* 9, no. 1 (2006): 93–177.

Baron, Cynthia, Diane Carson, and Mark Bernard. *Appetites and Anxieties: Food, Film, and the Politics of Representation*. Detroit: Wayne State University Press, 2014.

Barrier, J. Michael. *Hollywood Cartoons: American Animation in Its Golden Age*. New York: Oxford University Press, 2003.

Basinski, Sean. "Hot Dogs, Hipsters, and Xenophobia: Immigrant Street Food Vendors in New York." *Social Research* 81, no. 2 (2014): 397–408.

Bauer, Martin W., Nick Allum, and Steve Miller. "What Can We Learn from 25 Years of PUS Survey Research? Liberating and Expanding the Agenda." *Public Understanding of Science* 16, no. 1 (2007): 79–95.

Beckstein, Günther. "An Approach to the Guiding Culture." In *Germany in Transit: Nation and Migration, 1955–2005*, edited by Deniz Göktürk, David Gramling, and Anton Kaes, 303–305. Berkeley: University of California Press, 2007.

Beissel, Adam S., Michael Giardina, and Joshua I. Newman. "Men of Steel: Social Class, Masculinity, and Cultural Citizenship in Post-Industrial Pittsburgh." *Sport in Society* 17, no. 7 (2014): 953–976.

Belasco, Warren James, and Philip Scranton. *Food Nations: Selling Taste in Consumer Societies* New York: Routledge, 2002.

Bell, David, and Gill Valentine. *Consuming Geographies: We Are Where We Eat*. London: Routledge, 1997.

Beltrán, Mary C. "The Hollywood Latina Body as Site of Social Struggle: Media Constructions of Stardom and Jennifer Lopez's 'Cross-Over Butt.'" *Quarterly Review of Film & Video* 19, no. 1 (2002): 71–85.

——. "The New Hollywood Racelessness: Only the Fast, Furious (and Multiracial) Will Survive." *Cinema Journal* 44, no. 2 (2005): 50–67.

Bendazzi, Giannalberto. *Cartoons: One Hundred Years of Cinema Animation*. Bloomington: Indiana University Press, 1994.

Benhabib, Seyla. *The Claims of Culture: Equality and Diversity in the Global Era*. Princeton, NJ: Princeton University Press, 2002.

Benjamin, Walter. *Reflections: Essays, Aphorisms, Autobiographical Writings*. Edited by Peter Demetz. New York: Harcourt Brace Jovanovich, 1978.

Bentley, Amy. "From Culinary Other to Mainstream America: Meanings and Uses of Southwestern Cuisine." *Southern Folklore* 55, no. 3 (1998): 238–252.

Benwell, Bethan. "Ironic Discourse: Evasive Masculinity in Men's Lifestyle Magazines." *Men and Masculinities* 7, no. 1 (2004): 3–21.

Berardinelli, James. Review of *Julie & Julia*. ReelViews.net, August 8, 2009. www.reelviews.net/reelviews/julie-julia.

——. "*Like Water for Chocolate*: A Movie Review by James Berardinelli." n.d. ReelViews.net. www.reelviews.net/reelviews/like-water-for-chocolate.

Big Night. Internet Movie Database. www.imdb.com/title/tt0115678/?ref_=fn_al_tt_1.

Bingham, Dennis. *Acting Male: Masculinities in the Films of James Stewart, Jack Nicholson, and Clint Eastwood*. New Brunswick, NJ: Rutgers University Press, 1994.

Bitetti, Rosamaria. "Economics of Failure in Movies After the Big Crisis." *Mises Seminar*, Istituto Bruno Leoni, Turin, Oct. 7, 2012. https://prezi.com/qkpub8wkhnup /economics-of-failure-in-movies-after-the-big-crisis/.

Bordo, Susan. *The Male Body: A New Look at Men in Public and in Private*. New York: Farrar, Straus and Giroux, 1999.

——. *Unbearable Weight: Feminism, Western Culture, and the Body*. 10th anniv. ed. Berkeley: University of California Press, 2004.

Bovey, Shelley. *The Forbidden Body: Why Being Fat Is Not a Sin*. Rev., updated, and exp. ed. London: Pandora, 1994.

Brandes, Stanley, and Thor Anderson. "*Ratatouille*: An Animated Account of Cooking, Taste, and Human Evolution." *Ethnos* 76, no. 3 (2011): 277–299.

Brittan, Arthur. *Masculinity and Power*. Oxford: Basil Blackwell, 1989.

Brown, Catrina, and Karin Jasper. *Consuming Passions: Feminist Approaches to Weight Preoccupation and Eating Disorders*. Toronto: Second Story Press, 1993.

Browne, Nick. *Refiguring American Film Genres: History and Theory*. Berkeley: University of California Press, 1998.

Brownlie, Douglas, and Paul Hewer. "Prime Beef Cuts: Culinary Images for Thinking 'Men.'" *Consumption, Markets and Culture* 10, no. 3 (2007): 229–250.

Brumberg, Joan Jacobs. *Fasting Girls: The History of Anorexia Nervosa*. New York: Vintage, 2000.

Burgess, Jean E., Marcus Foth, and Helen G. Klaebe. "Everyday Creativity as Civic Engagement: A Cultural Citizenship View of New Media." In *Communications Policy & Research Forum*. Sydney, Australia: Network Insight Institute, 2006.

Butler, Judith. *The Psychic Life of Power: Theories in Subjection*. Stanford, CA: Stanford University Press, 1997.

Butler, Judith, and Joan Wallach Scott, eds. *Feminists Theorize the Political*. New York: Routledge, 1992.

Bynum, Caroline Walker. *Holy Feast and Holy Fast: The Religious Significance of Food to Medieval Women*. Berkeley: University of California Press, 1987.

Carlucci, Heather, Charlotte Druckman, Cheryl Smith, Mona Talbott, and Sue Torres. "Breaking the Mold: Women in Restaurant Kitchens." Conference panel. New School for Public Engagement, New York City, June 6, 2012.

Chagollan, Steve. "Eat Drink Make Movie: Hollywood's Next Course." *New York Times*, July 9, 2009.

Chan, Andrew. "*La grande bouffe*: Cooking Shows as Pornography." *Gastronomica* 3, no. 4 (2003): 47–53.

Chapman, James. *Cinemas of the World*. London: Reaktion, 2003.

Christensen, Jens. *Global Experience Industries: The Business of the Experience Economy*. Aarhus: Aarhus University Press, 2009.

Cockburn, Alexander. "Gastro-porn." *New York Review of Books* 24, no. 20 (1977): 15–18.

Cohan, Steven, and Ina Rae Hark. *Screening the Male: Exploring Masculinities in Hollywood Cinema*. London: Routledge, 1993.

Collins, Kathleen. *Watching What We Eat: The Evolution of Television Cooking Shows*. New York: Continuum, 2009.

Connell, R. W. *Masculinities*. Cambridge: Polity, 2005.

——. *The Men and the Boys*. Cambridge: Polity, 2000.

Counihan, Carole. *The Anthropology of Food and Body: Gender, Meaning, and Power*. New York: Routledge, 1999.

——, ed. *Food in the USA: A Reader*. New York: Routledge, 2002.

Counihan, Carole, and Penny Van Esterik, eds. *Food and Culture: A Reader*. 2nd ed. New York: Routledge, 2008.

Crary, Jonathan. *Techniques of the Observer: On Vision and Modernity in the Nineteenth Century*. Cambridge, MA: MIT Press, 1990.

Dávila, Arlene M. *Latino Spin: Public Image and the Whitewashing of Race*. New York: New York University Press, 2008.

——. *Latinos, Inc.: The Marketing and Making of a People*. Berkeley: University of California Press, 2001.

De Genova, Nicholas, and Ana Y. Ramos-Zayas. *Latino Crossings: Mexicans, Puerto Ricans, and the Politics of Race and Citizenship*. New York: Routledge, 2003.

Dermott, Esther. *Intimate Fatherhood*. Abingdon: Routledge, 2008.

Deutsch, Francine. "Undoing Gender." *Gender & Society* 21, no. 1 (2007): 106–127.

DeVault, Marjorie L. *Feeding the Family: The Social Organization of Caring as Gendered Work*. Chicago: University of Chicago Press, 1994.

Doane, Mary Ann, Patricia Mellencamp, and Linda Williams. *Re-vision: Essays in Feminist Film Criticism*. Frederick, MD: University Publications of America, 1984.

Doiron, Roger. "This Lawn Is Your Lawn." 2009. www.youtube.com/watch?v =dkMVTMoGszw.

Druckman, Charlotte. *Skirt Steak: Women Chefs on Standing the Heat and Staying in the Kitchen*. San Francisco: Chronicle, 2012.

Drummond, Murray J. N. "Men, Body Image, and Eating Disorders." *International Journal of Men's Health* 1, no. 1 (2002): 79–93.

Dudink, S., A. Clark, and K. Hagemann. *Representing Masculinity: Male Citizenship in Modern Western Culture*. New York: Palgrave Macmillan, 2007.

Dyer, Richard. *White*. London: Routledge, 1997.

Ebert, Roger. Review of *Big Night*. *Chicago Sun Times*, Sept. 27, 1996. www.rogerebert .com/reviews/big-night-1996.

——. Review of *Chocolat*. *Chicago Sun Times*, Dec. 22, 2000. www.rogerebert.com /reviews/chocolat-2000.

——. Review of *Julie & Julia*. *Chicago Sun Times*, August 5, 2009. www.rogerebert.com /reviews/julie-and-julia-2009.

——. Review of *No Reservations*. *Chicago Sun Times*, July 25, 2007. www.rogerebert .com/reviews/no-reservations-2007.

——. Review of *Simply Irresistible*. *Chicago Sun Times*, Feb. 5, 1999. www.rogerebert .com/reviews/simply-irresistible-1999.

——. Review of *Woman on Top*. *Chicago Sun Times*, Sept. 22, 2000. www.rogerebert .com/reviews/woman-on-top-2000.

Ehrenreich, Barbara, and Deirdre English. *For Her Own Good: 150 Years of the Experts' Advice to Women*. New York: Anchor, 1989.

Faludi, Susan. *Backlash: The Undeclared War Against American Women.* New York: Crown, 1991.

Fan, Maureen. "*Kung Fu Panda* Hits a Sore Spot in China." *Washington Post,* July 12, 2008. www.washingtonpost.com/wp-dyn/content/article/2008/07/11/AR2008071103281 .html.

Ferguson, Priscilla Parkhurst. *Accounting for Taste: The Triumph of French Cuisine.* Chicago: University of Chicago Press, 2004.

Ferrero, Sylvia. "Comida sin par. Consumption of Mexican Food in Los Angeles: 'Foodscapes' in a Transnational Consumer Society." In *Food Nations: Selling Taste in Consumer Societies,* edited by Warren James Belasco and Philip Scranton, 194–220. New York: Routledge, 2002.

Fine, Gary Alan. *Kitchens: The Culture of Restaurant Work.* Berkeley: University of California Press, 1996.

Finkelstein, Joanne. *Dining Out: A Sociology of Modern Manners.* New York: New York University Press, 1989.

Finz, Stacy. "Bay Area Flavors Food Tale: For Its New Film 'Ratatouille,' Pixar Explored Our Obsession with Cuisine." *San Francisco Chronicle,* June 28, 2007. www .sfgate.com/bayarea/article/BAY-AREA-FLAVORS-FOOD-TALE-For-its -new-film-2583956.php.

Fiske, John. *Television Culture.* London: Methuen, 1987.

Food Festival Amsterdam, 2015. http://foodfestivalamsterdam.nl/.

Fraser, Nancy. *Justice Interruptus: Critical Reflections on the Postsocialist Condition.* New York: Routledge, 1997.

Fusco, Coco. *English Is Broken Here: Notes on Cultural Fusion in the Americas.* New York: New Press, 1995.

Gabaccia, Donna R. *We Are What We Eat: Ethnic Food and the Making of Americans.* Cambridge, MA: Harvard University Press, 1998.

Gal, David, and James Wilkie. "Real Men Don't Eat Quiche: Regulation of Gender-Expressive Choices by Men." *Social Psychological and Personality Science* 1, no. 4 (2010): 291–301.

García Canclini, Néstor. *Consumers and Citizens: Globalization and Multicultural Conflicts* Minneapolis: University of Minnesota Press, 2001.

Garlick, Steve. "What Is a Man? Heterosexuality and the Technology of Masculinity." *Men and Masculinities* 6, no. 2 (2003): 156–172.

Gautier, Jacques, Roberto Santibañez, Mariana Suarez, and Maximo Tejada. "From Ethnic to Mainstream: Latino Chefs Conquering NYC." Conference panel. New School for Public Engagement, New York City, Nov. 7, 2011.

Ghoussoub, Mai, and Emma Sinclair-Webb. *Imagined Masculinities: Male Identity and Culture in the Modern Middle East.* London: Saqi, 2000.

Giroux, Henry. "Racial Politics and the Pedagogy of Whiteness." In Hill, *Whiteness,* 294–315.

Godenzi, Alberto. "Style or Substance: Men's Response to Feminist Challenge." *Men and Masculinities* 1, no. 4 (1999): 385–392.

Goldberg, David Theo, ed. *Multiculturalism: A Critical Reader.* Cambridge, MA: Blackwell, 1994.

Gough, Brendan. "Real Men Don't Diet: An Analysis of Contemporary Newspaper Representations of Men, Food and Health." *Social Science & Medicine* 64, no. 2 (2007): 326–337.

Gramsci, Antonio. *The Gramsci Reader: Selected Writings, 1916–1935.* Edited by David Forgacs. New York: New York University Press, 2000.

Gray, Herman. *Watching Race: Television and the Struggle for "Blackness."* Minneapolis: University of Minnesota Press, 1995.

Gross, Terri. Interview with Stanley Tucci. *Fresh Air.* Philadelphia: National Public Radio, 1997.

Grzanka, Patrick R., ed. *Intersectionality: A Foundations and Frontiers Reader.* Boulder, CO: Westview Press, 2014.

Guerrero, Ed. *Framing Blackness: The African American Image in Film.* Philadelphia: Temple University Press, 1993.

Guthman, Julie. *Weighing In: Obesity, Food Justice, and the Limits of Capitalism.* Berkeley: University of California Press, 2011.

Haemon Hoo, Ann Marie Fiore, and Miyoung Jeoung. "Measuring Experience Economy Concepts: Tourism Applications." *Journal of Travel Research* 46, no. 2 (2007): 119–132.

Hall, Stuart. "Encoding/Decoding." In *Culture, Media, Language: Working Papers in Cultural Studies, 1972–79,* edited by Stuart Hall, Dorothy Hobson, Andrew Lowe, and Paul Willis, 128–138. London: Hutchinson Centre for Contemporary Cultural Studies, University of Birmingham, 1980.

Halter, Marilyn. *Shopping for Identity: The Marketing of Ethnicity.* New York: Schocken, 2000.

Harris, Jennifer L., Marlene B. Schwartz, and Kelly D. Brownell. "Marketing Foods to Children and Adolescents: Licensed Characters and Other Promotions on Packaged Foods in the Supermarket." *Public Health Nutrition* 13, no. 3 (2010): 409–417.

Heldke, Lisa M. *Exotic Appetites: Ruminations of a Food Adventurer.* New York: Routledge, 2003.

Hill, Mike, ed. *Whiteness: A Critical Reader.* New York: New York University Press, 1997.

Hjalager, Anne-Mette, and Greg Richards. *Tourism and Gastronomy.* London: Routledge, 2003.

Hoecherl-Alden, Gisela, and Laura Lindenfeld. "Thawing the North: *Mostly Martha* as a German-Italian Eatopia." *Journal of International and Intercultural Communication* 3, no. 2 (2010): 114–135.

Hoffman, Anya. "Chef." In *Lights! Camera! Taste! Spotlight on Food & Film,* edited by James Beard Foundation, 14–18. New York: James Beard Foundation, 2013.

Hollinger, David A. *Postethnic America: Beyond Multiculturalism.* New York: Basic Books, 1995.

hooks, bell. "Eating the Other: Desire and Resistance." In Scapp and Seitz, *Eating Culture,* 181–200.

Hua, Anh. "Homing Desire, Cultural Citizenship, and Diasporic Imaginings." *Journal of International Women's Studies* 12, no. 4 (2011): 45–56.

Hunter, Stephen. "*Tortilla Soup*: A Combo Plate; In Remake of *Eat Drink Man Woman*, the Food Is the Star." *Washington Post*, Nov. 21, 2001, C12.

Jeffords, Susan. *Hard Bodies: Hollywood Masculinity in the Reagan Era*. New Brunswick, NJ: Rutgers University Press, 1994.

Johnston, Jose, and Shyon Baumann. "Democracy versus Distinction: A Study of Omnivorousness in Gourmet Food Writing." *American Journal of Sociology* 113, no. 1 (2007): 165–204.

Juffer, Jane. *At Home with Pornography: Women, Sex, and Everyday Life*. New York: New York University Press, 1998.

Kacen, Jaqueline. "Girrrl Power and Boyyy Nature: The Past, Present, and Paradisal Future of Consumer Gender Identity." *Marketing Intelligence and Planning* 18, no. 6/7 (2000): 345–355.

Kaufman, Frederick. "Debbie Does Salad: The Food Network at the Frontiers of Pornography." *Harper's Magazine*, Oct. 2005, 55–60.

Keen, Sam. *Fire in the Belly: On Being a Man*. New York: Bantam, 1991.

Keller, James R. *Food, Film and Culture: A Genre Study*. Jefferson, NC: McFarland, 2006.

Kelly, Nathan J. *The Politics of Income Inequality in the United States*. New York: Cambridge University Press, 2011.

Kempley, Rita. Review of *Babette's Feast*. *Washington Post*, April 8, 1988. www.washingtonpost.com/wp-srv/style/longterm/movies/videos/babettesfeastnrkempley_aoca1c.htm.

Ketchum, Cheri. "The Essence of Cooking Shows: How the Food Network Constructs Consumer Fantasies." *Journal of Communication Inquiry* 29, no. 3 (2005): 217–234.

Kimmel, Michael S. *The Gender of Desire: Essays on Male Sexuality*. Albany: State University of New York Press, 2005.

——. *The Politics of Manhood: Profeminist Men Respond to the Mythopoetic Men's Movement (and the Mythopoetic Leaders Answer)*. Philadelphia: Temple University Press, 1995.

Kirshenblatt-Gimblett, Barbara. "The Ethnographic Burlesque." *Drama Review* 42, no. 2 (1998): 175–180.

Klein, Richard. *Eat Fat*. New York: Pantheon, 1996.

Kristeva, Julia. *Desire in Language: A Semiotic Approach to Literature and Art*. New York: Columbia University Press, 1980.

Lair, Ann. "*Ratatouille*: An Historical Approach Toward Gastronomy." In *Diverse by Design*, edited by C. Bloom and M. Gascoigne, 121–130. Richmond, VA: Central States Conference on the Teaching of Foreign Languages, 2009.

Langford, Barry. *Film Genre: Hollywood and Beyond*. Edinburgh: Edinburgh University Press, 2005.

LaSalle, Mick. "Most of 'Simply's' Charms Are Easily Resistible but Gellar Shows She Can Play Grown-Up." *San Francisco Chronicle*, Feb. 5, 1999. www.sfgate.com/cgi-bin/article.cgi?f=/c/a/1999/02/05/DD13974.DTL.

Lawson, Nigella. *How to Be a Domestic Goddess: Baking and the Art of Comfort Cooking*. www.nigella.com/books/view/how-to-be-a-domestic-goddess-12.

Lehman, Peter. *Running Scared: Masculinity and the Representation of the Male Body.* New ed. Detroit: Wayne State University Press, 2007.

Lewis, Jon. *The New American Cinema.* Durham, NC: Duke University Press, 1998.

Lindenfeld, Laura. "On the Ethics of Food Television: Does Rachael Ray Really Promote Healthy Eating?" In *Whose Weight Is It Anyway? Essays on Ethics and Eating,* edited by Sofie Vandamme, Suzanne van de Vathorst, and Inez de Beaufort, 161–174. Brussels: Acco, 2010.

Long, Lucy M., ed. *Culinary Tourism.* Lexington: University Press of Kentucky, 2004.

——. "Culinary Tourism: A Folkloristic Perspective on Eating and Otherness." *Southern Folklore* 55, no. 3 (1998): 181–204.

MacCannell, Dean. *The Tourist: A New Theory of the Leisure Class.* New York: Schocken, 1976.

Mannur, Anita. "Model Minorities Can Cook: Fusion Cuisine in Asian America." In *East Main Street: Asian American Popular Culture,* edited by Shilpa Davé, LeiLani Nishime, and Tasha G. Oren, 72–94. New York: New York University Press, 2005.

——. "'Peeking Ducks' and 'Food Pornographers': Commodifying Culinary Chinese Americanness." In *Culture, Identity, Commodity: Chinese Diasporic Literatures in English,* edited by Tseen Khoo and Kam Louie, 19–38. Montreal: McGill-Queen's University Press, 2005.

Manring, Maurice M. *Slave in a Box: The Strange Career of Aunt Jemima.* Charlottesville: University Press of Virginia, 1998.

Marks, Laura U. *The Skin of the Film: Intercultural Cinema, Embodiment, and the Senses.* Durham, NC: Duke University Press, 2000.

Martin, Emily. "The Egg and the Sperm: How Science Has Constructed a Romance Based on Stereotypical Male-Female Roles." *Signs: Journal of Women in Culture and Society* 16, no. 3 (1991): 485–501.

McBride, Anne E. "Food Porn." *Gastronomica* 10, no. 1 (2010): 38–46.

McGuigan, Jim. "The Cultural Public Sphere." *European Journal of Cultural Studies* 8, no. 4 (2005): 427–443.

McLaughlin, Katy. "Food Truck Nation." *Wall Street Journal,* June 5, 2009.

McNary, Dave. "Lionsgate Hopes to Ride Moore's Wave." *Variety,* Sept. 18, 2009.

McRobbie, Angela. *The Aftermath of Feminism: Gender, Culture and Social Change.* Los Angeles: Sage, 2009.

Michael, Edwin, Afi Roshezry Abu Bakar, Ira Meilita Ibrahim, Geetha Veerappan, Norazleen Mohamad Noor, Lim Ean Heng, Taufik A. Latif, and Ng Kar Yann. "A Comparative Study of Gender Roles in Animated Films." *Global Journal of Human Social Science* 12, no. 5 (2012): 73–78.

Milkie, Melissa A., and Kathleen E. Denny. "Changes in the Cultural Model of Father Involvement: Descriptions of Benefits to Fathers, Children, Mothers in *Parents' Magazine,* 1926–2006." *Journal of Family Issues* 35, no. 2 (2014): 223–254.

Miller, Toby. *Cultural Citizenship: Cosmopolitanism, Consumerism, and Television in a Neoliberal Age.* Philadelphia: Temple University Press, 2007.

Milmo, Cahal. "The Curse of 'Man and Baby': Athena, and the Birth of a Legend." *Independent*, Jan. 16, 2007.

Mintz, Sidney Wilfred. *Tasting Food, Tasting Freedom: Excursions into Eating, Culture, and the Past*. Boston: Beacon, 1996.

Montgomery, Kathryn C., and Jeff Chester. "Interactive Food and Beverage Marketing: Targeting Adolescents in the Digital Age." *Journal of Adolescent Health* 45, no. 3 (2009): S18–S29.

Moss, Mark. *The Media and the Models of Masculinity*. Plymouth, UK: Lexington Books, 2012.

Mouffe, Chantal. "Feminism, Citizenship and Radical Democratic Politics." In Butler and Scott, *Feminists Theorize the Political*, 369–384.

Mowforth, Martin, and Ian Munt. *Tourism and Sustainability: Development, Globalisation and New Tourism in the Third World*. 3rd ed. London: Routledge, 2009.

Mulvey, Laura. "Visual Pleasure and Narrative Cinema." In *Issues in Feminist Film Criticism*, edited by Patricia Erens, 28–40. Bloomington: Indiana University Press, 1990.

Neale, Stephen. *Genre and Hollywood*. London: Routledge, 2000.

Negrón-Muntaner, Frances. *Boricua Pop: Puerto Ricans and the Latinization of American Culture*. New York: New York University Press, 2004.

Nestle, Marion. *Food Politics: How the Food Industry Influences Nutrition and Health*. Berkeley: University of California Press, 2002.

Neumann, Anne. "Ratatouille Edit Bay Visit!" *Comingsoon.net*, 2007. www.comingsoon.net/movies/features/19939-ratatouille-edit-bay-visit.

Nichols, Bill. *Movies and Methods: An Anthology*. 2 vols. Berkeley: University of California Press, 1976, 1985.

Nicholson, Mervyn. "My Dinner with Stanley: Kubrick, Food, and the Logic of Images." *Literature Film Quarterly* 29, no. 4 (2001): 279–289.

Niebylski, Dianna C. "Heartburn, Humor, and Hyperbole in *Like Water for Chocolate*." In *Performing Gender and Comedy: Theories, Texts and Contexts*, edited by Shannon Hengen, 179–197. Amsterdam, Netherlands: Gordon and Breach, 1998.

Noriega, Chon A., and Steven Ricci. *The Mexican Cinema Project*. Los Angeles: UCLA Film and Television Archive, 1994.

O'Neill, Molly. "Food Porn." *Columbia Journalism Review* 42, no. 3 (2003): 38–45.

Ono, Kent A., and John M. Sloop. *Shifting Borders: Rhetoric, Immigration, and California's Proposition 187*. Philadelphia: Temple University Press, 2002.

O'Sullivan, Michael. Review of *It's Complicated*. *Washington Post*, Dec. 25, 2009. www.washingtonpost.com/gog/movies/its-complicated,1158864.html.

Otten, Jennifer J., Eric B. Hekler, Rebecca A. Krukowski, Matthew P. Buman, Brian E. Saelens, Christopher D. Gardner, and Abby C. King. "Food Marketing to Children Through Toys: Response of Restaurants to the First U.S. Toy Ordinance." *American Journal of Preventive Medicine* 42, no. 1 (2012): 56–60.

Owen, Jenny, Alan Metcalfe, Caroline Cryden, and Geraldine Shipton. "'If They Don't Eat It, It's Not a Proper Meal': Images of Risk and Choice in Fathers' Accounts of Family Food Practices." *Health, Risk, and Society* 12, no. 4 (2010): 395–406.

Palermo, Mark. "The Odd Success of the Food Film." *On the Page Magazine*, no. 9 (Winter 2002–2003): www.onthepage.org/food/the_odd_success_of_the_food _film.htm.

Parasecoli, Fabio. *Bite Me: Food in Popular Culture*. Oxford: Berg, 2008.

Pfeil, Fred. "Getting up There with Tom: The Politics of American 'Nice.'" In *Masculinity Studies and Feminist Theory: New Directions*, edited by Judith K. Gardiner, 119–140. New York: Columbia University Press, 2002.

——. *White Guys: Studies in Postmodern Domination and Difference*. London: Verso, 1995.

Pine, B. Joseph II, and James H. Gilmore. *The Experience Economy: Work Is Theater and Every Business a Stage*. Boston: Harvard Business School Press, 1999.

——. "Welcome to the Experience Economy." *Harvard Business Review*, July-August 1998, 97–105.

Pixar. *Ratatouille* Podcast #7: Cooking up CG Food, 2007. www.youtube.com /watch?v=eu-7olnY6Xs.

Pollack, William S. *Real Boys: Rescuing Our Sons from the Myths of Boyhood*. New York: Henry Holt, 1999.

Pollan, Michael. *In Defense of Food: An Eater's Manifesto*. New York: Penguin, 2008.

Poole, Gaye. *Reel Meals, Set Meals: Food in Film and Theatre*. Sydney: Currency Press, 1999.

Pope, Harrison G., Katharine A. Phillips, and Roberto Olivardia. *The Adonis*. New York: Touchstone, 2000.

Probyn, Elspeth. *Carnal Appetites: Foodsexidentities*. London: Routledge, 2000.

——. "Choosing Choice: Images of Sexuality and 'Choiceoisie' in Popular Culture." In *Negotiating at the Margins: The Gendered Discourses of Power and Resistance*, edited by Sue Fisher and Kathy Davis, 278–294. New Brunswick, NJ: Rutgers University Press, 1993.

——. *Sexing the Self: Gendered Positions in Cultural Studies*. London: Routledge, 1993.

Quadri-Felitti, Donna, and Ann Marie Fiore. "Experience Economy Constructs as a Framework for Understanding Wine Tourism." *Journal of Vacation Marketing* 18, no. 1 (2012): 3–15.

Radway, Janice A. *Reading the Romance: Women, Patriarchy, and Popular Literature*. Chapel Hill: University of North Carolina Press, 1984.

Ray, Krishnendu. "Domesticating Cuisine: Food and Aesthetics on American Television." *Gastronomica* 7, no. 1 (2007): 50–63.

Ritzer, George. *The McDonaldization of Society: An Investigation into the Changing Character of Contemporary Social Life*. Rev. ed. Thousand Oaks, CA: Pine Forge Press, 1996.

Roberts, Shari. "The Lady in the Tutti-Frutti Hat: Carmen Miranda, a Spectacle of Ethnicity." *Cinema Journal* 32, no. 3 (1993): 3–23.

Roediger, David R. *The Wages of Whiteness: Race and the Making of the American Working Class*. Rev. ed. London: Verso, 2007.

Rojek, Chris, and John Urry. *Touring Cultures: Transformations of Travel and Theory*. London: Routledge, 1997.

Root, Deborah. *Cannibal Culture: Art, Appropriation, and the Commodification of Difference*. Boulder, CO: Westview Press, 1996.

Ross, Matthew. "Docs Drive Innovative Deals." *Variety*, Sept. 9, 2009. www.variety.com/article/VR1118008354.html?categoryid=3720&cs=1.

Rousseau, Signe. *Food Media: Celebrity Chefs and the Politics of Everyday Interference*. London, Berg, 2012.

Said, Edward W. *Orientalism*. New York: Pantheon, 1978.

Salkin, Allen. *From Scratch: Inside the Food Network*. New York: G. P. Putnam's Sons, 2013.

Santa Ana, Otto. *Brown Tide Rising: Metaphors of Latinos in Contemporary American Public Discourse*. Austin: University of Texas Press, 2002.

Scapp, Ron, and Brian Seitz, eds. *Eating Culture*. Albany: State University of New York Press, 1998.

Schlosser, Eric. *Fast Food Nation: The Dark Side of the All-American Meal*. Boston: Houghton Mifflin, 2001.

Segal, Lynne. *Slow Motion: Changing Masculinities, Changing Men*. New Brunswick, NJ: Rutgers University Press, 1990.

Sellaeg, Kari, and Gwen E. Chapman. "Masculinity and Food Ideals of Men Who Live Alone." *Appetite* 51, no. 1 (2008): 120–128.

Seung-ah, Lee. "Take a Culinary Trip at the Seoul Food Film Festival." Korea.net, July 9, 2015. www.korea.net/NewsFocus/Culture/view?articleId=128631.

Shaviro, Steven. *The Cinematic Body*. Minneapolis: University of Minnesota Press, 1993.

Shohat, Ella, and Robert Stam. "Contested Histories: Eurocentrism, Multiculturalism, and the Media." In Goldberg, *Multiculturalism*, 296–324.

——. *Unthinking Eurocentrism: Multiculturalism and the Media*. London: Routledge, 1995.

Simpkins, James B. "Two Rats in the Kitchen: *Ratatouille* and an American Culinary Dream." *Contemporary French and Francophone Studies* 14, no. 2 (2010): 205–211.

Sobchack, Vivian Carol. *The Address of the Eye: A Phenomenology of Film Experience*. Princeton, NJ: Princeton University Press, 1992.

——. *Carnal Thoughts: Embodiment and Moving Image Culture*. Berkeley: University of California Press, 2004.

Spelman, Elizabeth. *Inessential Woman: Problems of Exclusion in Feminist Thought*. Boston: Beacon, 1988.

Stack, Peter. "*Big Night*'s Winning Recipe: Tucci Whips up Delicious Food Film." *San Francisco Chronicle*, Sept. 27, 1996. www.sfgate.com/movies/article/Big-Night-s-Winning-Recipe-Tucci-whips-up-2964971.php.

Stam, Robert, and Louise Spence. "Colonialism, Racism and Representation." *Screen* 24, no. 2 (1983): 2–20.

Stark, Jim. "At the Movies: *Tortilla Soup*." *Gastronomica* 2, no. 1 (2002): 100–101.

Stearns, Peter N. *Fat History: Bodies and Beauty in the Modern West*. New York: New York University Press, 1997.

Suárez-Orozco, Marcelo M., and Mariela M. Páez, eds. *Latinos: Remaking America*. Berkeley: University of California Press, 2002.

Sullivan, Nikki. *A Critical Introduction to Queer Theory*. New York: New York University Press, 2003.

Swenson, Rebecca. "Domestic Divo? Televised Treatments of Masculinity, Femininity and Food." *Critical Studies in Media Communication* 26, no. 1 (2009): 36–53.

Szabo, Michelle. "'I'm a Real Catch': The Blurring of Alternative and Hegemonic Masculinities in Men's Talk About Home Cooking." *Women's Studies International Forum* 44 (May-June 2014): 228–235.

——. "Foodwork or Foodplay? Men's Domestic Cooking, Privilege and Leisure." *Sociology* 47, no. 4 (2012): 623–638.

Tate, Greg. *Everything but the Burden: What White People Are Taking from Black Culture*. New York: Broadway Books, 2003.

Three Black Chicks. Review of *Woman on Top*, 2000. www.3blackchicks.com /bamsontop.html.

Trubek, Amy B. *Haute Cuisine: How the French Invented the Culinary Profession*. Philadelphia: University of Pennsylvania Press, 2000.

Tucci, Joan Tropiano, Gianni Scappin, and Mimi Taft, *Cucina & Famiglia: Two Italian Families Share Their Stories, Recipes, and Traditions*. New York: William Morrow, 1999.

Turan, Kenneth. "'Big Night': A Feast of Fine Character." *Los Angeles Times*, Sept. 20, 1996. http://articles.latimes.com/1996-09-20/entertainment/ca-45581_1_big-night.

Urry, John. *The Tourist Gaze*. 2nd ed. London: Sage, 2002.

Valdivia, Angharad N. *A Latina in the Land of Hollywood and Other Essays on Media Culture*. Tucson: University of Arizona Press, 2000.

Varney, Wendy. "The Briar around the Strawberry Patch: Toys, Women, and Food." *Women's Studies International Forum* 19, no. 3 (1996): 267–272.

Watson, James L., and Melissa L. Caldwell. *The Cultural Politics of Food and Eating: A Reader*. Malden, MA: Blackwell, 2005.

Wein, Daryl. *Mister Lister Presents Consumed*, 2015. www.consumedthemovie.com/#intro.

Weinraub, Judith. "A 'Big Night' for Food Fans." *Washington Post*, Sept. 25, 1996. www .washingtonpost.com/wp-srv/style/longterm/review96/fbignight.htm.

Weiss, Michael J. "The Salsa Sectors." *Atlantic Monthly*, May 1997. www.theatlantic .com/magazine/archive/1997/05/the-salsa-sectors/376871/.

Welter, Barbara. "The Cult of True Womanhood: 1820–1860." *American Quarterly* 18, no. 2 (1966): 151–174.

Williams, Linda. "Film Bodies: Gender, Genre, and Excess." *Film Quarterly* 44, no. 4 (1991): 2–13.

——. *Hard Core: Power, Pleasure, and the "Frenzy of the Visible."* Berkeley: University of California Press, 1999.

Williams, Raymond. *Problems in Materialism and Culture: Selected Essays*. London: Verso, 1980.

Williams-Forson, Psyche. "Building Houses out of Chicken Legs: African American Women, Material Culture, and the Powers of Self-Definition." PhD diss., University of Maryland, College Park, 2002.

Wilson, Terrie L. "Tasty Selections: An Evaluation of Gourmet Food Magazines." *Journal of Agricultural & Food Information* 5, no. 2 (2003): 49–66.

Witt, Doris. *Black Hunger: Food and the Politics of U.S. Identity.* New York: Oxford University Press, 1999.

——. "Soul Food: Where the Chitterling Hits the (Primal) Pan." In Scapp and Seitz, *Eating Culture,* 258–287.

Zafar, Rafia. "The Signifying Dish: Autobiography and History in Two Black Women's Cookbooks." In Counihan, *Food in the USA,* 249–262.

Zimmerman, Steve, and Ken Weiss. *Food in the Movies.* Jefferson, NC: McFarland, 2005.

INDEX